Making It Their Own
Severn Ojibwe Communicative Practices

The Anihshininiwak, an Algonquian people who live in the remote subarctic forests of northwestern Ontario, speak a variety of Ojibwe that represents one of the most robust indigenous languages in North America. In this book, Lisa Valentine explores the language and discourse of the people of Lynx Lake, an Anihshininiwak community where every member uses the Severn Ojibwe language.

For the most part, anthropologists translate, interpret, and report the discourse of the peoples they study. In this study, the Anihshininiwak speak for themselves. Valentine presents their voices as the focus of her research and a guide to their culture, which she finds to be unique in its integration of contemporary ideas and technology into a traditional lifestyle. In adapting radio and television to community service and in their approach to Native-language literacy, this singular group confirms that new technologies are not necessarily precursors to enculturation. Culture-external institutions, including Christianity, have also been subject to active transformation by the people of Lynx Lake, who are the central actors of *Making It Their Own.*

In this fascinating ethnographic study, Valentine guides the reader through the language, geography, and sociology of the Lynx Lake community, yet we never lose sight of the emotional dimensions of daily life.

(Anthropological Horizons)

LISA PHILIPS VALENTINE is an assistant professor in the Department of Anthropology at the University of Western Ontario.

ANTHROPOLOGICAL HORIZONS
Editor: Michael Lambek, University of Toronto

This series, begun in 1991, focuses on theoretically informed ethnographic works addressing issues of mind and body, knowledge and power, equality and inequality, the individual and the collective. Interdisciplinary in its perspective, the series makes a unique contribution in several other academic disciplines: women's studies, history, philosophy, psychology, political science, and sociology.

Published to date:

Making It Their Own

Severn Ojibwe Communicative Practices

Lisa Philips Valentine

UNIVERSITY OF TORONTO PRESS
Toronto Buffalo London

© University of Toronto Press Incorporated 1995
Toronto Buffalo London
Printed in Canada

ISBN 0-8020-0643-4 (cloth)
ISBN 0-8020-7596-7 (paper)

Printed on acid-free paper

Canadian Cataloguing in Publication Data

Valentine, Lisa Philips, 1954–
  Making it their own : Severn Ojibwe communicative
  practices

  Includes bibliographical references and index.
  ISBN 0-8020-0643-4 (bound) ISBN 0-8020-7596-7 (pbk.)

  1. Ojibwa Indians – Communication. 2. Ojibwa language –
  Social aspects – Ontario. 3. Ojibwa language –
  Dialects – Ontario. 4. Communication and culture –
  Ontario. 5. Anthropological linguistics – Ontario.
  I. Title.

  E99.C6V35 1994   306.4'4'089973   C94-932321-7

University of Toronto Press acknowledges the financial assistance to its publishing program of the Canada Council and the Ontario Arts Council.

This book has been published with the help of a grant from the Social Science
Federation of Canada, using funds provided by the Social Sciences and Humani-
ties Research Council of Canada.

Contents

vi Contents

Preface

Using a discourse-centred approach to ethnography, this study provides an empirically based, synchronic overview of a rapidly changing First Nations village in Northern Ontario, Canada. It illustrates ways in which a society is indexed through its discourse, and how changes in society affect language use, making the book both an ethnography of speaking and an ethnography through speaking. The primary data collected for this research were naturally occurring discourses, most of which were presented by members of the Native community for the Native community itself.

The topics covered in the book are diverse, ranging from communication technologies to code switching between Ojibwe and Cree, and between Ojibwe and English; to literacy in both Cree syllabics and standard English; to the intersection of language and music; to a formal analysis of two narrative genres. These topics were selected as representative of the major linguistic forms found in the community – forms which are inextricably bound to the cultural context and social institutions of the Lynx Lake community. The diversity of topics covered led to the use of multiple analytic methodologies: techniques from ethnopoetics, conversational analysis, form–content parallelism, narrative analysis, and sociolinguistic quantitative analysis were employed in the search for understanding relationships between micro-level linguistic variation and macro-level social processes.

Because of its unique brand of self-determinism, the Severn Ojibwe community of Lynx Lake stands as a model for other Native communities, demonstrating that cultural change and the adoption of modern technology need not mean that a people must lose either their Native identity or their language. The people of Lynx Lake demonstrate a remarkable ability to integrate new ideas and technologies into their Native lifestyles.

Acknowledgments

The people of Lynx Lake taught me more about life and living than they can ever know. Among my many teachers, I want to thank the women who so kindly allowed me to join their beadworking sessions, where I sat, sewed, listened, and learned for anywhere from three to six hours weekly throughout my time in the community. Through the years, I had the excellent help of Anidia Memengwe, Jesse Pipoon, Ruth Pipoon, Mary Memengwe, and Mary Omakakii, who joined me in various labours from collecting data to transcription and translation. These are women who transformed work into play and, indeed, turned the world on its head continuously, causing me to rethink almost everything I thought I knew. Micah Pipoon taught me invaluable lessons about cultural roles and expectations in Ojibwe society.

This book, in its many incarnations, has had the benefit of some excellent input. Rand Valentine was an invaluable partner throughout many years of fieldwork. His insights into the more linguistic aspects of the Severn Ojibwe world have been foundational to my understanding of the subtleties of language use within the social context. Joel Sherzer was the initial filter for my scribbled musings. His version is that we would discuss my first draft, come up with a direction for the edits, and then I would write something entirely different from what had been planned. While this may be true (and I don't remember it this way at all), I do know that his input was enormous. John Nichols has been providing me insights into both English and Severn Ojibwe language and culture for the last thirteen years. Other readers of various portions of the manuscript who have contributed much to the final product include Dick Bauman, Tony Woodbury, Greg Urban, and Steve Feld. Regna Darnell, friend and colleague extraordinaire, gave me the push to make my work public: without her encouragement and sage advice, this book might still be mouldering in a filing cabinet. Later readers who helped me see the place of this book in a broader perspective include the anonymous readers for the Canadian Research Council book subvention committee, and Michael Lambeck, editor of the Anthropological Horizons series. I also wish to thank the copy-editor, Beverley Beetham Endersby, whose perseverance and keen eye have decidedly improved the quality of this manuscript. Dell Hymes made a key contribution by offering the title for this book. I carried around his suggestion, written on a yellow message sheet from the AAA conference in Washington, DC, for six months until, at last, I realized that this title really did tell the story of the book.

The field research in 1987–8 was financed by grants from the National Science Foundation and the Wenner-Gren Foundation. An earlier version of chapter 4 appeared in the *International Journal of American Linguistics*, and chapter 7 first appeared as an article in *Culture*.

Finally, I wish to thank my children, Whitney and Thibault (aka Tyler), who have shared the benefits and difficulties of living in Lynx Lake and other Native communities without the same motivations as their parents. Their presence in Lynx Lake gave substance to my claim to be a human being. They continue to reinforce my humanity and humility daily.

Making It Their Own

Severn Ojibwe Communicative Practices

Chapter One

Discourse and Ethnographic Research

While this study began as an ethnography *of* speaking, it soon evolved into an ethnography *through* speaking. In 1987, as I conducted my second term of fieldwork, I set out to produce an ethnography of speaking of Lynx Lake, documenting in particular linguistic genres and their use and distribution. However, it soon became apparent that by studying discourse in context, I was also exploring many aspects of the social organization of the community of Lynx Lake, one of the few truly viable Ojibwe speech communities, and indeed one of the few viable Native-language communities in all of North America. While contextualized discourse remains the centre-piece of this book, I expanded my initial design, using naturally occurring discourse as the empirical basis for analyses of several major aspects of social organization in the community. Thus, I present an ethnography *of* and *through* speaking. My data are taken from two years' residence in Lynx Lake, in 1981–3 and 1987, with a further visit in 1988; as a result, I describe a contemporary social situation with passing references to earlier situations only when they are overtly mentioned in discourses or are directly relevant to the presentation. Research on the Lynx Lake speech community, an Amerindian village in which the Native language is completely viable and used by every member of the Native community, is a particularly valuable addition to studies in ethnography of speaking. The topics covered in this book represent the major types of language use in the community, including literacy.

The fundamental premise behind my research at Lynx Lake is that, within any social organization, discourse, defined here as 'language in use,' plays a central role. (See the discussion of discourse models below.) This project has its roots in the tradition of the ethnography of speaking of the 1970s, in which naturally occurring discourse emerged as a focus of study. Today it is clear that discourse is not merely "[an invisible] glass through which the ethnographer comes to perceive the reality of social relations, of ecological practice, and of belief" (Sherzer and Urban 1986: 1); rather, discourse is the universe through which sociocultural relationships are most actively created, reinforced, negotiated, changed, and disseminated. As anthropologists move from studying societies as static objects to studying societies engaged in ongoing processes of interaction, discourse increasingly becomes central. For the most part, the discourse of other peoples has been translated, interpreted, and reported through the words of the anthropologist. In much of this study, however, the words of Severn Ojibwe people are presented so that they may speak for themselves. The voices of the Severn people are the cynosure of this book in two senses of the word: as the focal point of the research and as a guide to the Severn Ojibwe language/culture intersection.

The primary data for this study are naturally occurring discourses, most of which were presented by members of the Native community for the Native community itself. In working with these data, it became clear that such discourses provided the empirical basis for a synchronic ethnographic study of Lynx Lake. Thus, this book is a study both of the ways in which a society is indexed through discourse and of the ways in which changes in society influence language use. Throughout this study, my intent has been to provide a picture of modern community life in Lynx Lake. In this regard, I align myself with such anthropologists as Basso (1970, 1979), Philips (1983), and Scollon and Scollon (1979, 1981), all of whom attend to naturally occurring speech in their studies of contemporary Native American societies.

ETHNOGRAPHY OF SPEAKING

The ethnography of speaking is not a field or a discipline; rather, it is a perspective, an orientation towards the relationships among language, culture, and society. The development of the ethnography of speaking is closely tied to the unique history of anthropology and linguistics in the United States. At the turn of the century, the major force in American anthropology was Boas, who, along with his students (among the most notable, Sapir and Benedict), studied both language and culture. Indeed, many North American Indian languages were first described by Boas and his students; the resulting grammars, text collections, and ethnographies stand as eloquent testimonies to excellent research and scholarship. Cultural and linguistic relativism, in which each language/culture was studied on its own terms, was a central tenet of this research.

Between the First and Second World Wars, the ways in which language and anthropology fit together emerged as a major focus of inquiry. This was the era in which Sapir, and his student Whorf, struggled with the lexical, morphological, and syntactic encoding of culture-specific elements which appeared to structure the basic world-view of societies. The attempt to deal with linguistic evidence for cultural categories eventually led to what has become known as the Sapir-Whorf hypothesis: in the strong version of this hypothesis, language is said to determine culture; in the weak version, language is considered a major influence on people's perceptions of the world around them.

After, and perhaps resulting from, the Second World War, studies of languages outside of Native North America began to predominate, particularly those within the South Pacific and African areas. At the same time, linguistic and anthropological study became more compartmentalized. The studies from this period were predominantly empirical, often overly so. Thus, from the study of language in relation to culture came symbolic anthropology (through the examination of metaphors and metonyms), ethnoscience, sociolinguistics, and psycholinguistics. It was a time of high self-confidence that one could get at 'truth' through specific types of language study.

In the early to mid 1960s, Hymes (1964) and Gumperz (and Hymes 1974 [1964]) brought together ethnoscience (and symbolic anthropology), sociolinguistics, and communications in the newly created field of ethnography of communication. This field emerged during the era when linguistics in North America had become thoroughly compartmentalized, and language was studied almost exclusively outside its cultural context. Anthropologists, on the other hand, were learning and using Native languages only as tools for studying a culture, not as systems within the culture. The introduction of the ethnography of communication was an attempt by Hymes and Gumperz to bridge the gap that had widened, and continued to widen, between anthropology and linguistics. The somewhat narrower research endeavours of ethnography of speaking arose directly out of this initial work.

By the 1970s, and into the early 1980s, studies in the ethnography of speaking had become, if not common, then not uncommon. Among the excellent work done in this period were Basso's *Portraits of 'the Whiteman': Linguistic Play and Cultural Symbols among the Western Apache* (1979) and 'To Give Up on Words: Silence in Western Apache Culture' (1972 [1970]);

Bricker's *Ritual Humor in Highland Chiapas* (1973); Gossen's *Chamulas in the World of the Sun: Time and Space in a Maya Oral Tradition* (1974); and Sherzer's *Kuna Ways of Speaking: An Ethnographic Perspective* (1983), all of which address language use among Amerindian peoples.

These earlier works in the ethnography of speaking focused on ground rules for speaking, the principles needed to understand interchanges, verbal interactions, verbal art, and discourse acts and events. From the beginning, studies in the ethnography of speaking were based on the following set of assumptions:

1. All speech communities are heterogeneous: that is, multiple styles, languages, dialects, registers, levels, and the like are found in every speech community.
2. Speech communities overlap and intersect with one another. The isolated, discrete, and homogeneous speech community is a fiction.
3. One must attend to the overlapping and intersecting functions of language. Among the functions are social, phatic (establishing interpersonal relationships), and metacommunicative parameters, as well as the poetic function of language.
4. Languages and language usage include many components, such as the traditional linguistic levels of phonetics, phonology, morphology, and syntax, along with the added level, discourse.

In the 1980s and 1990s, studies in the ethnography of speaking expanded to include industrialized societies. In particular, the ethnography of speaking perspective has been applied to society, politics, and education within the United States. Methodologically, researchers concerned with the ethnography of speaking have advanced the ways in which discourse, or language in use, is collected, annotated, discussed, and analysed, in the process influencing both mainstream anthropology and linguistics. This research continues the general tradition within ethnography of speaking of systematically studying a community's language use in the context of its culture. And, while *Making It Their Own* focuses on an Amerindian community, as did much of the work done in the 1970s, the attention given here to modern communicative technologies moves this work into more contemporary paradigms.

DEFINITIONS OF DISCOURSE

For the purposes of this study, 'discourse' is defined as 'language used in social interactions.' This definition distinguishes discourse from text, which is a stretch of discourse as encapsulated in some static medium such as on the printed or written page or on audio or video tape. Discourse *is* social action; it *is* social practice. As such, discourse provides one of the most accessible arenas for studying emergent concerns of societies. Just as discourse is never static, neither is discourse context presumed to be static (cf. Plummer 1990, and the interactionist arguments); discourse study does not merely allow for social change; rather, it takes change as a given.

In Abu-Lughod and Lutz's (1990) book on language and the politics of emotion, they present '"discourse" [as] a concept that recognizes that what people say ... is inseparable from and interpenetrated with changing power relations in social life. There is a double movement implied in this notion. First, social and political life is to be seen as the product of interactions among individuals whose practices are informed by available discourses; second, language and culture are ... understood as part of social and political life' (p. 41). This definition, which has clear resonances with both Foucault and Bourdieu, is particularly appealing because it addresses discourse as both the locus and the means of social action.

My interests reside in both the grammatical and the social dimensions of discourse. Any given discourse is socially situated and fills some function which depends upon the social structure and nature of the society in which the discourse is presented. An excellent example of how discourse is socially (contextually) situated is the use of silence in a society (cf. Basso 1972). The discourse functions of silence in society are provocatively evident in such statements as 'He clammed up' or 'She gave him the silent treatment.' While silence has no *apparent* internal grammatical structure, it is interpretable if considered in the context of other discourse.

FORMAL LINGUISTIC FEATURES AND SOCIAL PROCESS

Integrating analyses of discourse-internal structuring (the analysis of formal linguistic features of discourse) and analyses of discourse-external structuring (the social role or function of discourse) has had somewhat minimal, local success. A variety of scholars are working on this integration from an Americanist perspective. Contemporary scholars attempting to address this particular issue include Bauman (1986a), from the field of folklore; Feld (1982), from the combined perspective of the anthropologist and ethnomusicologist; Urban (1991), from the vantage of linguistic anthropology; Wodak (1989), working in linguistics; and Thibault (1993), who combines text linguistics procedures with social semiotics. While these scholars have begun to address these issues with some success, they have been limited by the paucity of metalanguage available to talk about discourse in both realms. While this book attempts to address both micro-level formal analysis and macro-level social process, the focus is clearly on the side of the micro-level analysis, as research in Severn Ojibwe (as well as most Algonquian speech communities) has not begun to scratch the surface of the diversity and complexity of discourses and linguistic resources available.

LINGUISTIC DISCOURSE MODELS

I have used multiple analytic methodologies in an effort to understand Ojibwe discourse, to tease out connections between formal features and social processes. Most analysts use a single methodology, but I found no one model that was appropriate for dealing with the range of data that I wanted to address. One of the challenges of writing a book about discourse has been to clarify just what the terms 'discourse' and 'discourse analysis' mean at any given point in a discussion. One way to elucidate the terms that I am using is to give a brief overview of key analytic methodologies that inform this work. The following are six of the major schools of discourse analysis within lingusitics and linguistic anthropology :

1. *Text analysis*: The questions being asked by text analysts include what is being talked about? and how do we understand a given stretch of text as a unit? Thus the major focus has been on topic, comment, and text-internal relationships, including multiple cohesive devices. Text analysts often employ statistical methodologies, for example, Halliday and Hasan (1976), Longacre (1976), Halliday (1985), and Givon (1980, 1985).

2. *Conversation(al) analysis*: Those working on conversation analysis have had an enormous influence in two primary areas. The first and foremost has been in finely articulating transcriptional methodologies. Indeed, much of conversational analysis is based on discovering and naming recurring structures highlighted in detailed transcriptions of, in particular, dyadic conversations. Conversational materials are used to outline interactional routines found in conversational genres. The major proponents of conversation analysis were Sacks, Schegloff, and Jefferson (1974). The work of C. Goodwin (1981), M.H. Goodwin (1982, 1990), and Moer man (1988), among others, has extended this methodology into a broader ethnographic arena.

3. *Sociolinguistic research:* Sociolinguistics came about in an effort to discover reasons for linguistic variation within a speech community; that is, to account for language change synchronically. This was one of the earliest forms of research into the intersection of linguistic variation and, if not culture, then at least sociological categories. As defined in sociolinguistic research, discourse is considered to reflect differences in speakers' social and economic backgrounds and aspirations. Labov (1972a), a pioneer in sociolinguistics, expanded his inquiry into various aspects of discourse/text analysis (1972b), some of which are reflected in this book.

4. *Discourse as a social-interactional resource:* Discourse studied using this approach was not limited to spoken language but included other communicative strategies, including framing (Goffman 1974), physical and verbal joking (Basso 1979), and silence (Basso 1972). Miscommunication was also included as a major area of study (Gumperz 1982).

5. *Form–content parallelism:* In this approach researchers explore ways in which a variety of formal features interact to provide culturally specified, rhetorical structuring of texts. Hymes (1977, 1981, 1985) used this structuring to reconstruct performance features from texts collected by especially Boas's students (see also Bright 1982). Woodbury (1987) further explicated relationships between rhetorical devices used to look at contemporary Central Alaska Yupik texts. Hymes's focus on aspects of performance had three important results: it allowed contemporary students to study texts of extinct or moribund languages and discover oral features, especially of narratives; it presented an analysis of rhetorical structuring based on internal formal features of the text; and it provided yet more evidence that transcriptions themselves are theory-driven and not simply atheoretical descriptive artefacts.

6. *Ethnopoetics:* While related to form–content parallelism, ethnopoetics focuses in particular on artistic genres, giving details of translation and prosodic structuring primary emphasis. The structuring devices addressed are similar to those analysed by Jakobson (1960), as teasing out parallelism of forms at all levels is a major element. Primary works in this area include those by Tedlock (1971, 1977, 1984, and 1987), Hymes (1977, 1981, 1985), Bright (1982), and Rothenber g (1972).

I have used *all* these methodologies in my work: all have their amplifications and their reductions. While each is theoretically informed, none is sufficient as a theory of discourse. In each, descriptive exuberances are tempered by the limitations of scope. However, by using multiple models to study a single speech community through a period of twelve years, the resultant textual foundation of naturally occurring discourse is exquisite, one afforded to few anthropologists or linguists.

In addition to these types of discourse analysis, a variety of other 'textual analyses,' more familiar to anthropologists, exist. Indeed, the terminology adopted to describe language in social action has been appropriated in various anthropological models to sidestep language entirely. Geertz's (1973: 448–9) discussion of his use of text illustrates such a move:

Such an extension of the notion of a text beyond written material, and even beyond verbal, is, though metaphorical, not, of course, all that novel. The *interpretatio naturae* tradition of the Middle Ages, that, culminating in Spinoza, attempted to read nature as Scripture, the Nietzschean effort to treat value systems as glosses on the will to power (or the Marxian one to treat them as glosses on property relations), and the Freudian replacement of the enigmatic text of the manifest dream with the plain one of the latent, all offer precedents, if not equally recommendable ones. But the idea remains theoretically undeveloped; and the more profound corollary, so far as anthropology is concerned, that cultural forms can be treated as texts, as imaginative works built out of social materials, has yet to be systematically exploited.

By the 1990s, such usages of 'text' and 'discourse' *have* become systematically exploited in anthropological literature, causing some misunderstanding of specific usages of hitherto linguistic terms by those on either the sociocultural or the linguistic side of anthropological interpretation, writing, and analysis. While I am using the term 'discourse' in this study as specifically and literally language-centred, understanding the social context of such discourses, as addressed by more explicitly sociocultural anthropologists, *is* the point of this book. Thus, while my methods as a linguistic anthropologist may not always overlap with those of sociocultural anthropologists, my goals often do.

AN OVERVIEW OF THIS BOOK

The topics covered in this book were selected as representative of all major linguistic forms found in the community – forms which are inextricably bound to the cultural context and social institutions of the Lynx Lake community. While the topics are diverse, ranging from communication technologies to the intersection of language and music, to narrative genres, each topic is crucial for understanding the types and place of discourse within the community.

Chapter 2 provides an overview of the Severn Ojibwe language variety, relating it to the other Ojibwe varieties, and to the Algonquian language family in general. The Lynx Lake community is delineated as belonging to the eastern subdialect of Severn, and compared with other Severn communities in terms of population, reserve size, religious institutions, economics, literacy, and general language use. Included is an outline of Severn phonology and roman orthographic conventions.

In chapter 3, changes in communication networks induced by technological imports into Lynx Lake are outlined medium by medium. Included are discussions of trail radios, telephones (microwave relay system), the Native-produced newspaper, *Wawatay News*, the community radio station Wawatay Radio News, TVO North, and Wawatay TV. In each case, the history of the medium in the community is provided, with an ethnographic description of its place within Lynx Lake. In many cases, excerpts from larger discourses illustrate community use and attitudes towards each medium in an interesting metacommunicative discussion of information flow within a culture. Because the media have been in the hands of locals in this community from the start, they are viewed as emergent aspects of their own community. To a non-Native reader, the discussion of these Native media provides a unique view of the indigenization of 'Western' technology. An interesting side-effect of the now long-standing presence of these media in the Severn region is that information dissemination has become quite 'public' and thus more accessible to the outside researcher, lessening the effects of 'the observer's paradox.'

Chapter 4 provides an overview of the languages used in the community. In Lynx Lake, as in most of the Severn Ojibwe villages, Severn Ojibwe, Cree, and English are all codes heard within the confines of the community. Of these, only Severn Ojibwe is used by the entire Native population of Lynx Lake: Cree and English are used in relatively bounded social domains by a subset of community members. Cree is used in church and religious settings, usually by religious specialists over the age of forty. In the last fifteen years, English has become a factor in the areas of education and in relating to the Euro-Canadian matrix society in the areas of medicine, law, government, and commerce. In this chapter, three essentially monologic public discourses demonstrating different types of code switching, including phonological shift, lexical insertion, and full code substitution, are investigated in terms of both form and function: in just these few texts, a complex linguistic repertoire is used to index social systems and roles, in some cases overlaid by humour and irony.

In chapter 5, the focus is on written as opposed to oral codes, which again index complex social relationships between the Severn people and the Cree and the Canadian-English linguistic communities. Literacy in Lynx Lake is associated in the main with the community's three predominant institutions, religion, politics, and education: in the 1980s, the balance between religion and politics made the small village of Lynx Lake a model for other Severn communities. The people of Lynx Lake are unique in their level of literacy in the indigenous language, even among the Severn Ojibwe, who are known for high levels of literacy in Ojibwe using Cree syllabics. In Lynx Lake, the literacy rate in the indigenous language may be as high as 100 per cent for people over the age of thirty. The people of Lynx Lake use one of three recognized book standards of the Cree syllabic script for writing Ojibwe. The means of learning and teaching syllabics are explored, along with such issues as local definitions of literacy, motivations for literacy, and prospects for syllabic literacy. Uses of syllabics within the community are enumerated, and English literacy in the community is outlined and compared with Native literacy.

In chapter 6, an ethnographic overview of language and music is provided, covering such issues as who sings, who plays musical instruments, the place of singing in the community at large, and types of music found in Lynx Lake. The majority of musical expression in Lynx Lake can be tied to church contexts, where there appears to be a continuum between language and music. This continuum is described in some detail, moving from singing, to sing/chanting, to chanting, to oral reading, to a religious rhetorical style, to 'everyday' talk. These genres are particularly interesting as they represent socially constructed oral reading styles, which demonstrate yet another way in which literacy affects the linguistic repertoire of a people. At the far end of the scale are animated dialogues, which in many ways demonstrate musical features. All genres but the animated conversation occur in the context of the church, and many forms *only* within a church context: there is no chanting, little oral reading, and virtually no singing outside the religious context. As the Anglican church took hold in the Severn area by the turn of the century, these varieties represent relatively recent genres.

While religion is discussed more or less indirectly in chapters 4 through 6, chapter 7 addresses the institution directly through speeches and sermons delivered by people from Lynx Lake to their peers along with metacommentary about them. The previous chapters are predominantly descriptive, outlining a complex linguistic situation, focusing on linguistic resources and language use. Chapter 7 addresses issues of ethnographic research, demonstrating how, through the study of naturally occurring Native-to-Native discourse, an outsider can best gain access to the cultural insider's world-view. Previous analyses of Severn religious systems have neglected the discourse of the people and, in doing so, have skewed the published results, ironically in an effort to show the 'real' Native religion. The community of Lynx Lake is strongly Anglican (not to be read as 'Euro-Canadian Anglican'): this identification with Christianity has become an important part of the community's Native identity. The association with the Church of England provides many economic and social benefits to the community, which have given Lynx Lake prestige throughout the Severn region.

Included is a discussion of the 'folklorization of ethnicity,' the redefinition of Native identity on the basis of difference from some other group – in this case, Euro-Canadian society. The folklorization of ethnicity has been confined to more southerly Ojibwe groups, many of whom are in the process of losing their aboriginal languages. The two most salient cultural systems around which Amerindian groups build their identity are language and religion: as languages are lost, religion then becomes primary in ethnic identification. Thus, occasionally, Native groups of Southern Ontario look to the culturally Christian Natives in the north and declare them to be 'selling out to the White man' when, indeed, these people see no conflict in being Native and Christian. Indeed, being Christian is a part of being Native in Lynx Lake. However, with more contact between the groups, ethnicity may yet become an issue for the Severn Ojibwe people, with resulting redefinitions. Discourse is central throughout these discussions, as the focus of ethnographic methodology and in the working out of religious practice within the community.

Chapters 8 and 9 move from discourse within the community to discourse-internal structuring. In chapter 8, a first-person narrative is analysed using a Labovian model, with a further focus on rhetorical structures such as syntactic and semantic parallelism, chiasmus, and direct discourse. Also included are a discussion of metanarrative devices and a comparison of first-person narratives and myth and legends. In chapter 9, Severn emic categories of genre, overtly provided in the metanarrative frames of most narratives, are discussed along with other indexical devices which connect narrative with the here and now of the storytelling situation. Also addressed are transcription conventions, structuring and rhetorical devices associated with *aatisoohkaanan* (myth/legends), and extragrammatical features, including laughter, pauses, and storytelling tempo.

In the concluding chapter, the use of discourse as a tool in sociocultural analysis and the interplay between ethnographic research and discourse analysis are addressed. In light of these issues, methodologies of discourse analysis used in the earlier chapters are critically examined. Given the variation in discourse genre, context, and analytic goals, no one methodology is applicable. Thus, as researchers who focus on discourse, we must continue to expand and experiment with new techniques and methodologies to illuminate the place of discourse in society.

A formal linguistic study of discourse indexes crucial aspects of social life, just as the cultural context provides the key to understanding the discourse. By focusing on a community's discourse, the anthropologist avoids many of the problems inherent in ethnographic research. With an understanding of community life in Lynx Lake, opportunities for gathering naturally occurring discourses were easily found, and in fact, because of the interest in Native media, my services as an anthropologist, whose primary means of collecting data was with an 8-mm video camera, were often solicited by the Native community as a means to record events for their own use across the broader Severn community.

In studying a variety of discourse genres, the need for multiple analytic approaches became clear: approaches utilized here include conversational analysis; ethnopoetic investigation, including pause structuring and form–content parallelism; aspects of text analysis; a Labovian analysis of a first-person narrative; and a statistical sociolinguistic analysis of code switching. Given the range of data, no single approach is adequate.

CONTRIBUTIONS OF THIS STUDY

One of the advantages of conducting research through naturally occurring discourse is the lack of preconceived programs in conducting fieldwork. Instead of having the research agenda guide the discourse, the discourse guides the research. This discourse-guided and -centred study of the Lynx Lake community furthers linguistic, anthropological, and folkloric research in the following ways:

1. As a study in the ethnography of speaking, this research centres on a completely viable North American Indian community, one of few left today. Unlike other ethnography of speaking studies conducted in the Americas, this one focuses on a speech community whose verbal forms have not been considered particularly remarkable; that is, unlike Kuna, Chamula, and Afro-American English Vernacular traditions, where language variety and language play organize much

of the social life of the speakers, the generic repertoire of the Severn
Ojibwe tends to be more subtly marked. At most, the Severn people
are known for the content of a relatively modest corpus of myth/
legends; they are not yet known for their rhetorical style, their artistic
verbal forms, or, traditionally, for elaborated ceremonial language,
even at the level of curing ceremonies. This study demonstrates that,
although Severn Ojibwe people are not known for elaborated types of
talk, such elaboration exists. Because of this difference in the aware-
ness of centrality of language in social life, it was necessary to look at
many different aspects of language use in the community, giving the
book its particular character. So, though the variation in styles found
in Lynx Lake may be at some level more subtle than that among other
groups; this subtlety allows for a broader look at minor, but important
generic differences that may be missed in a group whose several
heavily marked genres are selected as the exclusive focus of research.

2. This study gives evidence that, within the context of change, through
   contact with other Native communities and with Euro-Canadians,
   linguistic forms have become more rather than less elaborated. In
   Lynx Lake, there are now evidently more linguistic genres than there
   were prior to contact. Some of these genres, although initially imported, have become central both to Lynx Lake and to the broader
   Severn community. These forms have been transformed and
   indigenized, and are now perceived as entirely local.

3. This study provides an interesting ethnographic study of literacy in a
   non-Indo-European tradition. Lynx Lake is of particular importance
   as the community is known as the centre of literacy for the entire
   Severn Ojibwe region. The syllabic literary tradition extends back to
   the turn of the century, long before the people of the Lynx Lake
   Band were settled into a community. This study not only outlines the
   place of literacy in the community, but also provides one of the first
   discussions of the oral aspects of literacy in a non-Western society.

4. This study documents a unique Amerindian community which has
   undergone major changes in social structure, economic base, and
   technology, all within just a couple of decades. By looking at the
   technology of talk, we discover insights into the indigenization of
   technology, which might otherwise be interpreted as acculturation
   towards a Western lifestyle.

5. A final, but important, issue addressed in this book involves the ethics
   of ethnographic reporting, in particular the obligation to accept and
   report accurately Native choices and changes in lifestyles. One change

addressed here is especially delicate: the people described here have adopted Christianity as their major religious paradigm. Ethnographers must allow for all types of religious expression that occur, even in ethnographic documentation where the tendency towards cathartic diatribes against non-Native religious systems seem so compelling. While we have the right to make judgments about aspects of our Western culture as members of that culture, and we have a right to judge people of our own culture on the way they interact with other cultures (e.g., the means by which missionaries have proselytized), we have no right to judge another culture on whether or not its members have adopted outside systems. As ethnographers, our responsibility is to provide an accurate representation of a culture, regardless of our personal biases. Through the study of discourse, one finds both the means of discovering how a community is presenting itself to itself and the means of describing the community.

In many ways, this was a difficult book to write – I found that I must speak with the voices of people whose words I can only imperfectly express, and I am making public the lives of a very private community, a community which allowed me to do research on the basis of a continuing friendship which I do not wish to betray. Throughout the writing of this study, I have attempted to present materials of interest to two audiences, to the people of Lynx Lake and to the academic community. When in the position of having to choose between the two, I have consistently chosen a Native audience as primary. In doing so, and in recognition of my role as a cultural outsider, I have often chosen description over generalization or symbolic analysis. I consider this an ethical decision which has arisen out of my deep respect for these people. Indeed, I have been faulted for presenting too optimistic a picture of this community, for focusing on the strengths rather than the weaknesses, unlike the trend that is so common in portrayals of contemporary First Nations peoples. However, given the plethora of materials presenting Native peoples of North America as broken by colonialism and lacking in hope, power, or dignity, I am willing to err on the side of positivity (though not positivism) in presenting a perspective of an empowered community of people, who, for the most part, view themselves as such.

The place of religion in the community of Lynx is unique in relation to other Severn Ojibwe communities of Northern Ontario. Whereas many of the Severn communities have a long history of missionization, resulting in the establishment of often multiple, and sometimes conflicting, churches in the communities, Lynx Lake has resisted efforts to divide the community's religious loyalties: these loyalties were unified many years before the group had settled into community life at Mihshamihkowiihsh in the 1930s. In light of the major role that the Anglican church plays in Lynx Lake, it is heavily represented here, although this was not what I intended or desired to do. This issue is even more complex than it might appear on the surface. Just as the power structures in Lynx Lake allow outsiders access to the community according to their goals and expectations, the fact that I had obtained permission to contact the community from the Anglican bishop in Kenora prior to approaching Lynx Lake was a primary factor in the willing and immediate acceptance of my presence in the community. My work within the community, which included, within the first month of arriving, working in the Band office on a proposal for a laundromat, was as a linguistic and anthropological researcher. Indeed, I entered the community to learn Ojibwe in order to conduct a dialect survey of all the Ojibwe dialects across Canada, a project which was funded by the National Museums of Canada (see R. Valentine 1994). Because of suspicion in many anthropological circles that someone who is willing to identify with a majority religion cannot do a legitimate ethnography, I initially did not want to deal with religion in the community at all. However, in order to do an ethnography of Lynx Lake, I realized that I had to deal with this extremely important institution, as would any ethnographer who came into that community.

The real difficulty in writing to an academic audience about the predominant religious system of Lynx Lake is that that system is defined by the audience as Christian. While Anglicanism in Lynx Lake is, as any religious system would be, locally constructed, the locality may not be immediately apparent to the reader who wishes to construe some external agenda. While I present the local religious organization in a positive way, I do so based on my understanding of the ways in which the Lynx Lake community views itself, and would like to be presented. Because of my experiences in Lynx Lake, I feel compelled to make a strong statement for the rights of Native people to make choices which may or may not reflect continuous Native traditions. This marks a deviation from tendencies of some anthropologists working in Native North America, who, professing to speak for the people, insist that the only legitimate expressions of Native religion are those of indigenous origin. This view has resulted in studies which downplay, ignore, or even denigrate any non-Native influences. Again, the issues are multilayered and extremely complex.

The members of the Lynx Lake Band are innovative and ingenious people who seek out changes that make life more fun, more productive, and easier. They are, in a very real sense, in charge of their own lives. Often they accept outside influences, occasionally they reject them outright, but the choice is always their own. In the midst of enormous changes, there is no indication that they feel they are losing their Native identity or even that they necessarily have or need to produce a 'Native' identity; rather, they are *actively* incorporating change into their lives. Contact with other people has increased the number of genres in Severn Ojibwe, in a sense strengthening the language while allowing for new genres. Lynx Lake is indeed unique.

This is not, however, an idyllic community: between 1987 and 1990 four young men hanged themselves, causing great concern to the community as a whole. As a result of these tragedies, one chief resigned his office, and several council members suffered bouts of depression. Such tragedies are not unique; the suicide rate among young men is at epidemic proportions across the Severn region. Successful suicides in the region were limited to the young male population until 1991, when the first young woman killed herself, opening up even more terrifying prospects for the young. Despite the evidence that underlying troubles are plaguing the young people who have not been grounded in the Severn landscape through life on the traplines, the people of Lynx Lake are overwhelmingly happy to remain in the community: very few people chose to leave the village. Lynx Lake is seen by other Severn communities as a model of good business administration and of strong church leadership, and as being at the vanguard in adopting and adapting new ideas and technologies to daily Severn life.

Ultimately, the aim of this research is to provide an empirically based, synchronic overview of a community in the midst of rapid social change. Through the study of discourses originating within the community, we are allowed a perspective on social and cultural change which is, for an outsider, at times surprising. The self-empowering adoption and adaptation of new technologies present unique reversals of expectation about change in a Native community where the importation of apparently Western technologies does not give rise to 'acculturation' or a loss of Native identity. Rather, we find in the community-directed discourses that originally external technologies are transformed to fit the world of the Lynx Lake people. It is just such transformations to a Native world-view that are documented in this book.

Chapter Two

Overview: Severn Ojibwe and the People of Lynx Lake

My first sight of Lynx Lake was from the window a Twin Otter plane as it circled over the village on a rainy morning in late summer. Inside the airplane was the entire cadre of Band administration workers, from the Band administrator to the chief and all the Band councillors. As we circled over the village in preparation for what was to be my first water landing, I was taken, first, by the sight of colourful houses interspersed with stands of spruce and birch; by the slender, drying tree trunks perched in conical stands that appeared as teepees to my uninitiated eyes; and by the sight of outhouses in various stages of ageing. As we approached the dock, I was intrigued by the faces of the people who lined it and who appeared to fill the entire hillside rising gently behind it. I still remember the older women, dressed in bright flower-print skirts, their heads covered by colourful scarves knotted beneath their chins. These women stood, hands outstretched, as my husband and I, carrying my two-year-old daughter, followed the Band officials from the airplane. The image of these women was so strongly etched in my mind that I was later able to name them in the order that they greeted me and shook my hand. I was amazed at the seeming quiet, given the number of people, at least 150, at the dock that day. It wasn't until years later that I realized the reception was not for the Band officials, but for us, these *kihci-moohkomaanak* (Americans) who were coming to live in their community – not as transient teachers, but simply as guests.

After being greeted by the elders, I noticed the people my age and younger – they were dressed in a uniform of wide-legged blue-jeans and Levi's blue-jean jackets that year. Except for one young woman who had been assigned the task of showing us around, none spoke to us, or to each other during that long walk up the hillside. It was during this walk that I became conscious of the combination of odours I have ever after associated with Lynx Lake – damp earth, woodsmoke, and spruce needles. During the next couple of years in the Lynx Lake community, I was gently and graciously tutored by these same people who had greeted us at the dock. To this day I still think of the flora and fauna of Ontario first in Ojibwe, then in English translation. But, more than just a language, I was taught about being connected to the land, to one's family, to one's community. It was this instruction that changed my outlook, and indeed my world, for ever.

INTRODUCTION TO OJIBWE

Despite pressures from governmental agencies, educational systems, White traders, missionaries, and even some Native peoples themselves, to use a majority language, Ojibwe remains one of the three most viable Native American languages spoken in North America today, alongside Cree and Inuktitut. Ojibwe and Cree are both members of the Algonquian language family, which is spoken over a wide area of central Canada and the United States. One common denominator among Ojibwe, Cree, and Inuktitut – perhaps the primary contributing factor for language viability – is the relative physical isolation from the matrix English- or French-speaking society. There are very few White people willing, or able, to endure life 'in the bush,' where amenities such as indoor plumbing, electricity, and proximity to commercial centres are rare. Where the Native people view the land as sustaining them, the typical Euro-Canadian has focused on only the harsh climate and social isolation, often to the benefit of the Native peoples who have made the northern Subarctic and Arctic their homes. However, even this is changing as resources as diverse as gold, oil, and water for hydro-electric power beckon the White entrepreneur to create extractive industries in the heart of Native lands. This tendency is evident even among researchers, whose work often benefits the academic world more than the Native people with whom they have lived and worked.

The physical isolation has been a very real deterrent to language loss among the Ojibwe. Estimates of Ojibwe population range from 41,000 to 52,000, with about a third of those coming from the United States, where they are more commonly called Chippewa (Chafe 1965). A recent study of aboriginal languages in Canada (Phillips 1985) gives a figure of 19,385 for those Native people who claim Ojibwe as their native tongue, with 13,440 of these currently using Ojibwe as the language of the home. Of those who use Ojibwe in the home, some 8,000 come from one of the seventeen Severn Ojibwe communities, none of which has a year-round road to link it with towns to the south. In fact, not one of these villages is serviced even by rail, which, elsewhere in Canada, is usually the first step in linking villages with the larger Euro-Canadian community. In more southerly Ojibwe reserves, the ones with the least access to White communities – for example, reserves along the Canadian National Railway which have no other roads; reserves in the Lake of the Woods area in the far southwest corner of Ontario, where there are relative few and widely separated Euro-Canadian towns in the vicinity; and reserves in the Berens River region, where again there are a few small and widely separated Euro-Canadian communities – have the strongest Native language use.

Ojibwe is one of seven Central Algonquian languages, which include Cree-Montagnais-Naskapi, Potawatomi, Menominee, Fox-Sauk-Kikapoo, Miami-Illinois, and Shawnee and Ojibwe, a grouping based more on historical geographic proximity than on genetic relationships. Of the Central Algonquian languages, only Ojibwe and Potawatomi may form a distinct genetic subgrouping; that is, they share a few innovations beyond Proto-Algonquian, which is assumed to have been spoken between 2,500 and 3,000 years ago (Goddard 1978).

Through many years of contact, beginning with White trappers and missionaries in the mid 1600s to the present, the Ojibwe have been designated by many different names, including Ojibwe (also spelled 'Ojibway' and 'Ojibwa'), Chippewa, Saulteaux, Ottawa (Odawa), Algonquin, Nipissing, Mississauga, Ojicree, and even Cree. At the time of contact, some of these names were already well established, but particularly in earlier documents, labels were given cavalierly, causing considerable confusion about identity of Ojibwe people. The phenomenon of one group's adopting another's name has compounded the historic confusion in determining which people were being referred to by a given designation. This tendency to adopt the name of a neighbouring group is found elsewhere among the Ojibwe: the Native peoples in the communities of Golden Lake and Maniwaki are called Algonquin, although they are clearly linguistically distinguishable from the Algonquin north of them; the Ottawa call themselves Ojibwe, but differ linguistically from other populations of Ojibwe in their vicinity; and some Severn peoples call themselves Cree in English (Rhodes and Todd 1981). In all these cases a southern group has adopted the name of the adjacent northern people, which is usually the more prestigious of the two dialects. The northern group also tends to be the one with the historically later European contact.

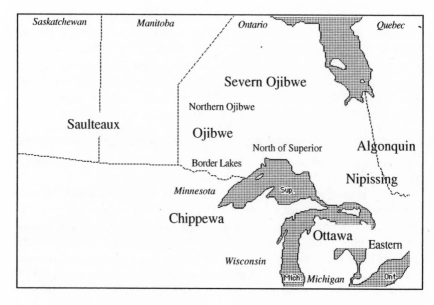

MAP 1 Ojibwe Linguistic Groups

INTRODUCTION TO OJIBWE LANGUAGE VARIATION

Recent linguistic work in Ojibwe language variation (R. Valentine 1994) suggests that Ojibwe falls into two primary groups, northern and southern. The primary northern grouping includes Algonquin and Severn Ojibwe. (See map 1 for rough locations.) The southern grouping includes Chippewa (and Eastern Ojibwe), Odawa, and Saulteaux. Between the northern and southern groups are transitional areas which, in some cases, form definable subdialects. Among these is a group of communities in northwestern Ontario which could be broadly grouped as Northern Ojibwe. In the east, the Nipissing dialect shows a mixture of northern and southern features. Note that any discussion of dialects is problematic as they are not homogeneous: in all cases one finds transitions within and across dialect boundaries. In addition, labelling dialects is extremely difficult as there continues to be no consensus as to the use of names, or an individual community's identification with a given dialect over another. However, of all the groupings mentioned, the Severn Ojibwe region is undoubtedly the most distinctive Ojibwe dialect on the basis of unique phonological, lexical, and morphological forms.

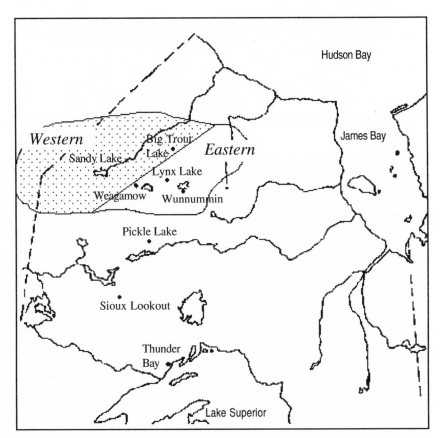

MAP 2 Severn Ojibwe Area

INTRODUCTION TO SEVERN OJIBWE

Severn Ojibwe, the most northern of all Ojibwe dialects, is linguistically the most distant and distinct from the others. The dialect is named for the Severn River drainage area, which covers much of inland Northern Ontario above the fiftieth parallel, extending from northeastern Manitoba east and north into Hudson Bay. (See map 2.)

Because the Severn River drainage system is marked by vast expanses of muskeg, sphagnum moss–covered bogs, lakes, and rivers, no Severn community is yet accessible by permanent road or rail: access to these communities is exclusively by air, except in particularly cold winters, when some communities forge temporary roads for heavy tractors and trailers which can only then safely travel the frozen waterways.

This forced insulation of the approximately 8,000 Severn Ojibwe people from heavy outside contact has been a major factor in maintaining the linguistic viability. Indeed, based on the figures for Ojibwe speakers in Canada, Severn Ojibwe people constitute more than half of the total number of Ojibwe speakers. The language used in the Berens River Ojibwe region is the next most viable; it is spoken in communities located immediately south of Severn, along the Berens River drainage system, which flows westward into Lake Winnipeg. Berens and Severn Ojibwe are mutually intelligible, despite major differences in intonation and somewhat less immediate differences in morphology, phonology and lexicon.

The two major subdialects of Severn Ojibwe, Winisk and Severn (terms used by Nichols [1975]), are differentiated by a few superficial features of phonology, morphology, and lexicon. (See map 2 for locations.) One such feature is the treatment of nasal and obstruent clusters. The western subdialect has nasal clusters only in verbs of thinking (e.g., *kitinentaan,* 'you think so'), a feature shared among other Ojibwe dialects *only* by some Algonquin communities, but in the eastern Severn subdialect, sometimes called the 'n-dialect,' nasal clusters are commonly found allowing for such shibboleths as the western *maak,* 'loon,' and the eastern *maank,* 'loon.' The western dialect without the nasal clusters is considered the prestige dialect, perhaps owing to the perceived similarity to Cree phonology. (See chapter 4 for further discussion.)

HISTORICAL BACKGROUND OF THE SEVERN OJIBWE

Early historical records of the Ojibwe in Canada, dating back to the mid 1600s, come from two primary sources, the Hudson's Bay Company and French Jesuit missionaries. The earliest of these records locates the Ojibwe in areas around Lake Superior across to the area north of Lake Huron and east to Georgian Bay. The geographic location of these Ojibwe appears to correspond with that of the Southern Ojibwe dialect group noted below. The westward movement of Ojibwe (Saulteaux) into Manitoba and Saskatchewan was well documented. Far less documentation of Northern Ojibwe groups is available, the most notable being reports of Algonquins in the border areas between Ontario and Quebec, the location of contemporary Algonquins. In these early written sources, there is little documentation of people living in the northwest woodland region of Ontario, the area occupied by the contemporary Severn Ojibwe group.

The early documents which discuss the northwest woodland area simply call the people of that region 'Cree.' In general, this name has been taken to indicate the specific linguistic and cultural group of Cree, either Swampy or Moose Cree. However, this may have been an error. Many contemporary Severn Ojibwe call themselves Cree, even though they recognize that their language is different from that of the Cree who live to north and east of them along Hudson Bay and James Bay. While Severn Ojibwe and Cree are substantially different from each other, they share some highly salient linguistic features, including aspects of morphology, many discourse particles, and a considerable corpus of lexical items. Thus, differences between Severn Ojibwe and southern Ojibwe groups lead to a perception by the latter that Severn Ojibwe is a form of Cree. With increased contact between Severn and other Ojibwe dialects recently introduced through media such as Native-language newspapers, radio and television, speakers of Severn Ojibwe seem to be shifting their linguistic identity more towards the Ojibwe than towards the Cree.[1]

INTRODUCTION TO THE LYNX LAKE BAND

The Lynx Lake Indian Reserve is located approximately 160 miles south of Hudson Bay and 250 miles north of Thunder Bay in north-central Ontario, Canada, within the Laurentian Plateau.[2] Lynx Lake and all other Severn Ojibwe communities are located in the boreal forest, a circumpolar ecological zone often referred to as 'the taiga.' Northern Ontario is covered by numerous lakes, created by retreating glaciers, which are surrounded by forests of black spruce, jack pine, and white birch interspersed with muskeg, bogs of sphagnum moss (Winterhalder 1983).

The Lynx Lake Indian Band is located on one of the smaller reservations, or reserves, as they are called in Canada, in Northern Ontario, covering an area of almost 17,300 acres, about half the area of the average of the seventeen Severn reserves. The community's population of about three hundred people is also considered somewhat small, even by Northern Ontario standards. Despite its small size, this is a community whose presence is felt across Northern Ontario. Not only was Lynx Lake the first Severn community to buy out the local Hudson's Bay Company store so that they might channel the monies back into the community for community-based projects which would train and employ local labour, it also boasts the highest-ranking Native Anglican minister, an archdeacon, in all Ontario dioceses. This tiny community is known even to members of Parliament in Ottawa, Canada's national capital, 840 miles away. Along with the Native population, there is usually a transient Euro-Canadian population of two or three teachers, occasionally accompanied by a spouse or child, who spend an average of two school years in the community. Since the fall of 1988, the school has been under Band control, so there may be fewer non-Native teachers in the future.

As is true of the Severn area generally, Lynx Lake is quite remote, located one hundred air miles north of the nearest paved road and accessible only by airplane. The physical remoteness described for Lynx Lake is representative of that of all Severn communities: its closest neighbour is another Severn village, Kaa-miskwaapihkaak Lake, thirty miles to the east. To the west, sixty miles distant, is Weagamow, and sixty miles north, Namekosipiink. Until the fall of 1987, when the Lynx Lake airport was unoffically opened, all incoming planes landed on the lake, either on pontoons in the short summers, or on skis on the three and a half feet of ice that forms on the lake in the winter. The airport is an important acquisition for the community as it allows easier access for the vast quantity of Euro-Canadian goods shipped in by plane each year. No longer is the flow stemmed by freeze-up, the transitional period in the fall when the lake freezes over, often lasting up to six weeks, or by break-up, the period during which the ice loses its stability, breaking up into millions of long crystal chimes which are swept across the lake by the brisk but warming winds of spring.

By 1965 the trees around the settlement on the south side of Mihshamihkowiihsh Lake, the location of a camp trade post for the Hudson's Bay Company, were almost gone, having been used to heat the dwellings of the people who lived there at different times during the year. The situation was so critical that the community had to relocate, and by April 1965, the last group of people moved from the settlement to the community of Lynx Lake, about six miles to the east. This was the beginning of a new way of life for many of the people. Whereas previously families had been widely separated, many living on their traplines for at least nine months of each year, suddenly they were congregated in a single settlement at Lynx Lake for all but a couple of months of the year. The catalysts for change were many, but the most far reaching was Canada's legislation of universal education, which resulted in a school being opened at Lynx Lake that year, with attendance mandatory.

Almost everyone in Lynx Lake aged thirty and older vividly remembers the move from Mihshamihkowiihsh to the present location. Originally, the community had planned to move across Lynx Lake to Mataapiitinaank ('Esker that goes into the water,' see map 3 for the location). However, the site of the current village was found to have all of the advantages of Mataapiitinaank, including visibility from atop an esker which created a

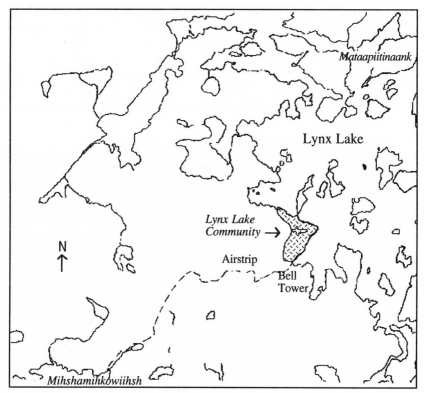

MAP 3 Lynx Lake

point extending into Lynx Lake. This location had good fishing and available wood, with the further advantage that it was on the near side of Lynx Lake, making the move that much easier. The community at Mihshamihkowiihsh was divided into two sections, roughly along family lines: one of the groups had become considerably more sedentary than the other, spending much of the year around the Hudson's Bay Company camp trade outlet established in a small log structure.[3] Members of this group were the initial settlers of the Lynx Lake community. The second group at Mihshamihkowiihsh, whose traplines were to the north of both Mihshamihkowiihsh and Lynx Lake, tended to continue their year-round hunting/trapping lifestyles through 1965, as a few members do even to the present. It was this latter group that completed the community move from Mihshamihkowiihsh to Lynx Lake, their belongings strapped to dog sleds and tied in canoes for the mass exodus on that spring day in 1965.

Evidence for the separation of these two groups is reflected even today in the arrangement of the Lynx Lake community, which is split along an approximately north–south axis. The first group which settled at Lynx Lake is the larger of the two, constituting about three-fourths of the population. This group lives to the south and east of the tip of the esker down to the shore of the lake. Almost all these frame houses are situated along three parallel dirt roads which ultimately intersect with the one leading westward to the airport, and beyond, to Mihshamihkowiihsh. Members of the second group settled along the northern shore of the point. Here the houses have been built farther apart along the inland side of the single, dead-end road which follows the lake northwest about a half-mile. This geographic division is echoed in several lexical items which distinguish the two groups as well.[4]

The people of Lynx Lake have seen enormous changes in their lives with the influx of new technology. As innovations became available to the people of the Severn area, they were eagerly incorporated into daily life. Rifles and mass-produced canoes were some of the earliest innovations which made life easier: now only the oldest members of the community remember using bows and arrows for hunting, and canoe building is a skill of the past. Steel traps from the Hudson's Bay Company were efficient and easier to use than traditional deadfalls and other hand-made wooden traps. Store-bought cloth blankets, while not necessarily warmer than the traditional hand-woven rabbit-skin blankets, were for the most part far easier to obtain, especially in years when rabbits were scarce. Many of these innovations meant the difference between starvation and death and survival in the harsh taiga. Indeed, the Severn Ojibwe people may have moved into the relatively harsh region of inland northwestern Ontario as a part of the general expansions caused by the fur trade. In this area, where vegetal resources are extremely scarce, both small and large game may be found, though local fluctuations in game have always been common, often causing temporary but severe hardships for individual families. The use of imported goods in hunting, fishing, and trapping has often meant the difference between life and death.

The more recent innovations, equal in scope to the availability of rifles, have also had enormous impact on the people of Lynx Lake. One young man, aged thirty-two, told me of his first sight of a snowmobile in about 1964. He and his family were on the trail, moving their campsite from one area in their territory to another. A messenger came by to break the exciting news that a young man from a neighbouring trapline was going to come along the road on his snowmobile. When the boy heard the sound of the motor in the distance, he jumped off the trail, expecting the enormous and powerful machine to run over him. When he finally saw "H. on this little red Bombardier," he laughed at how insignificant the snowmobile appeared. The impact of the machine was not insignificant, however: within five years, the snowmobile had rendered dog-sledding obsolete. Fifteen years later, I independently collected texts from two of the first men to purchase snowmobiles (called either *iskitoo* [pl. *-n*, inanimate], after the brand-name Skidoo, or *otaapaan* [pl. *-ak*, animate]). In their narratives each man was careful to establish his own position as being either the first or the second person to buy the machine, which was then, as now, a symbol of prestige. These statements were presented as points of pride for the far-sighted use of new technology.

Since the move to Lynx Lake in 1965, many other changes have come about in the lifestyles of the people of the community. Most of these changes are viewed positively by the people of Lynx Lake. There is no indication that by accepting the changes the people of Lynx Lake have 'given up' any part of their identity as Natives. When elders describe the old days, their stories recount instances of extreme hardship and are often closed with statements of how much easier and better life has become with chain-saws, snowmobiles, motor boats, insulated houses, and year-round access to the store food. If anyone yearns for the old days, he need only fly, boat, or snowmobile out to his trapline. That lifestyle is still available for those who desire it, and many families spend weeks, and even months, in the bush to this day – but from choice, not necessity.

Today, wages gained from local employment in the Band Office, Band store, as construction workers, in the school or church, or from social welfare finance most daily needs. Hunting and trapping are considered secondary income sources for all but a few members of the community. Today hunting for meat is considered of greater importance than hunting for furs, the cash crop of yesteryear (cf. Brody 1981). This situation has changed even within the last decade as animal-rights activism has helped drive the price of pelts to unforeseen lows. Government social-welfare money is particularly important for the elderly. At the Band level, governmental grants provide money for many large and small community projects, projects which have made Lynx Lake a model of economic development. So it is that, by 1988, the community of Lynx Lake had made a fundamental change from a disaggregating Band society to sedentary community life.

LINGUISTIC REPERTOIRE

The remote location of Lynx Lake has allowed for extreme viability of the aboriginal language, which may be illustrated by noting that every Native member of the community uses Severn Ojibwe within the home, and that most use it in *all* daily transactions. While Severn Ojibwe is the language of the home, and usually the language of all interaction, English has gained some foothold in the community. The school, initially set up in the 1960s, uses English in its teaching, thereby heavily exposing students from kindergarten through the ninth grade to this language. Certain members in the community use English in business transactions, especially the store personnel (in 1988 this included five males from ages twenty-five to forty-five) and Band office workers (approximately five females, aged twenty to thirty, and five males, aged thirty to forty-five.) However, it is only in these and two other positions (teacher's aide and medical worker) that English has been necessary, and even then it is needed only in interacting with White government workers, outside suppliers, medical personnel, and teachers.

Other languages used in the community are the Swampy, Moose, and Plains dialects of Cree, a language closely related to Ojibwe, but not necessarily mutually intelligible with it.[5] Moose and Plains Cree are liturgical languages, used in the local Anglican church. The Bible is written in Plains Cree, the *Anglican Prayer Book* used in worship services is in Moose Cree, and the two hymnals are in Plains and Moose Cree. Swampy Cree, spoken in the areas north of the Severn Ojibwe region along Hudson Bay, is also used by The Venerable William Pipoon, an archdeacon in the Anglican church. The Venerable William Pipoon is a Native Lynx Lake Band member who speaks both Severn Ojibwe and Swampy Cree. His facility in Cree has come through years of studying the Cree Bible and through extensive contact with Swampy Cree people in his capacity as catechist, then priest, and later archdeacon in Northern Ontario.

The Severn Ojibwe use a syllabic writing system originally designed for Ojibwe but now generally associated with Cree, which has a phonological system similar to, in particular, the Northern Ojibwe dialects such as Severn.[6] The use of the hymn-books, the prayer-book, and the Bible contributes to the reading proficiency in syllabics. Because of the number of important documents used by the Severn people that are written in Cree, Cree is held in extremely high esteem.[7] Especially through the efforts of The Venerable William Pipoon, the church has been instrumental in establishing a high rate of literacy in the Native language among the Lynx Lake population. (For further information on literacy in the community of Lynx Lake, see chapter 5. A brief typological sketch of key Severn Ojibwe linguistic structures is located in appendix 1.)

Chapter Three

Technology and Talk: Technological Change and Emerging Speech Events in Lynx Lake

Unlike many other Native communities in North America, Lynx Lake has not yet experienced Western contact through territorial encroachment so much as through selective instigation by the community itself. As noted in the previous chapter, the non-Native population in Lynx Lake is normally limited to two or three elementary-school teachers who reside in the community only while school is in session, from September through mid-December, and again from early January through June. During a typical year, perhaps ten to twenty different Euro-Canadians make their way into the community for visits ranging from a couple of hours to a couple of days. However, more than three times this number of locals fly out to different Euro-Canadian communities yearly. The favourite towns to visit are Thunder Bay and Sioux Lookout in Ontario, and Winnipeg, Manitoba. Young people who leave do so to attend secondary-school programs in one of several residential schools. Adults who leave Lynx Lake do so to attend various Native meetings, including chiefs' meetings, religious instructional seminars, and the like, and to shop for everything from groceries and toys to church organs and pick-up trucks – all items which are later flown into the community at a shipping rate of about fifty cents per pound. With few exceptions, the people of Lynx Lake who leave the community come back. Lynx Lake is seen as a haven by its inhabitants.

Technology has come into the village at the Band's discretion, not at the insistence of some White agency. For example, as early as 1980, Ontario Hydro – a major electric company – offered to electrify the village. The Lynx Lake Band administration refused the offer as they felt that, by allowing Ontario Hydro into the community, the Band would lose some control over its resources. In 1986, the Band bought several large generators and set up their own electrical system. They did not fear the technology; rather, their refusal was based on the rejection of the opening for Euro-Canadian control of the technology. By 1988, the Band had decided that perhaps the electrical system offered by Ontario Hydro might be cheaper for the Band overall, so were only then considering inviting Ontario Hydro's presence – but only if they could set the parameters within which Ontario Hydro would work. A similar situation occurred regarding the airstrip. The Band refused to put an airstrip in the community – despite the availability of funds for this purpose – until 1987, when they determined that the community was ready for the increased traffic the airstrip would allow. This is the same community that created a corporation and bought out the Hudson's Bay Company store – the only store in Lynx Lake – and turned it into a Band-owned and -operated enterprise which funnels tens of thousands of dollars back into the community in the form of new businesses and projects each year.

The significance of these economic decisions is that the community of Lynx Lake is hardly a powerless pawn being overrun by a Euro-Canadian presence. The level of self-determination seen in these areas is also evident in the adoption and adaptation of new media in the community. With this background in place, we now turn to the technology associated with talk.

In Lynx Lake – as in most societies – knowledge is power. The accumulation of knowledge comes with the years, giving elders a privileged position in the community. Much of the respect given to elders is a recognition of the wisdom accrued through their years on this earth. In Lynx Lake, both young and old still value the knowledge of the elders – knowledge of how to live on the earth, both physically and spiritually. In places where youths no longer show respect for elders, it tends to be the case that the young people no longer value or see as relevant to daily life the knowledge of the elders. In my own culture, this lack of respect for elders has become the norm. One reason that youth is so highly valued is that it is the young who understand and can manipulate new technologies and thereby control the world around them. In Lynx Lake, the important technologies are still controlled by the elders, and they maintain the power associated with knowledge of relevant technologies.

The term 'moccasin telegraph' was coined by someone impressed by how quickly and widely news travelled among Native people. This term is still used throughout North American Native communities, often as the title of news sheets distributed by Native groups. The movement of information within and outside a community continues to be a major concern among people in the Severn area and has been greatly aided in the last two decades by the Native-run organization Wawatay Native Communications Society.

The new technologies that have grown along with Severn communities have enabled many traditional forms of communication to continue despite changes in lifestyle from the seasonal migrations along family traplines to the relatively sedentary village life. Through community radio, younger people continue to learn from the stories told by elders, which earlier were narrated to the younger people lying around the fire inside a *matokwaan* (canvas-covered teepee) or *wiiskwehokaan* (canvas tent) in the evenings on the traplines. The intent of the storytelling sessions remains the same: the stories entertain while teaching moral values. The stories themselves are often unchanged, but the channel of communication has been greatly altered, providing even a wider audience for such narratives than before. As so many of the communication networks have become public in Lynx Lake, we have immediate access to data allowing for unique insights into community life that otherwise would not be so readily available.

The elder in his baseball cap and parka sits slightly hunched over, his eyes fixed on the table in front of him. His voice is quiet, with its intonational range compressed into an evenly paced monotone as he weaves his story, his *tipaacimowin.* Suddenly, the phone rings. The elder picks up the receiver and, after a very brief interchange, quickly reaches over to turn a dial on the console in front of him, then grasps his microphone a bit tighter and resumes his storytelling. Unbeknownst to him, the volume control at the radio station had been turned down between shows, but with his one minor adjustment, the elder's story was now heard clearly by the entire community.

The two institutions in the community of Lynx Lake that have had the greatest influence in creating new speech forms are the local Anglican church and the Wawatay Native Communications Society. Where the church has had its greatest influence on language in the areas of public oratory styles (see chapter 4), literacy (see chapter 5), and music (see chapter 6), the technological advances brought into the community by the Wawatay have influenced the more everyday speech events. This chapter focuses on communication flow in Lynx Lake, with particular emphasis on the technologies used, the history and place of each communication system within the community, the ways in which the systems are used within the village and across the broader Severn community, and the impact of these systems on language use. The investigation of Lynx Lake's adaptation of and to technological innovations provides insights into the cultural integrity that continues in all aspects of life despite rapid changes. This community welcomes technology as an extension of its own culture and explores new technology with an eye for its potential to improve the lives of its people. The old lifeways were simple but severe; the new ways may be complicated but in many ways are infinitely easier.

The study of communication networks in Lynx Lake opens a window into the working of social networks. In this region, information is viewed as a commodity to be shared judiciously: the person with the most knowledge has the most power in a situation. Hunters are powerful because they know the animals they are hunting and the land on which they hunt. Elders are powerful because, by the fact of their age, they are seen as having acquired a hard-won knowledge that has enabled them to live long on this earth. Older women are trusted with skinning the most prized game: their knowledge, gained through years of experience, allows them the privilege and right to skin the animal. Knowledge in all areas is typically gained through experience. The attendant authority is displayed and reinforced by public practice of that knowledge. Speaking publicly is considered a sign of authority, but, further, in its practice it accords more honour and authority to the speaker. People will speak publicly only about those areas of life in which they are recognized as authorities. This understanding of the authority of a public voice undergirds all discussions of individual discourses and the general discourse practices presented in this book.

WAWATAY TRAIL RADIOS (*Waawaahtewihkitowinan*)

One of the earliest innovations in communication to come to the Severn area was the high-frequency radio, known more commonly as the 'Wawatay trail radio.' The first high-frequency radio available to the members of Lynx Lake Band was owned by the Hudson's Bay Company and operated by the Euro-Canadian Bay manager, 'Willie,' back in the 1950s, when the community was still located at Mihshamihkowiihsh. Radios across the north became somewhat more common in the 1960s and 1970s, when the less expensive citizen-band radios came into popular use in Southern Ontario, and when the Sioux Lookout Friendship Centre began a pilot communication program in the early 1970s with the placement of six high-frequency radios in northern communities. This pilot project matured into the Wawatay Native Communications Society in 1974, which continued to support and distribute high-frequency and trail radios.

Trail radios are used in the most stereotypically traditional setting – on the trapline. The material value of this communication system is quite evident: the trail radios allow the hunters to maintain contact with primary communication networks. The following are some of the primary uses of the trail radio on the trapline:

1. Given an emergency medical situation on the trapline, the radio is used to signal for help. An airplane is usually only one call away from a sick or injured hunter.
2. Starvation is no longer a major threat in the bush. If supplies run low and game is scarce, the trail radio is used to arrange to have more supplies flown into camp, however remote it is.
3. With the new cash economy, men are usually employed in the village, making extended trips into the bush economically unreasonable. With charter airplanes readily accessible, the men can quickly transport themselves and their gear in and out of remote areas. As most men have jobs in the community, the duration of hunting trips tends to be tightly constrained, with both the beginning and ending dates of hunting trips set in advance. If the hunters are lucky in their hunting, however, there is no need to remain in the bush for the designated time, and the trail radio can be used to change scheduled pick-up times.

Wawatay rents out trail radios that are monitored in the community. In Lynx Lake in 1988, these units were located in the homes of the priest and the archdeacon. They were turned on at given times each day, times established by trappers on their way out to their traplines. The location of the radios in the homes of the foremost religious figures in the community reflects some of the importance that the church has in monitoring and influencing the communications networks throughout the Lynx Lake community. However, in May 1988, the Band got a licence to use a radio phone to contact other communities: the radio phone had been acquired eight years earlier, when the SocioEconomic Development Corporation of Lynx Lake bought out the local Hudson's Bay store. The radio has four bands: the first, band A, was the channel for the Thunder Bay operator; band B was the Hudson's Bay Company channel; and the other two bands were not pre-set.

In addition to the radio phone, citizen-band radios are also used on occasion. In the following excerpt from an account of a forest fire that broke out in 1981 near the community of Lynx Lake, we find that both the community FM radio and the citizen-band radio hold prominent positions. The radios mentioned in this discourse about a forest fire that broke out near the Lynx Lake village were crucial to the event, structuring the movements of many people mentioned in the text. This excerpt begins about a third of the way through the narrative:[1]

1981 kaa-kii-niipink kiih-sahkitepan ohomaa piko pehshonc naanta piko maasehsik peshikotipahaahkan kaah-piihsinaakwanikwen ihiwe ishkote. Mekwaac eh-aapihtaakiishikaakipan kaa-mate-onci-wiincikaatek antohtamowikamikonk "Mate-sahkite akaamink kahkiiw," mate-ihkitonaaniwan ...

In the summer of 1981, there was a forest fire near here, only about a mile away. During the noon hour it was announced at the radio station, "There is a fire across the way on the other side of the lake," it was said ...

Peshikwaa kiih-piishaamakanitok kaa-kiinikwaanaahkonikepanihoomakahk. Niishin wemihtikooshiwak kii-takohshinoopaniik, nahke piko aaniin kaa-tootamowaakopanen. Ohomaa ohsha wiin iko okii-ontinaanaa waakaa-kii-aahtawehikewaac naapewak aapacihcikanan. Siipii-kitowinan okiih-aapacihtoonaawaa kaa-aahtawehikewaac. Mii himaa wenci-kaah-kanoonitoowaac.

A helicopter came maybe one time. Two White men arrived, but I really don't know what they might have done. Th(e) [helicopter] was where the men who put the fire out got their tools. They used citizen-band radios when they put the fire out. That's what they called each other on.

The citizen-band radio was so important for the local fire-fighters in battling the fire that, when batteries ran low, it was necessary for the narrator to go by plane to the nearest community, thirty miles to the east of Lynx Lake, for replacement batteries:

Mekwaac ihiwe kaa-sahkitek ninkii-pasikwahominaapan Wanimanisaa-kihikaninink e-kii-naacipaatinihsiwey-aankipan. Mii hsha tahsh ihi kaa-pi-kiiweyaank nikiih-kiinikwaanii-minaapan ihimaa kaa-ishi-sahkitek ...

While the fire was still burning, we flew off to Kaa-miskwaapihkaak Lake to get batteries. And so when we came back home here, we flew around where the fire was burning ...

A very non-Native conception of the trail radio can be seen in the November 1988 edition of the *Wawatay News*, which led with a front-page article on the 'misuse' of trail radios, stating that "… some people with trail radios are abusing the HF (high frequency) radio system by using it as a telephone instead of an emergency communications tool."[2] Compare this perception with the following discourse, which provides a clear example of how the use of trail radios has become indigenized. The narrative portion presented here, taped off the local Lynx Lake radio station in 1983, was embedded within a story about the speaker's travels to several other Severn Ojibwe communities. The narrator is an outgoing, middle-aged woman, noted for her singing and her humour. She was scheduled to 'sit' (*api*) with her husband, but as he could not come to the radio station, she spent the entire hour alone, chatting easily about whatever came to mind. This excerpt begins about thirty-five minutes into the hour:

Kaawin hsha wiin aha piiwite kaa-kii-wiiciyaamak. Ehaa hsha otaanihsan Taaniyan Mihkinaak ohomaa kaa-kii-pi-ishaahpan. M-ohsha ahaweti kaa-kii-wiicihaamak.

Ekaa hsha-sh iko anihshaa e-okitowinic. Mii cika ahpan e-kaa-wiihkaa kaa-ponci-kanoonihshihpan: kaawin hsha okitowinihsiin. Ohoweni tawiin kaa-kiinikwaanaahkowe-panikaatenik. Kiihsh—Ayaan oti caakihsewan ankitaahsonan, ihkito. Kii-kiishkaapihkenikaatenikopan kaana hi okitowin; kaa-kii-onci-otaahpinikaatenik otankitaahson. Niishiniipaniin hsha ontan-kitaahsonan <Cough>wetawiin miina kaa-kii-ishaayaankipan. Ekwa ehta acina otayaan ehaa toohkaan Saayman kaa-ayaac kitowinini waawaahtewiyaahii. Mii iwe ani-eyaac ehta. Shaakoc amii maawac e-minwentaakwahk.

Keniin ahko eni-onci-ayantoht-amaan ahko kaa— kaa-ni-papimaahkohshinaan kaa-ani-tipihkaak e-antohtamakwaa ahko kaa-kakitowaac. <Laughter> Aana hsha

It was no stranger that I stayed with. She was the daughter of that guy Daniel Mihkinaak who came here. It was this one that I stayed with.

It is just that she didn't have a telephone. That's why she never called me: there was no telephone. That is, the kind that is dialled. It was— It was because the [telephone] numbers [available for the community] are used up, it's said. Her phone was disconnected; that was why her number was taken. She'd had two numbers <Cough> when we went there last time. But she does have something [of a phone], the kind that Saayman has, it's a Wawatay radio. That is all that she has. But it's the best you could get.

I usually listen to it after I lie down at night, listening to those who called. <Laughter> Although attempts were made to call Lynx Lake, nobody ever answered.

*ahko aana-mate-ayishikitonaaniwan
ohomaa Okiishkimanihsiiwaaponk,
kwaan hsha hshiin awiya wiihkaa ci-
mate-kitoc. <Laughing> Kwaa kaana
piko wiihkaa otawaahkonaanaawaa.
Ahpin oti ehaa nitawemaa hsha
peshikwaa ninkii-onci-ayamihaapan
ihimaa kitowinan.*

*Naanta piko kaa-maatinwekii-
shikaanik, ninkii-onci-ayamihaapan
mate-kitohpan oti. Nikii-onci-
kanoonaa. (Pause) Kii-onci-
kanooncikehtamaakowaampaan.
"Ayamihekiishikaak nika-maacaa"
hsha mate-ihkitoopan.*

*Cehpin hsha-hsh miina peshikwaa
ninkii-onci-ayamihaapan himaa oti
emaa waawaahte-kitowinink. "Mii
cika-hpan ci-noontawihshiyan" hsha-
hsh nimate-ikopan, kaa-ishi-ayaac.
Wiinikwahk kaa-kii-wanimoc.
<Cough> Wiipac ahko kaa-
kishepaayaanik amii hawe niikaan
kaa-mate-kakitoc ahko, kaa-ani-
ayintinaaniwank e— eh-ani-waa-
wiintamaatiwaac. Aanti piko eh-
tanowewitamowaac. <Cough>*

*Waahkaahikan hsha kii-mate-
sahkitepan ihimaa ohowe kaa-mate-
aanimootank taawinini
Apwaanaahkosaakahikan kaa-ihkitoc,
kaa-mate-ihkitoc. Waahkaahikan hsha
kii-mate-sahkite naanta piko kaa-
maatinawekiishikaa. Naanta hsha
kaye—naanta-hsh kaye kaa-
pahkweshikanikiishikaak, mate-
sahkitepan hsha waahkaahikan.
Ketaht ahpan e-mate-mohci-
aanoocihtaakosiwaahpan.*

<Laughing> Maybe they never had it turned on.

But I heard my brother once over this radio. It just might have been on Saturday that I heard him talking. I called him from there. (Pause) They called him for me. "I'll leave on Monday" was what he said.

I was also talking to Cehpin once there on the trail radio. "It so happens that you will hear me" was what he said, where he was. It is his character to talk nonsense. <Cough> He's the one who talks there first, early in the morning, when they start telling each other about what is happening to them. They were calling from all over the place. <Cough>

A house was burning there in the village of Ponask Lake, he said, he was saying there. The house burned there maybe on Saturday. Or maybe— or maybe it was on Friday, the house burned. Suddenly there was a big uproar.

Naanta hshiin ohomaa ekaa wenic-
nooncikaatekopanen, ohomaa tawiin
waawaahtekitowin.

Mii hsha tahsh ihi—ontami-
maacaawaakopan hsha-ntiko, ontami-
amihcikewaac ikweniwak kaa-
owaahkaahikaniwaac. Papihshik-
wahtekopan hsha-hsh iko ihiwe
waahkaahikan kaa-kii-sahkitek. Awiya
oti kaye caakisokwen ntiko e-mate-
inentamowaahpan. Saaken hsha mate-
aanooncihtaakosiipaniik. Wiipac
hsha-hsh iko nintawaac okii-kakwe-
kehcinaahtaanaawaapan ikweniwak
kaa-onantohtamowiniwaac. Wiipac
hsha-hsh okii-kakihkentaanaawaa
ekaa awiya e-caakisonic. Paniskwe piko
ahpan waahkaahikan ehta. "Mate-
ihkitonaaniwan," ihkitoopaniik.
<Cough>

M-ohsha enaacimoyaan ahaweti eh-
okitowinic.

Ekwa tahsh ihkito peshikopiihsim
mitaahs—ayenaanewmitana hsha-
ntiko ihkitoopan eshi-tipahank,
naanta pankii awahshime, peshi-
kopiihsim, ekaa tawiin e-misiwe-
aapihkanaank. Kaa-misiwe-
tipahikaatek hsha-win iko, kaana
wiin iko ahpan eni-piici-otaahpinak
awiya kaa-misiwe-tipahank. Mii hsha-
ntiko hi.

Nintayinaa hsha wiin kaa—kaa-
wiitapimak, "Aahtinci kekiinawint ka-
kakwe-ayaamin," hsha nintinaa.
Maawac e-minwentamaan eh-antoh-
tamaan ahko kaa-papimihshinaan eh-
tahtepihtawakwaa awiya.

Mochi-paatinihs-ihkancikaateni
hsha ihiweni kaa-ayaac; kwaaniin iko

Maybe they didn't hear about it
here, through the Wawatay radio.

So then it was— while they were
gone, perhaps while the owners of
the house were out praying. So it
was empty, this house that burned.
They were wondering if some
person had been burned as well.
There was such a commotion
there. There were trying to find
out for sure that no one had been
burned. Right away they figured
out that no one had been burned.
It was just the house. "That's what
was said," they said. <Cough>

That's all I'll say about the one
who owns the radio.

And so for one month he says
it's one hundr— I think he said it
costs eighty, maybe a little more
per month, if he doesn't pay it in
full. When it is fully paid, then he
actually owns it. I think that is how
it is.

I was telling the one— the one
with whom I sit (my spouse), "We
should try to get one," I say to
him. I really enjoy hearing other
people talking when I am lying
down [lying around].

The one he has just runs on
batteries; not on the big batteries,

kihci-paatinihsan ehaa hsha piko,
naanta kaana nawac kaa-mintitonic
paatinihsan. <Cough> Ekaa tahshiin
eh-tahtipahikaaniwank kaa-
ayamihitinaaniwank. Mii-hsha eshi-
maa-mino-ayaatok ihiwe.
   M-ohsha enaacimoyaan.

the medium-sized batteries.
<Cough> It doesn't cost anything
when people are talking. That's
what makes them so nice.

That is all I'm going to say.

We find evidence for the emergency use of the radio in this text, but obviously the local view of the trail radio is that it is used primarily for entertainment. This medium has opened up new opportunities for talk – especially for storytelling. Humour is extremely important in this community, as I suspect it is in most Native American communities. Telling a good story is important, but telling a good story that is funny (as are most *aatisohkaanan*, 'traditional stories') is the mark of real social facility. Despite the value of the radio in emergency situations, its primary use is for making contact with people. Most of the transmissions on the trail radios involve storytelling, joking, and swapping news of all kinds. Particularly funny stories broadcast on the trail radios are often told and retold around the village, and even get repeated on the community radio station. This access to multiple media has given rise to some interesting variations on the 'moccasin telegraph.' It is not uncommon for a story to be told face-to-face, then to be repeated over the phone to a person sitting at the radio station. The person at the station may then repeat the story over the air – and the people listening will often run to the phone to discuss the story with someone else, perhaps even the original storyteller. Thus storytelling is no longer limited to the context of the tent or the home.

TELEPHONES (*Maacikitowinan*)

In the previous discourse, we also found the telephone to be a prominent part of the discussion. Several aspects of telephone usage were indexed in this discourse:

1. A telephone is considered an essential piece of equipment in a home.
2. People often have more than one telephone line in their home.
3. Telephones cost money to operate.
4. Telephones are the primary channel of communication between people in different communities.

Not quite so explicitly stated in this discourse is the fact that middle-aged and elder adults make the greatest number of phone calls. As will be seen in the discourses below, the persons with the most power tend to speak most often in telephone conversation, just as they speak most often in face-to-face interactions. Teenagers are considered too shy to talk around adults, and even around peers tend to be less talkative than the stereotypical Euro-Canadian teenager. This cultural difference extends also to telephone behaviour.

History of Telephone Service in the Community

In 1977 construction began on the 'Bell Tower,' (*mihtikohkaan*, lit. 'man-made tree'), the microwave relay station, located about a mile southwest of the centre of the Lynx Lake village, and by 1978 telephone service was available in the village. This system, with seven lines connecting the village to outside phones, is still operating in Lynx Lake, although it is now considered quite outdated, and was upgraded in 1991. Until then, there were a maximum of ninety two-digit telephone numbers in the community, ranging from the number ten to ninety-nine. While community phones could be dialled directly, access into or out of the community was handled through an operator by dialling zero.

While the phone service is through Bell Canada, Wawatay Native Communications Society is intimately involved with the northern phone service through its 'Wawatay' program. In this program, a Native speaker can dial an outside operator and, when the operator answers, say the word 'Wawatay' to signal that he or she needs a Native translator–operator. The bilingual Wawatay operator then aids the Native speaker in making the desired call. As most of the people in Lynx Lake often use English terms for numbers over twenty, this service is not used as frequently as it might otherwise be. Usually, if a call needs to be made to the English-speaking world, a monolingual Severn speaker will ask a younger member of the family to make the call. Acting as an intermediary between two people is a role that is commonly assumed, so that such a request is not viewed as an imposition.

Despite its brief tenure in the village, the telephone has become a major factor in community life. The telephone in a very real sense provides a window to the world inside and outside of Lynx Lake. Aside from normal conversations (discussed below), the primary use of the telephone is for engaging services such as plane rides to meetings or for hunting trips, and for buying goods from catalogue outlets – an important source of otherwise hard-to-locate items in a village with only one store.

In the community's Band office and store, and the church office, the telephone is an extremely important resource for conducting business. In the Severn area, face-to-face contact can be maintained only on the most immediate, community level. As the business community began to include more and more territory, the contacts between people remained just as important, but the opportunities for such contact were lessened, that is, until the import of telephones. Today the emphasis on interpersonal contact is reflected in the heavy use of the telephone in business (Band business and store and church business included), where a premium continues to be placed on personal interaction. In respect to telephone contacts, the community businesses appear much more 'urban' than many, less remote, Euro-Canadian communities in Ontario. In Lynx Lake, the heavy use of this piece of technology allows for a continuation of a form of face-to-face interaction, but on a much larger scale than otherwise would be possible, extending across the Severn area and into the Canadian matrix society.

Current Use of the Telephone in the Community

The telephone in Lynx Lake is viewed as an essential piece of home equipment by almost all members of the community. Most homes have at least one telephone line. The few people without phones tend to be elders over the age of sixty and families whose phones have been disconnected because of overwhelming long-distance charges. (Note, above, the discussion of trail radios for circumventing telephone charges.) Because of this last factor, telephone numbers change quite often throughout the community. High monthly telephone bills, in excess of five hundred dollars, are not uncommon and are often not the fault of the person to whom the phone is registered. Typically, friends and relatives make collect calls from outside the community which are almost invariably accepted by the one answering the phone. Another common problem for a bill payer is the person who uses other people's telephone numbers in billing his or her calls or who uses the phones for long-distance calls while the owner is away from the house. While the high phone bills from these outside sources are occasionally considered problematic, direct confrontations are rare, and most people would rather pay the bills than cause friction by asking for repayment.

The young woman opened up the lid to her woodstove and put three medium-sized spruce logs on the fire. After putting the lid back on, she closed down the two vents on top, then grabbed her parka and beaded gloves from the table in preparation for going out. After she put on her coat, she unhooked her telephone from the jack, wound the cord around the phone, and buried it in a box of clothing positioned in a corner of the room. She put on her gloves and boots at the door and was gone.

This event presents a creative means used to deal with a potentially problematic situation: the misuse of her telephone by her neighbour, a relative. When the young woman hid the telephone, it was a statement and a safeguard against the improper use of her phone. She stated that such extreme measures were being used only because her husband had to have a phone for his work with the Band. In a community where sharing resources remains the ideal, telephones are source of endless trouble. Rather than risk offending those calling collect, or those who use another's phone for multiple long-distance calls, people will allow their phone bills to run up so high that the phone company disconnects the line – often a blessing in disguise to the person with the phone number. One of the two public displays of anger and aggression that I witnessed in my years in the community was over the (mis)use of a telephone. In the days on the traplines, the scarcity of resources limited the extent of giving to one's kin. The limits set by the phone company on the size of a telephone bill often exceed the resources available to the person with the phone.

When a telephone is disconnected in Lynx Lake, a new line is often connected within a month or so under the name of another member of the family, creating a situation in which telephone numbers are quite fluid within the community. However, in such a small village, the resulting wrong numbers are only a minor inconvenience. In cases where a person cannot be located over the phone directly, a call to the radio station with a message for that person will usually get the desired response. The following excerpt from a radio text provides just such an example. This example is somewhat unique as the message was given in English, but the discourse before and after are in Severn Ojibwe, as indicated. (See chapter 4 for a discussion of this and other cases of code switching.)

Awekwen nikii-pi-kanoonik?	Who was it that called me here?
Stiiban Pipoon, you're supposed to call seven three seven two six seven six.	[Text in English.]
Mii we enaacimohtawinaan kaa-kii-apihihshiyan.	That is what I am saying to the one who had me sit.

Telephone usage, heavy among the people of Lynx Lake, is associated with a unique telephone etiquette. The three telephone calls presented below were recorded directly off the radio. The first two are quite brief but typical phone calls in which a person calls to get some finite bit of information. Most telephone calls that I observed in my two years' residence in the village were of this sort, not particularly lengthy, often spanning only a few seconds or a few minutes. The first two phone calls were conducted by the same person, in the first case as the instigator of the call and, in the second, as the recipient of the call. Owing to the nature of the recordings, only one side of the conversation can be heard, but, as can be seen by the examples, the instigator of the calls is generally expected to provide the content and to control the closing, with the recipient providing primarily back-channel cues.

CALL #1

The person at the station dials a two-digit number, a local call.

Kitayap iicika tawihsh.	So you're home. [Short pause for response.]
Kitayap iicika tawihsh.	So you're home. [Somewhat longer pause.]
<Laughter> Amii cika hi.	<Laughter> Is that right? [Short pause for response.]
Waa? Ohomaa piko antohta-mowikamikonk. Nitayap [___].	What? Here at the radio station. We are just sitting [unintelligible]. [Hangs up.] [Whispered to partner at the station:]
Coohsap mate-onci-kitoc.	Coohsap answered the phone.

CALL #2

[Phone rings.]

Maa. Aaniin oho saaken.	[To audience:] Listen! Who is leaving?
Anoo? <Pause>	[Picks up phone:] Hello? <Pause>
Amii tahsh wiin ahko miina ehkitoc. Ci-wa-oshaahshihshinan hsa [___].	That's what she usually says. That you'll slip (unintelligible).
Ekwa tahsh ociipaahkwaanahkihkonk ci-ishi-shikic. <Laughter>	And to pee in her cooking pot. <Laughter> [In reference to a joking story just told.]

Aaw. Mii tahsh ihi.	Okay. That is it.

[Hangs up. To audience:]

Aanii S. hsha kaa-mate-inihshic.	Aanii S. called me from there. "But
"Shaakooc wiin iko ahko. Miina ekaa	she goes out when it's not daylight
mahshi e-waapaninik e-saakahamok-	yet," she says. [She goes outside
wen," hsha mate-ihkito.	despite the slippery conditions.]

The following telephone call is actually quite long for a call at the radio station. The woman responding to the call is the person who earlier discussed the trail radio; the telephone call came some time later, near the end of the broadcast hour. What we find in this one-sided transcription of the phone call is a virtual lexicon of back-channel cues. Notice that the speaker provides very little referential information, although she is clearly involved in the interaction. After the call ends, she provides a brief summary of the interchange, shorter but similar to the one found in the last example. In the following text, asterisks are used to indicate pause length. A single asterisk indicates a very brief pause, a double asterisk indicates a pause of between 1.5 seconds' and 3 seconds' duration, and a triple asterisk indicates a pause that is more than 3 seconds long.

CALL #3:
Answers phone.

Hello? Hello?<**, clears throat>	Hello? Hello?
Waa? <clears throat, *>	What did you say?
Ehe. <**>	Yes.
Mii na hi? <*>	Is that so?
Eh, mii cika hi. <**>	Yes, that's right.
Amii na hi? <*>	Is that so?
Amii cika hi. <*>	Really?
Eh, anihshaa. <*>	Uh huh, at the last minute.
Eh, mii cika hi. <*>	Uh huh, really?
Eh, <*>	Uh huh,
eh, <***>	uh huh,
ehe. <**>	uh huh.
Ehe. <**>	Uh huh.
Ehe. <***>	Uh huh.

Ehe. <**>	Uh huh.
Ehe. <***>	Uh huh.
Amii na? <**>	Is that so?
Amii cika hi. <**>	Really?
Hm. <**>	Oh.
Mii t-ohsha hi. <*>	That's is it.
Eh, <Laughs>	Uh huh,
Oshkipiimakaa hsha-sh-iin iko noonkom.	Leaves are budding on the trees now.
Oshkipiimakaa hsha-wiin iko noonkom <*>	Leaves are budding on the trees now.
Ehe. <*>	Yes.
Amii cika hi. <*>	Really.
Huh. <***>	Hm.
Amii na hi? Kaawin iicika. A m-ohsha e-ishinaakwahk ntiko. Eh-paahpiihtawepiyaak ota kaye eshinaakwahk. <*>	Really? Not really! That's what it looks like. I guess when the water is really foamy, it looks so.
Amohsha hi. <*, short laugh, *>	Is that all?
Enh. <**>	Yeah.
Eh. <*>	Uh huh.
Mii na hi? Amoh— <*>	Really? Is that al—
Amii himaa? Mii cika hi. <**>	Oh there? Really!
Eh. <*>	Uh huh.
Eh. <***>	Uh huh.
Ehe. <**>	Yes.
Eh. <*>	Uh huh.
Hm. <*>	Huh.
Mii himaa kaa-ishi-nipaayan. Mii cika hi. <*>	So that's where you slept. Really!
Eh. <***>	Hm.
Eh? <*>	Hnh?
Mii na hi? <*>	Is that so?
Eh. <*>	Uh huh.
Amii cika hi? <*>	Really!

<Louder> Aw. Amii ta-hsha hi.
<Hangs up.>

Okay, that's it.

*<Sighs, says to audience:> Noohkomihs hsha wiin aha kaa-pi-kanoonihshic. "Kinantohtawin iko niin hsha nimateinik." Heh heh. <Sniff, *> Ninantohtaak hsha ho kaatatipaacimowak. Amohsha hi enaacimoyaan. <Cough>*

<Sigh.> It was my uncle indeed who had called me. "I can hear you," he said to me from there. <Sniff, *> Ha ha. He heard me, indeed, when I told the news [pertaining to him]. That is all I'm going to say. <Cough>

This call came in response to a story the woman had told on the air about the travels of several people who attended a Native Anglican church leaders' meeting in another Severn community. Notice that, as the recipient of the call, the woman at the radio station is relatively passive throughout: this mirrors many types of interchanges during which one person holds the floor with few interruptions but many back-channel prompts, and, at the close of the discourse, is followed by another interlocutor who then takes the floor. As the short summary indicates, the person instigating the call responded to the initial story with a story of his own. Thus, a look at telephone behaviour provides a window on other speech events typically encountered within the community.

Notice that greetings and leave-takings in each of these three conversations seem quite truncated by Euro-Canadian standards. In the initial conversation, the first words spoken by the caller after making a connection were *"Kitayap iicika tawihsh"* ('So you're home'), with no other opening. The closing was just as abrupt, as the caller's last turn at talk – *"Waa? Ohomaa piko antohtamowikamikonk. Nitayap- [___]."* ('What? Here at the radio station. We're just sitting here [unintelligible]') – indicates no closure whatever.

In the second phone conversation involving the same woman, this time as the recipient of a call, the openings and closings are somewhat elaborated. The phone is answered with *"Anoo?"* ('Hello?'), obviously adapted from the English usage. The caller was responding to a funny story told on the air by the speaker, involving the hilarious but ridiculous suggestion that her aged mother urinate into a cooking pot rather than risk going to the outhouse in dangerously slippery conditions.

In the third conversation, the greeting was the phonetically more English *"Hello?"* spoken twice. Less frequent but still heard is a passive greeting by the one answering the phone; in this case, the summoned will pick up a phone and merely listen as the one calling immediately says what he or she needs to say. I have witnessed this only with middle-aged or older community members who are answering the phone in their own homes, but I imagine that the latter factor, of being in one's own home, may be the more important of the two. If there is a simple message to give, there is no apparent need to open and close such a conversation using routines familiar to American and Canadian English speakers. The message itself provides the opening and the closing. In this way we again find telephone behaviour mirroring face-to-face encounters, in which verbal greetings and leave-takings in everyday community life are at best minimal, and usually non-existent. However, in face-to-face situations, the usual verbal greeting is either *'Pooshoo'* (originally from the French, *'Bon jour'*) or '*Waaciye,*' which was borrowed from the Cree (originally borrowed from English, '*What cheer*') initially for use in religious settings but in the last few years has also been used in many other contexts. There is no standard verbal formula used for leave-taking, outside of the church setting where a *'Waaciye'* at the door of the church suffices.

Within the last ten years, the telephone has become a major factor in maintaining relationships in the domains of the family and friends and in conducting Band and church business outside of the community. Telephone etiquette follows many of the rules found in Severn Ojibwe face-to-face interaction, which once again highlights how the people of Lynx Lake have adapted the telephone to their ends. This is somewhat different from the analysis of Dicks (1977: 129), which indicates that the telephone in Inuit society has caused real changes in the social structure: "An area of interest in this regard is the effect of the telephone on patterns of association. In closely-knit Inuit communities, the telephone permits instantaneous, random access to other members; and this association can neither be observed nor controlled by third parties. Anecdotal information gathered during fieldwork suggests that the telephone is thus facilitating a re-structuring of communications patterns."

I would argue that, in Lynx Lake, communication patterns have not changed so much as has the frequency of the interchanges. In a community where literacy has been a major factor for many years, contact with people outside of one's own village was actually quite common before the advent of electronic communications systems, so that even in terms of extracommunity contact, we find a continuation of communication patterns that were already in place.

Another medium with an impact in the community is the Wawatay newspaper. This monthly paper began in 1972 as the newsletter *Keesis*, published by the Sioux Lookout Friendship Centre, and was taken over by the fledgling Wawatay Native Communications Society in 1974. Until 1994, articles were presented in either Ojibwe *or* Cree, using only syllabic orthographies, and in English. In most cases, the Native-language articles were written initially in English then translated into Ojibwe or Cree, depending on the story's language of origin, and printed using a syllabic font. This format limited the audience of the Native-language sections to those who were literate in syllabics, primarily people from Severn Ojibwe, some from Berens Ojibwe, and those from the Swampy and Moose Cree communities. The newspaper is usually sold out within a day after appearing in Lynx Lake, attesting to the popularity of the publication.

Those who can, usually read the articles in English, in part because of the way the publication was prepared. Many of the reporters are younger Native people from communities in which syllabic education is minimal, so that when they interview people in the Native language for the *Wawatay News*, they take notes in English. Articles were prepared in English to be translated back into the Native language, usually by another person, which resulted in somewhat awkward Cree or Ojibwe output. The newspaper remains at its best covering sports, politics, and community events but, ironically, seems to be least culturally acute when discussing mental health and education, and when trying to define 'what is Indian.' In these latter cases, a 'southern agenda' appears to take over, where outward appearances (such as attending certain types of events; declaring 'traditional' a finite group of artefacts, which may or may not be; telling particular types of stories to the exclusion of others) take precedence over content. The irony is that the intended audience, at least for the Native-language sections written in syllabics, consists of those least in need of such outward definitions and who often reject outright some of the symbols being touted as most Native. For most of the Severn area, this has included pow-wows, smoking peace-pipes, and ceremonies involving sweetgrass. (For further discussion of ethnic definition, see chapter 7.) The change to an exlusively English format is reported to be financial – the costs of translation and typesetting became, apparently, prohibitive.

Despite its difficulties, the Wawatay newspaper remains a valuable contribution to the Severn area. It is the only newspaper of its kind, geared for the Native community, and it certainly addresses many issues considered important by the people. Through the newspaper, community members can keep abreast of political happenings which involve Native peoples, ranging from community matters to international concerns, or they can learn the airline schedules across the Severn area for the coming month. They can learn who in the northern communities had babies in the last couple of months, or find out the standings of the northern hockey teams. Looking through the paper, one can pick out the picture of a relative or friend; sooner or later, one's own picture is bound to show up.

THE COMMUNITY RADIO STATION

While it would be very difficult to say which of the Wawatay services is considered most essential by the people of Lynx Lake, it is clear that in the recent past the community radio station has had the greatest impact on language use. The ten-watt FM radio station arrived in the community in 1979, shortly after the first telephones came into the village. The radio station is the smallest public building in the community, consisting of a tiny ante-room just large enough to accommodate a wood stove; a smaller, closet-sized office off this room, normally locked and inaccessible to the public; and the larger main room in which the radio equipment, the console, and a tape deck, record player, and two microphones are situated along the east wall. Two telephones, each with its own number, flank the microphones on the far ends of the table. A simple wooden bench in front of the table seats the broadcasters. More wooden benches line the rest of the room; these are provided especially for the choir, who regularly sing at the radio station on Sunday afternoons, but they are also used by children and teens who occasionally drop in at the radio station. Friday- and Saturday-night Bingo games played over the air are also a popular draw for 'live audiences.'

Scheduling

The radio station is operated daily from 8:00 a.m. to 10:00 p.m., with a one-hour break at 1:00 p.m. for cleaning. Until 1986, the entire daily schedule was filled by locals. In 1986, in connection with the CBC Northern Radio Network and CBC Northern Television Network satellite systems, Lynx Lake was linked up to the Wawatay Native-language (news) programs out of Sioux Lookout. As explained by Hudson (1977: 133), "When CBC service reaches their community, local stations may elect to become CBC affiliates. Under an agreement with the CBC they carry a certain amount of CBC programming per week (one station may choose 56 hours, another 100 hours), but maintain control over their local production."

In Lynx Lake, the CBC programs are broadcast for a total of three hours daily: two broadcasts in Ojibwe (Severn and Berens both heavily represented), the first at 12:00 noon and the second at 5:00 p.m., and one Cree broadcast at 4:00 p.m. Outside of these hours, the radio-station programming remains exclusively local. There are no other radio stations on AM or FM bands available to community members, although on particularly clear nights Radio Moscow and the occasional Chicago station can be heard.

The radio station fulfils many communicative functions in the community. It is used to inform the community of Band business affairs, and of community events such as feasts, rummage sales, meetings, and church activities. Community members use the radio to announce deaths and births in the village and across villages of the Severn region. The radio station is used as a phone-call referral service, to send messages to those with no phones, to call children home in the evening. Officials visiting Lynx Lake and community leaders returning from meetings outside the community use the radio station as a medium for introducing new concepts to the general community. Aside from these rather serious functions, the radio station also provides an outlet for entertainment through the airing of jokes, stories and legends, and music of all kinds. Community-wide Bingo games are a regular weekend feature, tuned in by participants and non-participants alike.

This focus on the radio as a source of news and entertainment is consistent with the programming choices reported by Hudson (1977: 136) for Cree and Inuit listeners throughout northern Canada: "More news about the North was the first choice. Radio for entertainment was the second priority: respondents wanted more music, with Inuit generally favouring Inuit popular musicians and Cree asking for more country and western, particularly by Cree performers. The third choice, stories and legends, indicates that radio is also viewed as an important vehicle for transmission of oral culture and history." The programming on the radio in Lynx Lake, outside of the three hours provided by the CBC, demonstrates similar interests, although the priority would be news first, stories of the old days and legends second, and music, religious and country and western about equally represented, third. (See sample schedules below for a more detailed, representative breakdown of programming on a weekly basis.)

Each evening, by 7:00 or 8:00 p.m., the station manager or a person of his choice writes up a schedule of 'volunteers' to sit (*api*) the next day.

Depending on the one who makes the schedule, it will be written in English or in syllabics. Each person is scheduled for one hour during the day. Normally volunteers sit in pairs, usually of peers of the same sex or married couples. Less common are same-sex pairs with a generational age difference. Particularly among women, the members of different-generation pairs are often related, so that mother/daughter and mother-in-law/daughter-in-law teams are not uncommon. When men of different generations sit together, they tend to be related socially, that is, both are on the Band council or are hunting partners. The only unmarried different-sex pairs that I have heard on the radio were couples whose marriages were imminent.

Only members of a select group of elder men, known for their ability to talk through an entire hour-long program, are scheduled to sit alone. Two of the handful of men who are regularly scheduled to sit this way are the church leaders, the archdeacon and his brother, a priest. Of the other men regularly scheduled to sit alone, two are brothers whose children and grandchildren make up about half the population of Lynx Lake. The ability to carry a whole hour's program alone is considered a point of honour and pride. While it is rare to schedule someone singly, that is, outside the group of elder men, it is common for one half of a scheduled pair to miss the hour.

Typical Weekly Broadcast Schedule

Weekday schedule

8:00 a.m.–11:00 a.m.	Single elder, elder couples – stories of old days, current events
11:00 a.m.–12:00 noon	Church leaders, official visitors – church, Band business
12:00 noon–1:00 p.m.	Wawatay news
2:00 p.m.–4:00 p.m.	Non-working women, youths – music, talk
4:00 p.m.–6:00 p.m.	Wawatay news (Ojibwe, Cree)
6:00 p.m.–10:00 p.m.	Business reports, working people (especially those who work for the Band), Band councillors (most likely to have male broadcasters) – music, talk, reports

Saturday

8:00 a.m.–12:00 noon	Elders, working people
12:00 noon–1:00 p.m.	Wawatay news
2:00 p.m.–4:00 p.m.	General (youths, etc.)

4:00 p.m.–6:00 p.m.	Wawatay news (Ojibwe, Cree)
7:00 p.m.–8:00 p.m.	Adult males, middle-aged couples
8:00 p.m.–10:00 p.m.	Bingo game (on Friday or Saturday evening)

Sunday

8:00 a.m.–9:00 a.m.	Minister
1:00 p.m.–2:00 p.m.	Lay readers, church leaders – religious content, often singing
5:00 p.m.–6:00 p.m.	Senior church choir (women) with a few elder men – hymn singing; or the group from the 1:00 p.m.–2:00 p.m. segment, lay readers, church leaders, etc.
7:00 p.m.–9:00 p.m.	See 1:00 p.m.–2:00 p.m.

The younger the single person at the station, the more likely he or she will be to fill up the hour with recorded music. The older people who find themselves running the station alone often talk through the entire hour.

Ideally, the daily radio broadcast schedule is opened and closed with songs and prayers from the liturgy throughout the week, so that the persons scheduled for the first and last positions of the day are ones who are also recognized for their strong church connections. As this group includes most of the elder population of the community and those in leadership positions, such a consideration poses no problem for the one making up the schedule.

The schedule of 'those who are sitting' is typically read at the beginning and end of the hour throughout the day by the one currently broadcasting. The reading of the schedule is usually the only means by which volunteers are given formal notification of their expected duties. The schedule is often discussed privately, and those who are scheduled to sit are often informed of the fact by friends who have been listening to the radio. It is rare that one who is expected to sit is unaware of it, so absences tend to be deliberate, often resulting from personal schedule conflicts. Despite the many 'no-shows,' there are very few hours in which neither member of the scheduled pair attends. On the occasions when this happens, it is not uncommon that, on his or her own initiative, someone from the community will go to the radio station to fill in – or at least to pointedly read the schedule.

Each volunteer is expected to contribute two dollars each time he or she sits; this amount was double what it had been in the period between 1981 and 1986. The money from the volunteers is used for maintenance and upkeep of the radio station, covering such expenses as wood for heating the building, and housekeeping. For some of the elders who are regularly scheduled to sit, the cost is not insignificant, as can be seen in the following joking remarks between a husband (H) and wife (W) at the radio station:

H: *Mii kaana ahpan ekaa ci-kii-tipahikeyaan. Maawin. Ekaa ota mahshi e-na-naantawi-acitamooyaan. Kwaa kaana wiin kaye piko kaa-ni-miinikohsiinaan ...*
     I don't think I'll (be able to) pay. Perhaps. I haven't yet gone out to look for squirrels. No, probably not ...

H: *Peshikwaapihk takiin ehta homaa ninkii-tipahikenaapan miinawaa kaa-kii-apiyaan.* <*>
     I only paid one dollar the last time that I sat here.

W: *Mii hsha tahsh ihiwe.* <*>
     That's right.

| H: *Ekaa* [OVERLAP] | W: *Amii keniin e-inentamaan—* <*> |
| Not [__] | That's what I think too. |

H: *Kaawin kaye waawaac acitamoo nikii-nihsaahsiin.*
     I also can't kill a squirrel either. [Explaining that he's now a poor trapper]

W: *Keniin i ...*
     I, too ...

As with most conversational fragments, this short segment appears quite cryptic to the uninitiated. In this society, where fur-bearing animals were traditionally the closest equivalent to a cash crop, the reference to killing squirrels indexes the speaker's continuing poor financial situation. A single squirrel pelt is worth about one dollar and is the smallest saleable fur. Thus, the excerpt touches on what a hardship the two-dollar 'sitting fee' imposes on those without ready cash, particularly the elderly. On occasion, a person making out a schedule will subsidize the cost, paying perhaps half or the full amount anticipated for the day. In these cases, the person scheduled to 'sit' will be informed, either by a note attached to the schedule or by a phone call from the scheduler, that his or her contribution has been paid. The subsidies are one way of demonstrating generosity, and are taken as a sign of sharing one's good fortune with others in a very public way.

Show Formats

There are several standard formats heard during an hour's broadcast. The format followed depends on a combination of factors, including the age, sex, and social role(s) of the individuals involved in a given 'show' (the English term; the Ojibwe term is *apinaaniwank*, which carries the meaning '[people are] sitting'). The formats may be divided into two main categories: programs in which music is primary and those in which talk takes precedence.

Music programs involve either live performances or recorded selections. Performances always include religious music and are usually heard on Sundays, during the first broadcasting hour of the day, and on special religious occasions, such as every evening during the Advent season. Performances during the weekday-morning programs are limited to solos or duets by elders who are involved in the church hierarchy. Evening performances almost invariably involve groups singing Cree hymns, usually members of the exclusively female choirs, the 'junior' and 'senior' church choirs, accompanied and joined by one or more of the male song leaders and organists (see chapter 6 for further explanations of these categories) and male elders. On Sundays, performances vary somewhat, as some younger people, either females or mixed couples, will sing, in English or Cree, religious songs not found in the songbooks used in the local church, often in two-part harmony, a type of performance rarely if ever heard during the week.

Young people, between the ages of sixteen and thirty, tend to play recorded songs throughout their scheduled hour. For the most part, the only speech heard during these shows is a reading of the daily radio schedule; an announcement of the current time; the name of the selection being played; after the half hour, a plea for the next scheduled people to come to the radio station; and the occasional cryptic phrase followed by laughter. Adult males over the age of forty-five may play a few country and western or bluegrass songs during an hour. Women of this age group tend to play far less music, but those few who do play recordings tend to choose Mennonite renditions of religious songs, which have a decidedly mountain-traditional flavour.

Most radio shows involve talk. Men and women over the age of forty-five will give an hour's monologue if they find themselves alone at the radio station. This format was the original one, which started with the opening of the radio station, and this monologic format was adhered to even when two people sat together. All speakers at the station talked directly to the audience on the other side of the microphone. The now-common conversational format came about some time after the radio station had been in use, when two men, one then in his twenties and the other about ten years older, came to the station in the midst of moving the younger one into a new house. The relaxed camaraderie of the joint effort carried through the broadcast when, breaking all precedent, they began talking to each other, sitting there in front of the live mikes. The joking interaction became a popular format, one adopted by many of those paired up for a show, and even by the audience, as many people listening to their friends call in with retorts, jokes, and stories which may be repeated or summarized for the benefit of the general audience.

Common interactional arrangements of speaker and hearer heard on the Lynx Lake radio include:

1. single speaker with radio audience (unidirectional interaction);
2. single speaker with radio audience, phone-in interaction (bidirectional interaction);
3. two sequentially monologic speakers with radio audience (similar to 1, above, but with two speakers);
4. two speakers with phone-in interaction (two simultaneous but non-interacting conversations held between the radio broadcasters and members of the listening audience);
5. two speakers interacting with or without audience participation (conversational format).

These arrangements are quite fluid; during one section of a show the speaker may give a monologue pertaining to his or her community role, for example, a twenty-minute discussion of current policies and programs by the councillor for drug and alcohol abuse, which may be followed by an informal conversation with the Band chief, who then gives a report about a local situation, which is actively punctuated by calls from concerned community members.

While the conversational format is highly valued, the more traditional monologue is still viewed as an important means of imparting knowledge from elders to younger members of the community. Elders are scheduled for several hours each morning with the expressed intent that, through the elder's monologues, the younger people will have the opportunity to hear and learn from stories of the old days. These stories range from first- or third-person narratives to excerpts and discussions of myths/legends. Other extended monologues heard on the radio include sermons, lectures, discussions of current events, reports of travel, Band reports, and discussions of government and Band policies.

WAWATAY NEWS BROADCASTS

CBC North radio news broadcasts, presented by the Wawatay Native Communications Society, came to Severn communities in 1984 when TVO

(TVOntario) set up satellite disks in many of the northern communities. As noted earlier, the Wawatay radio network is broadcast in Lynx Lake from noon to 1:00 p.m. and from 4:00 to 6:00 p.m. The noon and 5:00 p.m. broadcasts are in Severn Ojibwe and the 4:00 p.m. broadcast is in Cree. The noon-hour broadcast tends to be a fast-paced mixture of northern news, announcements, telephone interviews, music, and weather. Aside from the weather report, all other speaking is in Ojibwe, mostly Severn. The weather report, which originates at the Big Trout Lake weather station, run by Euro-Canadians, is in English, as are most songs played over the air. The evening report is similar to the noon broadcast, but often the interviews and editorials are longer, going into more detail than the noon report. These formats are quite flexible; the hour may be wholly dedicated to one item, such as the accidental death of a prominent member of a northern community, an event sadly witnessed in the winter of 1987. The Cree and Ojibwe broadcasts are comparable, although the impression is that more music is played during the Cree hour than during the other two.

In their brief tenure, the radio broadcasts have had interesting effects on language attitudes in Lynx. With the broadcasts and television shows, Severn people have had much more contact with Berens and other Ojibwe dialects, with the result that, at least in Lynx Lake, intelligibility between these dialects is now perceived much differently than it was just a few years ago. In 1981, people in the community universally called their language 'Cree' in English, although the Severn term for the Native language, *anihshininiimowin*, differs from both the Cree *ininiimowin* and the more southerly Ojibwe *anihshinaapemowin*. At that time, people of Lynx were quite adamant that their language was not Ojibwe and that, in fact, Ojibwe was only minimally intelligible to them. In 1987 and 1988, a shift towards identification with Ojibwe was evident. While many people still called their language Cree, the informal designation for Severn, Ojicree, was becoming more and more popular, especially among the younger speakers. This term retains some of the identification with Cree while simultaneously demonstrating a growing identity of the language as Ojibwe.

WAWATAY TV

The latest venture of the Wawatay Native Communications Society has been the creation of a television network which produces a weekly half-hour Native-language television program aired on Sunday afternoons, preempting regular TVO programming. The television program, called *Keenawint* (*'kiinawint'* is the first-person-plural inclusive pronoun meaning 'us [including you]'), began in January 1987 and enjoyed instant success. The program is highly valued; its only limitation is that it is on the air only one half-hour each week. The show often has a different format from week to week, depending on the news gathered. Native reporters and camera operators, most in their twenties, travel across the Severn and northwestern Ojibwe areas conducting interviews and filming special events, providing an array of long and short stories to broadcast. Many broadcasts include brief messages from students who have left northern communities to attend high school in Sioux Lookout. In early broadcasts there were sections on teaching syllabics in a *Sesame Street* format, but, in late 1987, this portion of the programming was absent. At Hallowe'en, there was a comedy talk-show format, with all participants in costume and speaking in character. Other shows focused on particular communities and associated activities, for example, the program on Lynx Lake was dedicated to a Native Bible camp held in the bush at the north end of Mihshamihkowiihsh Lake and attended by many people from a number of Severn communities.

Keenawint is the source of great discussions, primarily about content rather than form, although performances of particular stories and plays are readily evaluated. In the radio excerpt below, a husband and wife discuss the latest show in which an elder of another community told some stories at the request of a Wawatay reporter. The setting for the storytelling event was quite typical of such events in 1987: the man was sitting on a couch beside a woman of his own age who prompted him several times during the narration. Not so typical was the presence of another a woman who lay on a couch to the narrator's other side, also providing back-channel cues. While the specific incidence of the two women provides the focus of the particular discussion below, this interchange is typical in flavour, giving some indication of the entertainment value that these brief programs give, often long after they have been aired.

H: *Ah. Waawaahten oka-tawaahkonaan.=*
     She'll turn the Wawatay [radio] broadcast on.

W: *=Hm. Waawaahten oka-tawaahkonaan.* <**>
     She'll turn on the Wawatay.

H: *Waawaahte ka— Os—osaam saaken ahko acina masinaahtehse. Osaam.*
     The Wawatay [TV] program is always too short. Always.

W: *Maanamihi e-wii-opwaakaniwahtek.*
     There's a strong smell of pipe here.

H: *M-ohsha hi. Osaam hsa acina masinaahtehse ahko.* <**>

That's it. It's usually too short, the television show.

W: *Opwaakanik e-ishimaahtek.*
It smells like a pipe.

H: *Kaanika, kaanika kanake pe—pe—peshiko tipahikan.=*
It should be on for an hour.

W: <=Loud yawn>

H: *Kaa-tahtipaacimowaac ahko kaa—* <**>
When they talk/tell stories, usually—

W: *Kaa-kii-paahpihakipan peshikwaa kaa-mate-tahtipaacimoohpan.*
I laughed at [the man on *Keenawint*] once when he was telling a
story.

H: *Kehi saaken niishoohkwewetok kaa—*
I wonder if he lives with two women—

W: <Laughter> *Niishoohkwewe kiniin=*
It's impossible that he's living with two women.

H: *=eh-taa-tahkamik.*
It's unbelievable.

W: *Eh-taa-tahkamik.*
Unbelievable!

H: *Naanta kaana ihi kihci-ahaawikamikonk kaa— kaa-ishi—* <**> *Naanta
kaana, mii himaa kaa-ishi-masinaahtehsec ot.* <**> *Kaawiniin kekoon
ntay-inaacimohsiin.*
It must be at the old folks home where— It must have been there
where they filmed. I don't have any [other] news.

The filming of events by Wawatay reporters has had some interesting
repercussions for the communities. Many of the communities are now very
interested in visual recordings of meetings and community events, including rummage sales, school programs, church services, storytelling, and
carnivals. The elders find these Native videos an excellent way to record
cultural knowledge in a medium that is availabe to young people to use
whenever they are ready to learn stories and skills. This desire to record
local activities gave an interesting boost to my fieldwork as I was in con-
stant demand to videotape numerous events that I might not have even
heard about otherwise. The Native Wawatay reporters and camera operators had taught the people what to expect with taping, so the people knew
what they wanted, and often told me exactly what to tape, when to tape,

and where to stand when I did it. Copies of these tapes were given to the appropriate person(s) in the community afterward, and many of these tapes made the rounds through the mail to many other Severn communities. In the summer of 1988, the Lynx Lake Band bought its own camcorder with the expressed intent of taping meetings outside the community to be broadcast in Lynx for the benefit of the community members.

The long-standing presence of these now Native media has made information dissemination quite public and thus more accessible to the outsider. The 'observer's paradox' is greatly lessened through active use of microphones by self-selected cultural experts who have become comfortable in front of microphones and cameras. These people fully visualize the audience to whom they speak and clearly address them, often treating the recorder/researcher either as an extension of the recording device or as a representative of the group being addressed. Because the media has been in the hands of Natives in this community from the start, they are viewed as an emerging aspect of *their own culture*.

CONCLUSIONS

The importance of writing lies in its creating a new medium of communication between men ... In this material form speech can be transmitted over space and preserved over time from the transitoriness of oral communications.

The range of human intercourse can now be greatly extended both in time and in space. The potentialities of this new instrument of communication can effect the gamut of human activity, political, economic, legal and religious. (Goody 1968: 1–2)

This statement outlining the effects of literacy could just as easily apply to any of the media discussed in this chapter, which have been adopted and adapted to fit the changing lifestyle(s) of the Lynx Lake people. Trail radios and telephones allow for immediate and widespread contact between people. The community radio station and CBC North radio and television give insights into the wider Native and Euro-Canadian societies. Video and cassette tapes have become primary means of recording and preserving cultural information. All these media have changed the shape of communication in Lynx Lake, broadening the scope, allowing for more interaction between groups, and opening up new avenues for younger members of the speech community to hone speaking skills. In this last area we find more opportunities inside Lynx Lake for 'youngers,' adults not yet elders, to use speech to direct the community in political and social directions; for younger adults to practise storytelling skills at the radio station, and at the level of the broader Severn community; and for young people to become newspaper, radio, and television reporters, changing the traditional locus of news from the elder to the youth. However, elders are not being replaced through these electronic media; rather, they now have wider audiences for their acknowledged areas of expertise. The boom in communications technology has opened up more avenues for discourse, all of which have been embraced and exploited by a community who treasures information as a most valuable commodity.

One winter afternoon, standing in a snowy pathway in the middle of the village, an elder engaged my husband in an impromptu discussion of the powers of the shaman of long ago. After he explained how disembodied voices came from the shaking tent (*kosaapancikan*) to communicate with the shaman, he concluded by saying, "You know, it's the same basic principle as the telephone."[3]

Chapter Four

Use of Multiple Codes: Code Switching, Language Levelling, and Language Attitudes

Until the late 1980s, almost all Severn people referred to themselves in English as Crees and to their language as a variety of Cree. The Severn ethnonym *Anihshininiwak* is unique among Ojibwe dialects – all other Ojibwe dialects uniformly use *Anihshinaapek* as a self-designation. The closest analogue to the Severn form is perhaps an apparent cognate in the Plains Cree ethnonym *Ayisininiwak.* Close scrutiny of the linguistic codes used in the Severn Ojibwe community of Lynx Lake provides a great deal of information about the social relationships that have been forged among the Ojibwes to the south and the Crees to the north and east of the Severn people. As well, an examination of the codes reveals a great deal about the relationships between Severn people and the Euro-Canadian matrix culture. Within this one remote and seemingly isolated village located in the broad expanse of the subarctic taiga, one finds two subdialects of Severn Ojibwe, three dialects of Cree (Swampy, Plains, and Moose), and two varieties of English available as linguistic resources.

Most studies of code switching have involved peoples living in industrialized societies, having extensive, daily contact with other speech communities. In most of these situations, the languages being switched are Indo-European, and often closely related to one another (see Woolard 1988; Heller 1988b; Blom and Gumperz 1972; Gumperz and Hernandez-Chavez 1970; Gal 1978; Poplack 1977 and 1979; and Timm 1975, among others). In the few studies of code switching among non-industrialized groups, the focus has been on language shift from a minority to a majority language (see McConvell 1988).[1]

This study examines a completely viable Native North American language situation in which code switching occurs between two Algonquian languages as well as between an Amerindian language and English, in that rare situation where English poses no immediate threat to the viability of the indigenous language. Thus, the Lynx Lake community provides a unique opportunity to study code switching within the paradigm of another, non-Indo-European, language family. The use of Cree and English in this Ojibwe setting is particularly notable in that there is in general little face-to-face contact with speakers of either Cree or English. In addition to these unusual aspects of multilingualism, we also find the speech community of Lynx Lake to be linguistically stable; that is, there do not appear to be signs of incipient language shift away from Severn Ojibwe. The textual data used in this study are also unique in that the discourses from which the examples are taken are essentially monologic as opposed to the more typical conversational data found in studies of this sort. Such monologic texts are particularly useful as it is much easier for the analyst to control such variables as participant, role, setting, and even genre.

All examples of code switching, from Severn Ojibwe to English or Cree, used in this book are found in discourses collected from just two speakers. Even in this small sample of three discourses, we find elaborately structured relationships in the use of multiple varieties of these languages, relationships which are consistent with the general pattern of language use in Lynx Lake. The first monologue is an hour-long radio discourse presented by the Lynx Lake Band chief one evening in November 1987 at the community's ten-watt FM radio station. In this monologue we find only two examples of code switching involving interchanges with other people, both of which are triggered by phone calls. All other examples of code switching in this text occur during monologic discourse where there are no such overt interactional exchanges. Following the discussion of code switching into two styles of English and into Cree in the chief's report, we will investigate excerpts from two public monologues provided by another influential member of the Lynx Lake community, the Native Anglican archdeacon. This man's prominence is not limited to the village of Lynx Lake; it extends to all the denominationally Anglican villages in the Severn area, a fact which is critical in understanding the social meaning attached to the code switching found in his discourse. The priest's first discourse is a sermon delivered as part of the morning service at Lynx Lake's St Paul's Church, in late 1982; the second is a twenty-minute radio monologue, recorded five years later, in the fall of 1987. The audience for both these public discourses included most of the adult community of Lynx Lake.

CODE SWITCHING BETWEEN ENGLISH AND OJIBWE

Two varieties of English are used in the community, the Standard Canadian English used in such social spheres as government, business, and education, and 'Indian English,' an Algonquian version of an informal, nonstandard Canadian English, marked particularly by the influence of Algonquian phonology and syntactic processes. In practical terms, this nonstandard English is the primary vehicle of English-language communication within the community. Standard Canadian English is rarely heard in intracommunity communication, but is very important in the interface between bureaucratic agencies and those in administrative roles within the Band. This variety may also be manipulated for humorous ends, as illustrated below.

The first stretch of discourse examined here comes from a session in which the Band chief and one of two Band councillors were scheduled to sit at the radio station, though, as it turned out, only the chief managed to make it to the station. As noted in the previous chapter, the radio station is central to public communication within the village. In the radio schedule, which is drawn up each day, two people of typically equal social rank are scheduled to sit together for an hour's time. Sitting at the radio station is considered an honour; being on the radio denotes a position of considerable public prominence. Those sitting typically conclude their sessions with an appreciative, "*Miikwehc kaa-kiih-apihihshiyan*" ('Thank you [the daily schedule-maker] for your seating me here').

The first two examples of code switching presented here fit Gumperz's (1982) category of 'situational code switching,' that is, where the presence of particularly salient aspects of the situations provide motivation for the shifts from Severn Ojibwe to English. The first case of code switching of this sort, from Severn to English, occurred about five minutes into the chief's radio discourse when a brief call interrupted his report of a recently held chiefs' meeting which he had attended in the south.

In each of the transcriptions of the chief's discourses, the column on the right provides an English translation in those places where Severn Ojibwe was used in the discourse, along with non-textual information, including, within parentheses, the timing of pauses in tenths of seconds between lines of speech[2] and notations of the speaker's actions.

	[Answers phone]
Hello.	(11.4)
Just a minute, I'll write it.	(0.7)

Seven, three, seven, twenty six, seven six.   (1.0)

That's Steven.   (1.8)

Okay!   (0.5)

I'll do it.   [Hangs up phone]
                                                                                 (4.3)

Umm,   (1.5)

Steven, Steven Pipoon, if you're listening,   (0.8)
you're supposed to call seven three seven
two six seven six.   (1.1)

Steven Pipoon, if you're listening,   (1.1)
you're supposed to call seven three seven
two six seven six.   (1.2)

Mii we pi-ihkitoc ahawe kaa-mate-kitoc.   That's what the person who called
                                             said.   (5.1)

                                             (Loud exhalation after 2.0)

Ekwa ahii kaa-aanimootamaampaan …   And, uh, what I had been rel-
                                             ating …   (1.7)

Many situational elements may trigger a switch into English. The two that we find in this phone call are: first, the use of English at the prompting of the caller, and second, the message being written down in English. Both of these factors are sufficient triggers for the use of English in this initial transmission and in the repetitions of the message (presented below). Several other situational elements found in these messages may contribute to the use of English. The first is the presence of the telephone number. While there are Severn terms for most numbers, numbers above twenty tend to be linguistically cumbersome, such that in most situations English numbers are used, even by otherwise monolingual Severn speakers. This practice extends to all units of time, including dates and other time phrases, such as week, month, and year. The only consistent exception to the use of English numbers is found in the church, where page numbers, chapter and verse numbers, and hymn numbers are all given in Severn Ojibwe. Thus, if a person is functional in English, the use of numbers could trigger the use of English through a given utterance, although normally this switch would extend maximally only a sentence or two.

Another important factor here is the English proficiency of the person to whom the message is addressed. As not all members in the Lynx Lake community share proficiency in English, English code switching indexes not only situations and topics (cf. Blom and Gumperz 1972: 424–5), but also age, cross-referenced with sex. Prior to 1965, the time when the community moved from Mihshamihkowiihsh and established itself at Lynx Lake, schooling was sporadic, and even functional proficiency in English was limited to those men who had left the community for a time to work in the mines in Anglo communities to the south, or to those who had spent extended time in hospital.[3] Until 1987, most women over the age of thirty-five were monolingual, with several women in their twenties functionally so. Only a handful of men over forty had any facility in English, with functional bilingualism evident only in those between the ages of fifteen and thirty-seven.[4]

In practice, the use of English between members of the Lynx Lake community is most likely between two males of the same generation. The use of English among women of Lynx Lake is far less likely, despite the apparent similarities with males in education among those between the ages of fifteen and thirty-five. Proportionally fewer of the young women leave the community to continue their education (the community offers public education only through grade eight), although, of those attending high school outside the community, women are just as likely to complete their programs as are their male peers. However, once finished with school, the women of Lynx Lake have less need to use English since most positions in the community involving heavy contact with Euro-Canadians are filled by men.[5]

Although all the elements for switching from Severn into English noted here may be present, such switches are not automatic on the radio. Even in the maximally compelling situation for code switching to English, that is, speaking with a monolingual Euro-Canadian, members of the community may use Severn Ojibwe. In this latter case, the key element is the presence of other Native community members, which can trigger a metaphorical switch to Severn. The radio is treated as a wholly Native medium, so that the presence of a Euro-Canadian, even as co-participant at the radio station, may not override the use of Severn. Only in cases where the intended audience can understand English is code switching into English a factor.

The interplay of situational and metaphorical switching is particularly interesting in radio messages aimed at the few resident non-Ojibwe-speaking Euro-Canadians, many of which are not given in English, but in Severn Ojibwe. In the years 1981–3, non-Native teachers, since they had a prominent role in the community, were often scheduled to sit at the radio station. However, when Native radio-station participants read the daily radio-station sitting schedule, rather than reading the actual name of a teacher from the schedule, they used the Ojibwe term for the school teacher's role, *otishkoonihiwe* ('teacher'), to inform the listeners who was to sit at the station. This meant that, even in the unlikely event that the teachers were listening to the radio station, they would not know to come during their scheduled hour. Ultimately, some member of the community would call them and, in English, inform the appropriate teacher that he or she was supposed to be at the radio station, often to his or her surprise and consternation. The use of the names of roles in place of given names actually demonstrates a measure of respect, adding yet another layer of complexity to the situation. In showing respect by using Severn terms for roles, a situation is established in which Ojibwe may be used as a means of 'non-communication' with the non-Native members of the community, that is, as a way of creating communicative distance with Euro-Canadians. Thus, the great irony is that, by using respectful designations, the Ojibwe terms for roles, the speaker can avoid communicating with the monolingual English speaker while simultaneously creating a situation in which the Euro-Canadian will not be able to fulfil community responsibilities.

Other situations in which members of Lynx Lake use Severn for purposes of non-communication include temporary and fleeting visits to the community by Euro-Canadians in capacities such as educational administrators, government officials, and the like. In the presence of such strangers, very few people would volunteer knowledge of English, unless the Native individual were involved in the meeting in an official capacity, and hence was under a social obligation to facilitate communication. Thus we find that the use of English also indexes immediate social roles and responsibilities in interethnic communication within the community.

The next two examples of code switching are repetitions of the message given above. The first repetition of the message is found about thirty minutes into the broadcast, with the second occurring about five minutes later.

First repetition of message:

Mii we ci-kihkentamek,	That is it, for your information,
	(0.1)
ekwa Mike pi-ishaan, aashay ani-	and Mike, come here! It's already
ayinaanewi-tipahikaneyaa.	beginning the eight o'clock hour.
	(1.2)
And uh, I have a,	(1.4)
I have something here, mm,	(1.8)
Steven Pipoon	(0.9)

if you're listening, you're supposed to   [Phone is ringing]   (1.6)
call seven three seven, two six seven six.
Two seven six seven, six ...
Hello?   (10.0+)

[The microphone is turned off. The discourse is continued in Severn after the microphone turned on.]

Second repetition of the message:

Awekwen[6] *nikii-pi-kanoonik?*   [Quietly:] Who was it that called
                                         me here?   (1.6)
Steven Pipoon, you're supposed to call [Louder]   (4.0)
seven three seven two six seven six.
Mii we enaacimohtawinaan kaa-kii—   [Quietly, then loudly:] That is what
                                          I am telling you, the one who—
                                                                          (1.4)
apihihshiyan.   had me sit.   (0.6)
Mii iwe.   That's it.   (0.3)

   Given all the parameters which might effect, and would allow, a shift into English, it would appear that in these situations the primary reason for using English is to mark the interruption of the ongoing radio-station discourse otherwise conducted in Severn. Thus, the use of English here effectively brackets information which lies outside the speaker–audience frame that had been previously established.

   The final example of English code switching found in this text is separated from the above example only by three sentences; although temporally close to the earlier English statements, the intent, style, intonation phrasing, and even amplitude of the next example is markedly different.[7]

English bureaucratese:

Mike, ekwa kekiin pi-ishaan.   [Loudly, quickly:]
                                         Mike, you come here too!   (0.7)

I want you to come up here   [Loud, slow, staccato]   (4.7)

to speak on behalf ... <u>hm hm heh heh heh.</u>   (0.4)
Ah, am-ohsha hi.   [Quieter:] Well, that's it. (1.1)

This example illustrates a very different use of English. Here, the addresser (the chief) and addressee (one of the Band councillors) were scheduled to sit together at the radio station. While the two men were not of the same age, they were of the same generation and closely associated through their occupations. The offices of chief and councillor carry authority and dignity; both men were well regarded by the community and, despite their youth, accorded a measure of respect usually reserved for elders. These men were to speak during the last broadcast hour of the day, a time slot given only to those with good standing in both the political and the religious spheres of community life. The religious standing is particularly important, as the broadcast day is concluded with prayers for the community. Both of these men speak English and, in their roles with the Band administration, are called upon to use English on a regular basis.

This token of English highlights another important aspect of life on the Lynx Lake reserve: the community's primary contacts with Euro-Canadian society have been with formal political and religious entities (such as the Department of Indian Affairs and Northern Development), which negotiate their business with the Native community using highly formal registers of English. Thus, officials representing the Band – in this case, the bilingual chief and councillor – are expected, and even required, by those agencies to have some facility in 'bureaucratese.'

In this brief instance of code switching, the chief indexes multiple aspects of the chief/Band councillor relationships to the world of Euro-Canadian bureaucrats. The chief perceived this hour as one in which the two representatives of the Band administration would relay information they had obtained in conferences held outside the community to the members of the Lynx Lake Band. Indeed, in the half-hour discourse which preceded this announcement, the chief had given a detailed report of a piece of pending legislation designated as Bill 31-C, which had been of particular interest during a regional chiefs' meeting he had just attended. In the following half-hour, the chief continued his report on the meeting, with discourses on a proposal for a dam initiated by the provincial electrical administration, Ontario Hydro, with details about upcoming meetings he was to attend, and concluding with a discussion of officials slated to visit Lynx Lake. Thus the formal style which the chief uses to entreat the councillor to join him at the radio station echoes the genre of discourse used in the formal business meetings being discussed during the broadcast hour.

However, the high level of English being imitated is somewhat beyond the chief's control as he leaves his sentence unfinished, closing it with quiet laughter followed by the statement "*Ah, am-ohsha hi*" ('Well, that's it') in

Severn. In his very brief metaphorical switch into bureaucratic English, the chief accomplished a pointed request to have the councillor join him at the station, but because of the marked nature of a performance of this style of English, made the request humorous and, hence, non-threatening. While a direct imperative in Ojibwe may be appropriate for requests (and, indeed, is considered polite), the same form in English turns into a threatening command. However, the use of indirect language for requests in English masks potentially powerful commands, a fact which is manipulated by the chief in this brief statement. This playful use of style allows the chief to frame a polite, but clear command to his missing partner: however, as the 'command' is unfinished and terminated with laughter, we are provided with the frame for interpreting the statement as a joking request, mitigating any potential threat.

Immediately following these instances of English code switching, the chief provides a metanarrational statement of his performance.

M-ohsha piko aasha kekaat ahpin iko peshiko-tipahikan e-ishihsek.	[Quickly:] Well, the whole hour is almost up. (1.6)
Nika-tepi-kipihcii kaana piko.	I think I'll be able to finish (the whole hour). (0.7)
Kwaaniin mihshiin awiya nikihkenim-aahsiin eh-tepi-kipihciic peshiko-tipahikan ahko kaa-mate-apic.	I don't know of many who could sit here and talk for the full time. (1.3)
Kaawiniin mihshiin awiya nikihkenimaahsii.	I don't know of many who could. (2.7)
Mii kaana tahsh hi keniin ci-tepi-kipihciiyaan ci-isihsek. Taapishkooc ekaa wiin niin ci-kiih-tepi-kipihciiyaan e-inentamaan.	It looks like I'm going to make it the full hour even though I wasn't sure I'd be able to. (1.3)
Mii hsha piko aashay eh-paakontashkwemoyaan hiwe inikohk kaa-naa-noontaakosiyaan.	It is just that my throat is already dry from talking so much. (1.9)
	<Cough> (0.3)

In this statement, the chief makes explicit his verbal facility by directing the audience to the length of time he has been able to carry out a solo discourse performance. The ability to speak unaccompanied for an hour or longer is highly respected, and usually accomplished only by a select group of elders. Throughout this hour, the chief displays his ability to translate difficult, technical information into Severn Ojibwe, and during announcements, such as those just presented, demonstrates his ability in English (two levels), and even attempts to use a variety of Cree (discussed later).

Burnaby's (1981) overview of the place of bilingualism in communities like Lynx Lake, in which the use of English tends to be limited to relatively few situations and to relatively few people, is consistent for most of the Severn region: "In certain communities in which the Native language is used for almost every function in the community, such as Kingfisher Lake or Webequie, it appears that only certain individuals become bilingual and that their bilingualism is related to the fact that they need to use English for their jobs – teacher's aide, Band manager, airport manager and so on" (pp. 116–17). The strategic placement of bilinguals in the Band office and community store insulates the rest of the community from the need for fluency in English. However, functional bilingualism is becoming more and more a necessity, as can be seen in the following announcement for English-language classes for elders that had been originally scheduled to commence in the fall of 1987. (Note that the bold-faced word in the text is spoken first in Cree, then given in Ojibwe, with the change in bold type.)

Mii we, mii we pankiiciihs ehan— e-naa-noontaakosiyaan howe kaa-ani-tipihkaak.

Mii tahsh kaye aashay e-saankahso-tipahikaneyaak. Kaawin awiya mate-inaakaniwihsiin ihaa, ihaa Mike.[8]

Ekwa miina homaa keniiniko pankiiciihs niwii-ishi-tatipaacim oti. Howe, aasha piko nawac weshkac nikii-pi-wiintamaakonaapan howeti kaa-aacihtawi-ayaanimihsekipan ahii aacihtawi kaawin tepwe ahko kwayahkohse[9] ishi— ishi-inentaa-kwanoopan ahii aatiht homaa kihci-ahaak wii- … wii-ishkoonoowiipaniik oti aasha ota piko maacii-ishkoono-waahpan.

Ekwa tahsh, mii-hsh aasha e-kii-mate-shaapohsek hiwe tootamowin kiyaam iko hiwe ci-toocikaatek. Ekwa tahsh a— kaawin mahshi mitoni kii-

That's all, that's a little, ah— that I've talked about this evening.

So it's almost nine o'clock. It doesn't appear that, uh, uh, Mike was told.

So I'm going to talk a little more about [things] around here. I was told about this a while ago, about the problems regarding the adult training school. It's not really going smoothly, it seems; some elders were going to go to the school [class] which could have been started already.

And now, it's already gone through, that activity to be undertaken. Things are still not quite ready yet, for instance, the paper

*ishi-osihsehsinoon kekoon toohkaan
pepanoowi-ishiihcikewin, ekwa miina
ta-piishaa awiya. Ekwa tahshiin iko
homaa ta-oncii ke-kihkinoohamaakec.*

*Aasha nikii-wiintamawaa howeni.
Ekwa miina aasha okii-ayamihaan
wiin iko inweniwan kaa-kiih-pi-
kanoonihshinic. Wiin iko ke-
kihkinoohamaakec iko homaa piko ci-
onciic kii-ihkitonaaniwanoopan, ci-
anihshinaapemoc iko tako, ci-wii-nt—
ci-wii-ishkoonihiwec. Tepwe tahshiin
iko ta-minwaahshin ihiwe.*

*Hiwe ka-ishi-maamitonentaa-
naawaa kaa-wii-ishkoonoowiyek oti.
Nikihkentaan, nikihkentaan wiin iko,
aasha wiin iko awiya e-ani-kihci-
ahaawic oti, ikweniwak oti kaa-wii-
ishkoonoowiwaac. Shaakooc eshkam
isihse kiyaapic e-onci-isihsek ahpin e-
maaciwinaakaniwic oti awiya. Ekwa
tahsh a— taapishkooc a— ihaa
Waashahook, Waashahoonk kaa-kii—
kaa-kii-wanihsec, mii iwe kaawin hiwe
e-kii-onci-kihkentank aaniin ke-
tootank, miina kaye, ekaa piko e-kii-
onci-nihtaa-wemihtikooshiimoc oti, ci-
kii— ci-kii-kitoohtamaasoc oti. Mii we
toohkaan kaa-isihsekwen haweti.*

*Mii tahsh hiwe toohkaan himaa ke-
onci-maamitonentamek aatiht wiin iko
isihsetok kehcin eshkam e-ishiwini-
kooyek oti taawinink, naanta kaye
aahkosiiwikamikonk kaa-ishaayek,
pankii wiin iko himaa ci-kii-onci-
waawiicihitisoyek wiin iko naanta kaa-
ishi-pimi-ayaayek. Mii we toohkaanan
ke— ke-ishi-kihkinoohamaakaaniwahk
oti, kehcin ke-isihsek. Mii we.*

work, and someone will be coming
here [from outside the community
to help set up the course]. But the
instructor will be from here.

I have already told her this and
she already spoken to the person
that called me. It was suggested
that the instructor should be from
here, and that she should speak
Ojibwe,[10] in order to teach [using
the Native language]. Really, that
would be nice.

And for you that are going to
school, you should keep this in
mind. I know that people are
getting older. These are the ones
who want to go to school. But
sometimes it happens that someone is taken from here. Like the
Fort Severn man who got lost [and
died], it's because he didn't know
what to do, and it's just [because
he didn't] know how to speak
English, to communicate for
himself. This is the sort of thing
that happened to that guy.

So you should keep that in
mind, when some of you are
occasionally taken to town, or also
perhaps if you go to the hospital,
so that you can help yourself a
little during your travels. It's things
like this that will be taught [in the
class], if it happens.

Mii we, pankiiciihsh e-wiintamaan.
Mii wiin iko howe ci-ani-mamaatihsek
kehcin mamaashi wiipac hiwe. Nikii-
antawi—nikii—nikii-aanimoo-
cikaat—nikii-aanimootaanaapan
homaa peshikwaa mii—nayi—e-
ohkwapiwaahpan kihci-ahaa ota wiin
iko. Hiweni toohkaan ci-kii-
ayaamakahkipan ci-an—paaskaan iko
ci-ani-ayisihsek hiwe.

That's it. I've told a little about it. This will start soon. I discussed this once already at the elders' meeting, that this should be done for the first time here [?uncertain]. That's it. That's for your information.

Mii we. Mii we ci-kihkentamek.
Mii wiin iko aasha e-kii-shaapohsec
wiin iko hawe shooniyaan ke-
aapacihaakaniwic. Ke-tipahaamawic
haweti ke-kihkinoohaamaakec.

The money that will be used for [the class] has already come through to pay the instructor. <Clears throat>

The chief's statement is only partially consistent with Burnaby's analysis "that native people in the study area are prepared to learn a second language for instrumental purposes, but that they are not motivated to learn the language in anticipation of need and use of the second language under such conditions does not spread from the instrumental use into other aspects of their lives" (ibid: 117). Obviously, the nine people who attended the course were learning English in anticipation of a need, but it is true that the use of English was only minimal after the course was completed.

The most productive type of code switching to English in this radio text involves lexical insertion, where an English word is used when there is no immediately accessible Severn equivalent. The English lexical items used are included in the following list in order of their first appearance:

radio station*	1 token
one week*	1 token
44 reserves*	1 token
Ontario	5 tokens
Ontario government	5 tokens
social services	2 tokens
federal government	1 token
Canada	2 tokens
federal	1 token

across Canada	1.5 tokens, changed to *misiwe Kanata*
numerals	5 tokens: 130, 200, 600, 23, and 44
Bill 31-C	2 tokens
OPP, Ontario provincial police	1 token
provincial	1 token
provincial law	1 token
by-laws	1 token
policy	1 token
our own police force, police force	1 token
Hello*	2 tokens
Ontario Hydro	5 tokens
Manitoba	2 tokens
Hydro, power	1 token
Sioux Lookout	7 tokens
Toronto regional director	1 token
Band office*	1 token*

*Indicates there is a Severn equivalent; Severn is rarely used in these cases.

Thus we have a total of fifty-one and a half tokens of English lexical insertion in an hour's radio broadcast. The only cases where English code switching is longer than a noun or prepositional phrase are those where the chief directly addresses a single individual. In most other cases, the shift to English either fills a lexical gap in Severn (as with 'Toronto regional director' and 'Bill 31-C'), or is used in place names ('Ontario,' 'Canada,' 'Sioux Lookout,' 'Toronto,' 'Manitoba,' 'radio station' and 'Band office'), numbers over thirty,[11] and in a very few prepositional phrases ('across Canada,' 'for one week').

CODE SWITCHING INTO CREE

The last type of code switching found in this hour's text is an attempt to use Cree, indicated below by bold-faced type. This section occurs within two minutes after the attempt at bureaucratic English, and only one sentence after completing a phone call.

[The section begins at the end of phone call]

Kaawin awiya?	He's not there?	(0.5)
Aaw.	Okay.	(0.9)
	<end of call>	
Kwaan awiya inaakaniwihsiin Mike	Mike wasn't told to sit.	(0.1)
ci-apic.		
Moona—	No—	(0.1)
nimoona-ihtaw, nimoon— matew	I am not going, I am not— Mike is	
Mike. (?Mihshiin) nimatew.	not here. (Many) I am not here.	
		(1.3)
Ahii miina kotak kika-	And, uh, there is another thing I'm	
tatipaacimohtawinaawaa ahii.	going to report.	(2.0)

Once again the chief switches from Ojibwe to another code to bracket metalevel discursive information. In this case, his Cree may not be eloquent, nor in places grammatically correct, but the chief's attempt to use this code illustrates the community value placed on even symbolic multilingualism.

Cree and English have completely different roles within the Lynx Lake community. English has come in as the language of politics, education, medicine, and commerce. Cree has had a much longer influence in the community, initially in the areas of trading and commerce, and later in the area of religion; it is in this last domain that Cree maintains its importance in Lynx Lake.

In this radio text, we find that code switching into English occurs at either the discourse level, where a speaker would switch fully into English, or at the lexical-insertion level, in cases where Severn Ojibwe had a lexical gap. Code switching into Cree, while more situationally limited, tends to be less syntactically limited than code switching into English. This may be attributable in large part to the close relationship between Cree and Ojibwe within the Algonquian language family. Because the languages are structurally similar, code switching below the discourse level may be expected and is, in fact, found. The sermon analysed here (a transcription of the first six minutes is found at the end of the chapter) was taped one Sunday morning in the winter of 1982 at Lynx Lake's St Paul's Anglican Church. In the sermon we find several layers of code switching, including phonological and morphological shifts alongside lexical *substitution*, as opposed to lexical *insertion*, which occurs where there is no Native equivalent.

Phonologically, both Severn Ojibwe and the Western Cree dialects have simple consonant inventories and quite severe constraints on allowable syllable shapes. As noted in chapter 2, the Severn dialect of Ojibwe actually consists of two subdialects: the eastern subdialect (to which Lynx Lake belongs) aligns with other Ojibwe dialects[12] in permitting consonant clusters of nasal plus obstruent; the western subdialect exhibits nasal clusters only in a handful of morphemes, having lost the nasal clusters elsewhere. Eastern Severn, *onci-*, 'from,' corresponds to Western Severn, *oci-*. Cree, like the western dialect, permits nasal clusters only in a very restricted set of morphemes, for example, *taante*, 'where,' and *anta*, 'there.' The nasal clusters found in Ojibwe correspond to Cree hC (e.g., Ojibwe, *onci*, 'from,' corresponds to Cree *ohci-*) or _C. Thus, *nanaantawaapantan*, 'look for it,' as used in Lynx, is *nanaatawaapatan* in Western Severn and *nanaatawaapahta* in Cree. In many cases, then, a phonological move towards the Western Severn by Eastern Severn speakers may also be a move towards Cree pronunciation and vice versa. As illustrated, in most cases the differences between the Western Severn form and the Cree entail more than the absence of a nasal in a cluster, for example, the Lynx word *pinkote*, 'ashes,' has as its equivalent in Western Severn *pikote*, but in Swampy Cree, *pihkotew*, which is distinguishable from the Western Severn form in having *h* in the place of the nasal but also in having a final *w*. However, the important point here is that the deletion of nasals may be used by the eastern varieties of Severn as a symbol of more Cree-like speech.[13]

What I describe here under the heading of phonological code switching is actually the demonstration of a linguistic variable related to a particular discourse genre. The genre, religious speech, is greatly influenced by the use of Cree in all religious contexts, which dates back over a century in this area. All printed materials used in the Lynx Lake church are Cree. These materials include the Bible written in Plains Cree; the two hymn-books, one written in Plains Cree and the other in Moose Cree; and the prayer-book, which is Moose Cree, making Cree a *de facto* liturgical language. Because of the relationship of Cree to religious contexts, we would expect to find more of these phonological shifts in religion-related discourse, which is indeed the case. The variables under consideration here involve the denasalization of clusters of the type seen in *maank*, 'loon' → *maak* in Western Severn, and the substitution of the Cree (also Western Severn) *-(y)ahk* for *-(y)ank* in morphological categories such as the conjunct 21 (first person plural inclusive) verb ending, which is particularly found in religious hortatory discourse.[14] The denasalized forms are represented by _C or hC throughout the Ojibwe text; in places where the nasal has been maintained, the nasal clusters are provided in bold-face type.

The analysis of code switching on the phonological level is primarily statistical (cf. Labov 1972a). As noted above, this is the most difficult level of code switching to analyse because the phonological system of Western Severn often echoes the Cree phonological system. Thus when an Eastern Severn speaker employs what appears to be a Cree phonological system, such a tendency may be analysed alternatively as a move towards the prestige Western Severn dialect. In either case, we are looking at a situation in which heteronomy, looking to a prestige standard, is clearly the motivating factor for variation (see Chambers and Trudgill 1980). Because the two languages in focus in this discourse are Eastern Severn as the language spoken in the community and Cree as the language of literacy referred to in the discourse, it is likely that the prestige language triggering the phonological changes here is Cree rather than Western Severn.

In the first six minutes of the sermon we find eighty-three potential nasal-cluster tokens, of which only forty-two (just over half) were realized with nasals. The other forty-one tokens were realized as h$\underline{C}$ or $\underline{C}$. Five of the forty-one 'denasalized' tokens demonstrate varying degrees of nasalization and/or devoicing, but each is clearly marked in relation to the normal nasalized cluster, and hence is included in the denasalized category. In these cases, I have retained the nasal but underlined the cluster to mark that it has undergone a degree of change towards the non-nasal equivalent. In a few cases, at the end of an intonational phrase, we find total devoicing, which often obscures the nasalization. These cases are marked by a dotted underline.

In a twenty-minute radio text by the same speaker given five years after the sermon, seventy possible nasal-cluster tokens were found. In this case forty-four (about 63 per cent) were realized as nasal clusters with the other twenty-six changed to the non-nasal, and often preaspirated, equivalent. An impressive display of this trend away from nasal clusters in religious discourse is found in the radio text where, of twenty-six forms without nasals, twenty occur in 'moralizing' (i.e., particularly religious) sections of the discourse. This leaves the total number of potential nasal clusters at forty-five in the non-moralizing sections, with only five (11 per cent) realized as non-nasals. (See figure 1)

The five-year time difference between the two samples may account for the higher percentage of denasalized clusters in the religious sections of the radio discourse and the sermon. This increase over time correlates with the increased usage of the Cree greeting "*Waaciye*," discussed below. I have used the term 'moralizing' discourse to index another aspect of language use in these religious samples – that of an increase in conjunct first person inclusive forms (as might be translated by 'that we [including the one spoken to] do X'), which in Eastern Severn have the form -*(y)a̲n̲k̲*. The increased use of these forms, which, as a *de facto* hortative, mark moral discourse (as in 'we should be thankful,' etc.), gives rise to a greater number

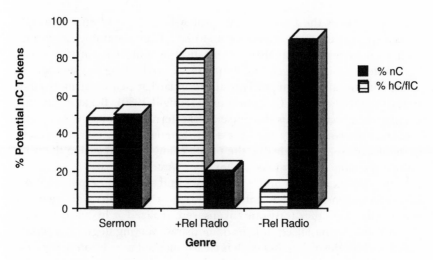

FIGURE 1 Relationship of nC to Genre

of potential nasal clusters. In fact, this single environment provides the greatest number of denasalized tokens in both religious discourses.

When the Cree Bible is read, the opposite situation to that of the Ojibwe section is found: here nasals are occasionally added, creating nasal clusters where one would not expect them in Cree. The interplay between Cree and Ojibwe is particularly interesting in the word *kaa-Tipencikec* ('the one who owns, sustains, or rules,' i.e., 'God'), which is realized as *kaa-Tipencikec* in Ojibwe and as *kaa-Tipeyihcikec* in Plains Cree. Within this discourse we find the word *kaa-Tipehcikec* without the nasal cluster in the Ojibwe section and even one case of the unabashedly Cree form, *kaa-Tipeyihcikec*, whereas we find *kaa-Tipencikec* (the fully Eastern Severn form) in the section where the priest was reading directly from the Cree Bible, creating an interesting type of language levelling.

Finally, Cree influences on phonology are most evident in this particular speaker's idiolect. His standing in the Severn community is unparalleled as the first Native Anglican archdeacon in the diocese. He is considered an expert in Severn literacy by both Native and Anglo scholars. He is functionally bilingual in Swampy Cree, underlining his qualifications as a religious leader. Because of these factors, discourses provided by this man give the most extreme examples of what has been observed as a tendency among lay readers in Lynx Lake.

The second level of code switching is morphological, seen in the phrase *Kaawin niminoyaa,* 'I don't feel well,' where the expected form for Severn is *Kaawin niminoyaahsiin.* The final negative morpheme, *-hsiin,* diagnostic of the Severn dialect, is not found in Cree. There are few examples of this type of switching in the sermon, and none in the radio text. However, in the chief's radio text there were several examples where the negative suffix was not present in its appropriate environment. Another example is found in *okosihsa,* 'his son,' where the expected Severn animate obviative[15] singular suffix */-an/* is replaced by the equivalent Cree form, */-a/*.[16]

The third level of code switching is the use of lexical items from Cree such as the word *peyak,* 'one,' which is *peshik* in Severn, and the greeting, "*Waaciye,*" which substitutes for the Severn *pooshoo*[17] (neither found in this particular section of the sermon). In 1981 through 1983, the greeting "*Waaciye*" was used only by the priest and lay readers at the end of Sunday services to greet people as they filed out of the church. By 1988, this greeting had become quite generalized, used by most adult members of the community in any context where a greeting was deemed appropriate. Indeed, such contexts seem to have become far more common in the last five years. Within the text, we find such lexical substitution in the terms *kaa-Tipeyihcikec* (God) noted above and in *ootenaw* ('town,' *ootena* in Severn).

The influence of English is also seen in the sermon in the pronunciation of the names 'Jeremiah' and 'Israel,' which retain the /r/ sound not present in Plains, Swampy, or Moose Cree, or in Ojibwe. The words *Jeremiah* and *Israel* (with special syllabic symbols for /r/, and /l/, the latter of which *is* found in Moose Cree) are found in the Cree Bible, translated from English into Cree at the turn of the century. With these vestiges of English retained, we find the three languages (Cree, Ojibwe, and English) represented within a single text – as we did in the chief's text.

In talking with members of the community about the priest's sermon style, younger people complained that he sounded like he was 'talking half-Cree, half-Ojibwe' and that it was sometimes hard to understand. While somewhat vague, this statement points up the marked nature of religious speech, as noted by members of the community themselves.

Further study is needed to gain a full picture of code switching in Lynx Lake, but even in this brief overview, we have found code switching on the sentential, morphological, lexical, and phonological levels used to create frames for understanding, to interrupt an ongoing discourse, to fill lexical gaps, to provide humour, and to mark genre. The use of different linguistic levels in Lynx Lake is manipulated along with the choice of code, creating a richly elaborated linguistic system, often overlooked in studies of Native American speech communities.

As it stands, this study adds to the literature on code switching in several important ways: this research of code switching came out of naturally occurring discourse, which means that rather than trying to find examples to fit some theoretical stance, I have attempted to explain why code switching occurs within particular extended discourses. The ongoing study of discourse of a single speech community allows for social, interactional, and personal linguistic contextualization rarely found in other studies of code switching. The physical isolation of Lynx Lake, along with its small population, has allowed for study of individuals' code usage, so that such variables as gender and role are well established. This study also puts the Labovian sociolinguistic variable (in this case, a combination of a morphological and a phonological rule) within the continuum of code switching. I also demonstrate that such a linguistic variable must be accounted for in terms of discourse genre as opposed to 'style' (cf. Labov's formal style, which in Lynx would cover both non-religious and religious radio speech). This study demonstrates that some of the same types of discourse strategies common in Indo-European languages – that is, code switching and style shifting – are used as interactional devices by Amerindian people for marking frames and providing keys to understanding discourse. Finally, this study presents a rare glimpse of just one aspect of the linguistic complexity and genius found in this viable and vital Amerindian speech community.

Sermon by The Venerable William Pipoon, October 1982, Lynx Lake, Ontario[18]

Ntootemak, nookom kaa-kekishepaayaak,	(3.3)
My friends, today	
kiminoyaamin	(2.9)
we are in good health	
kahkina.	(0.8)
all of us.	

Aana wiiniko	(0.8)
Oh,	
aanta awiya, "Kaawin nimino-ayaa̲a̲," enenta̲k.	(2.7)
some people might think, "I am not well."	

Ekwa tahsh kimino-ayaamin kahkina. (3.6)
Even so we are all healthy.

Ekwa miina (2.7)
And also
    kahkina ohomaa kaa-ayaayahk, (3.4)
    all of us here (in the community)
    kaawin ci-wanihitiyahk ohowe mekwaac, (1.0)
    we have not lost anyone of late
    ohowe mekwaat, (0.8)
    at this time
    kiiniko kaa-kiishikaak. (2.7)
    in this day.

Mii-hsh eshihsek (2.3)
It is at just such a time (as this)
    ci-kii-nanaahkomoyahk (1.8)
    that we should be thankful
    kaye ci-kiih-tepinawesiyahk (2.0)
    and that we should be satisfied
    kaye ci-kii-inentama k kiyaapac iicika eshihsek (1.5)
    and we should think how this has come to be,
    ci-kii-tootamaa**mp**aan (2.1)
    how I should act
kaa-ishi-nantawentaakosiyaan ci-tootamaan, kaa-ishi-nantawenimihshic
kaa-Tipencikec ci-tootamawak. (1.7)
in the way in which I am expected, to do what is God's will.

Ishinaakwan ci-kii-inentamahkipan (2.0)
· It appears that we should have thought about this
    kiyaapac iicika eshihsek (2.0)
    there evidently still is time
    kiyaapac iicika ci-taawaak, iwe ci-kiih-tootamaank. (3.7)
    and evidently continues to be time for us to do this.

Ekwa tahsh (3.5)
And so
    pa kiiciihsh nka-ayamihtoon— (1.1)
    I am going to read a portion
    —aanimootaan— (1.4)
    —discuss it—

Kayaashi-Testamant   (1.8)
of the Old Testament
kaa-kii-ayamihcikaatek   (1.8)
that which has been read
kwayahk wiin iko   (1.8)
so very carefully
oka-ayamihtoonaawaa okoweniwak, niishin awiyak,   (1.1)
those two people will read it
kaa-kii-amihtoowaac[19]   (2.0)
who read it
Kayaashi-Testamant miina Kihci-Masinahikewin.   (5.9)
the Old Testament and the Writings.

Ihkitoomakan   (5.7)
It says
  e-kii-maacii-kihci-okimaawic   (3.0)
  that he became ruler
  Cihaahikim okosihsa Caahsaaya,   (2.3)
  Johiyakim, the son of Josiah
  eshi-kihci-okimaahkantawaac Ishreyal,   (0.8)
  to rule there over Israel
  Coota-anishininiwan.   (3.6)
  the people of Judah.

Ihkitoomakan   (1.0)
It says
  otihkitowin kaa-Tipeyihcikec   (1.7)
  the word of the Lord
  kiih-takohshinoomakanini.   (6.2)
  has arrived.

Ahawe Cerimaaya   (1.7)
That one, Jeremiah,
  kaa-kii-anoonaakaniwic   (1.9)
  who was asked to [proclaim it]
  ci-niipaawic imaa maawacihitookamiko k,   (2.4)
  to stand up in the meeting place
  kaa-Tipencikenic owaahkaahikaniminiink.   (2.6)
  in the house of the Lord.

E-kii-anoonikoc ci-ayamihaac,   (3.3)

He was asked [by the Lord] to pray,
kaa-otahkiinic (1.6)
for the land
miina ihimaa kaa-otaawininit, Coota-ootena kaa-icikaatek, (3.2)
and for the settlement there, the City of Judah as it was called,
ekwa miin ikiweniwak ahko (1.5)
and for those also
kaa-pi-a̱tawi-amihcikewaakopanen (1.7)
who evidently used to come and pray
owaahkaahikanimink kaa-Tipe̱h̲cikec. (2.2)
in the house of the Lord.

"Wiintamaw," kii-inaakaniwi, (3.7)
He was told, "Tell them,
"kahkina piko mitoni wiintamawik (2.0)
tell every single one of them,
kaa-inahshowaaninaan (1.2)
what I have commanded you,
ci-ishi-wii̱tamawatwaa (0.6)
what I have commanded you to tell them,
ishi-wiintamawik. (2.3)
tell them!

Kaawin kanake peshik ihkitowin (2.4)
By no means [must] even one word
kaa-ishi-wii̱tamawinaan ci-ishi-wiintamawatwaa – kaawin kanake
peshik-ihkitowin (1.5)
that I tell you to tell them – not one word
manaa-wiintamawik." (4.9)
be left out that you have been told."

Mii kekiinawint eshi-antawentaakosiya̱h̲k (1.0)
So then, it is incumbent on us
kaa-anoonikowa̱h̲k (2.8)
when we are asked
ci-wiintama̱h̲k, ci-inwe̱tamawaatama̱h̲k Kihci-Masinahikan. (3.4)
to proclaim, (and) to interpret the Bible.

Mitoni piko mayaam (0.9)
Completely everything
ciih— ci-wii̱tamawakwaa – kahkina kekoon— kaa-masinahikaatenik

otayamowinink kaa-Tipencikec onci.   (3.4)
we are to tell them— everything – that comes from the word
of the Lord.

Taapishkooc alaaya—, taapishkooc Ceramaaya kaa-kii-ishi-wii̱ tamaakoc   (1.6)
Just as Alayaa—, Just as Jeremiah was told to do so by Him,
> *iniweniwan kaa-Tipencikenic,*   (2.4)
> by the Kind One (God),
> *e-kii-ikoc oncita ohsa piko*   (1.8)
> as He told him, it is the case that
> *aanta oka-nantohtaanaawaa*   (2.4)
> some will not listen to it
> *oncita ohsa piko aanta oka-tootaanaawaa.*   (6.1)
> but it is also the case that some will do it.

Wiintamawik, kahkina anihshininiwak,   (3.1)
Tell them, everyone,
> *kahkina kaa-tahshic anihshinini ci-poonihtooc omaci-ishiihcikewin.*   (8.5)
> each and every person to stop his evil deeds.

Kiishpin poonihtooc omaci-ishiihcikewin   (1.0)
If he stops his evil deeds
> *anihshinini, kii-ihkito kaa-Tipencikec,*   (2.8)
> [this] person, the Lord said,
> *"Nka-poonentaan maci-kekoon*   (2.7)
> "I will forgive these terrible things
> *kaa-wii-tootawaakwaapan omaci-tootamowiniwaa o̱ ci."*   (3.8)
> that I intended to do to them because of their terrible deeds."

Amii peshikwan kekiinawi̱nt. [-wint^h]   (2.5)
It is the same for us as well.

Kitayaamin maci-tootamowinan   (2.1)
We have evil deeds
> *e-kikishkaakoya̱ kin*   (2.0)
> with which we are clothed
> *miina e-pimi-tootaama̱hkin maci-tootamowinan.*   (2.7)
> and [still] we continue along doing these evil deeds.

[Slightly increased tempo]
Kaa-Tipencikec amii peshikwan kekiinawint e-ikoya̱hk: (2.9)

The Lord says the same thing to us:

"Wiintamawik ci-poonihtoowaac kahkina omaci-tootamowininiwaa   (1.0)
"Tell them to stop all their evil deeds,
anihshininiwak."   (5.3)
[tell] the people."

Ekwa tahsh, kitishi-wii_tamaakoomin   (1.7)
And so-o-o-o,we are told
   kekiinawint   (1.0)
   if we also
   kiishpin ekaa poonihtoowahk kimaci-tootamowininaan   (5.4)
   do not stop our evil doings
[Slightly louder]
   ci-ani-nihshowinaacihikoyahk kimaci-tootamowininaan.   (3.9)
   our evil deeds will destroy us.

Miina piko mayaam ki-wii_tamaakoomin, ke-ishihsek   (2.3)
This is precisely what we are told that will happen
   kiishpin ekaa poonihtoowahk kimaci-tootamowininaan   (3.1)
   if we do not stop our evil doing
   ohowe kii-inaakaniwiwak okoweniwak kaa-ayamihintwaa.   (5.1)
   just as it was told to those who were spoken to.

"Kiishpin ekaa wii-na_tohtawihshiyek   (4.0)
"If you do not want to listen to me
   ci-pimohsaatamek ntinahshowewininink   (1.1)
   to walk in my counsel,
   kaa-ishi-onahtamawinakok.   (2.1)
   in the way I have set up for you.

Kiishpin miina ekaa wii-nantohtawaayekwaa   (1.8)
Again, if you do not want to hear
   otihkitowininwaan ntanohkiinaakanak   (1.9)
   the words of my servants
   miinawaa okihkiiwek— okihkiwehikewinininiwak   (1.0)
   and the proph— prophets
   kaa-ishi-nihshahamawinikok, kiishpin ekaa wii-nantohtawaayekwaa,   (1.2)
   who I have sent to you, if you do not intend to listen to them
   wii-nantohtawekwaa,   (6.3)
   [so] listen to them!
   owe kiwaakaahikaniwaa   (3.0)

this house of yours
taapishkooc Saahiloo   (3.1)
just like Shiloh
nka-ishiihtoon   (6.5)
I will make it look like that
ci-ishinaakwahk kitaawiniwaa   (1.2)
so that your community looks
taapishkooc Saahiloo.   (6.6)
just like Shiloh.

Kitaawiniwaa   (3.5)
[It will be] your community
ci-macakintamowaac awiyak.   (3.2)
that people will bring condemnation upon.

[Louder]
Kahkina kaa-tahsohkaanesiwaac awiyak ci-macakintamowaat kitaawinini; (1.2)
All kinds of people will bring condemnation on your community;
nka-ishiihtoon.   (2.0)
I will make it so.

Taapishkooc kaa-kii-ishinaakwahk (owe?) otaanaank Saahiloo."   (3.0)
Just like Shiloh looked in the past."

Amii kaa-ihkitoc awe kaa-Tipencikec.   (3.3)
That is what the Lord said.

Masinahikaate imaa peshik   (2.0)
It is written there in one
masinahikanink,   (0.8)
book,
omasinahikanink Caahshowaa.   (4.7)
in the Book of Joshua.

Ekwa ayinaanewishaap maatinamaakanink.   (6.6)
In the eighteenth chapter.

[Pages rustle, Cough]   (6.1)
Ayamihtoowan iwe ayinaanewishaap maatinimaakanink   (2.5)
If you read that eighteenth chapter
ka-waapantaan imaa ci-aanimoocikaatek Saahiloo.   (3.2)
you will see Shiloh spoken of there.

Caahshowaa (2.1)
Joshua

    ahpin kaa-pii̱takec (0.7)
    when he enters
    ashotamaakowiniyahkii̱k (5.6)
    the Promised Land
    mii-hsa hiwe Saahiloo, <u>ootenaw</u>, ci-nihshowanaatahk̲. (12.0)
    it is that city of Shiloh that is to be destroyed.

Nka-amihtoon imaa (1.6)
I am going to read from there
    Caahshowaa masinahikanink (0.7)
    in the Book of Joshua
    ayinaanewishaap · (2.0)
    in the eighteenth
    maatinamaakani̱k, shaa̱kahso piskatasinahikan: (1.7)
    chapter, the ninth verse:

[Reading in Cree]
"*Aniki maaka naapewak* (2.6)
"Then those men
    kii-na<u>n</u>tawi-shaapoo-pimosewak askiik, (1.2)
    walked through the land
    ekosi kii-aatohtamowak eshi-ootenaawaninik masinahikani<u>nk</u> (1.0)
    and they were told about what the cities were like in that book
    tepakop tahtwaayak ishi, (1.8)
    ʔin the seventh part,
    ekosi kii-otihtewak Caashowaa kapehshiwinihk Shaalooihk. (1.8)
    until they came to Joshua at the camp of Shiloh.

Caashowaa maaka kii-wepinamowak kishkeyihtaakohkewin (0.9)
Joshua then cast lots for a revelation
    ekota Saalooink. (1.8)
    there in Shiloh.

Otishkaw kaa-Tipe<u>n</u>cikec. Ekota maaka Caashowaa kii-papehkihshinamew,
    askiiniw Isreyil otawaahshimihsa, eshi-papeskitisinic." (2.9)
[ʔHe inquired] of the Lord. And then Joshua distributed the land to the
    children of Israel; there he distributed it."

[End of reading]

Ahpin Caashowaa kihci-okimaa   (4.5)
Then Joshua, the leader,
    kaa-kii-piikonank ohoweni Saahiloo.   (2.2)
    divided up this Shiloh.

    ...

Chapter Five

PᴏᴄC ⊲ᴏꜱᴏᴏ·⊲ᴘᴏ"Δ9 ᴏ
(Can You Write Syllabics?):
Literacy in Lynx Lake[1]

Near the main dock of the village, visitors are met by a large, white wooden sign painted with red letters, which reads:

> ## LYNX LAKE, ONT
>
> RESIDENTS AND NONRESIDENTS
>
> DO NOT BRING LIQUOR INTO THIS RESERVE. ᏏΔᐧ ᏟᐱᏂᏏᏌ Γᴏᐁᐧᴏᐧ ᐅᐅL ΔᐣdᴏᏏᴏᐧ
>
> BY
>
> CHIEF
>
> BAND COUNCIL

(Syllabics: *Kaawin taa-piintikaate minihkwewin ohomaa ishkonikaninink.*)

This brief message, written in two languages with completely different writing systems, gives a glimpse into a yet another fascinating and complex aspect of language use in the community: literacy. There are, in fact, two literacy traditions in Lynx Lake: English literacy, which uses a standard Euro-Canadian *roman* writing system, and the Native writing system called *syllabics*. This chapter provides a brief ethnographic exploration of the two systems and the attendant multilingualism indexed through the systems.

In the last thirty years, many studies of literacy among minority peoples have focused on 'orality versus literacy,' purporting to type cultures as 'oral' or 'literate' with attendant implications for the capacity to reason abstractly (Goody and Watt 1963; Goody 1968; and Ong 1982). This theoretical position has been repeatedly attacked for its implied ethnocentrism and overly simplistic rationale. Rather than continuing the attack against what has become an untenable position, I will immediately align myself with Finnegan (1988), Cole and Scribner (1981), Heath (1982a, 1982b, 1983), and Street (1984), some of the most vocal and eloquent debunkers of the oral/literate dichotomy, who all agree that literacy is variably defined and manifested around the world. Representing this newer trend in the study of literacy, Heath (1982b: 74) writes that only through ethnography is "further progress ... possible towards understanding cross-cultural patterns of oral and written language uses." This is my rationale for including a discussion of literacy in this book about language use in the community of Lynx Lake. I further consider the following four points of Street's (1984: 8) outline of an ideological model of literacy fundamental to any investigation of literacy, including the present:

1. ... the meaning of literacy depends upon the social institutions in which it is embedded;
2. literacy can only be known to us in forms which already have political and ideological significance and it cannot, therefore, be helpfully separated from that significance and treated as though it were an 'autonomous' thing;
3. the particular practices of reading and writing that are taught in any context depend upon such aspects of social structure as stratificational (such as where certain social groups may be taught only to read), and the role of educational institutions (such as in Graff's [1979] example from nineteenth-century Canada where they function as a form of social control);
4. the processes whereby reading and writing are learnt are what construct the meaning of it for particular practitioners ...

The discussion here will focus on the social (ideological) significance of literacy in Lynx Lake, the practices of the literacies within the community, and the processes by which community members learn and transmit literacy skills.[2]

LITERACY IN ENGLISH

As noted above, there are two primary literacy traditions used in Lynx Lake, syllabics and roman. Only within the last twenty-five years have English and the roman writing system made inroads into the social life of the people of

Lynx Lake; their introduction and uses are predictable and well defined. English was brought into the area initially by traders working with the Hudson's Bay Company, and later by educators, both religious and secular. Most non-Native 'Company' agents who lived for extended periods in the north learned enough of the local languages to conduct business, but often, one or two Native people served as translators and middlemen for the trader, making knowledge of English unnecessary for the general aboriginal population.

From the 1950s to the present, literacy has been taught to children in formal school settings presided over exclusively, until only very recently, by Euro-Canadian teachers. In the 1950s, a school was built in Mihshamihkowiihsh, attended by some of the children only at those times when their parents were in the village: this was the first time that English literacy had a real impact upon the people inside the community. In the 1960s and 1970s, many students in even the middle-school grades went outside the community to attend boarding-schools, where Native language use was actively discouraged with threats of punishment. In this environment, English literacy was learned and became the norm for young people. In the 1980s, only students continuing past the tenth grade attended boarding-schools which continued to insist upon heavy English use both inside and outside the classroom.

Within the community, English literacy is closely tied to education, but the definition of what constitutes literacy in English is more closely tied to the Severn ideal than to the Euro-Canadian ideal, which is minimally expressed as "people be[ing] able to read and write all ranges of material" (Rice 1985: 175) and maximally as "being able to decode a message at approximately the same rate at which one speaks (if not more rapidly) ..." (Mailhot 1985: 17). In Lynx Lake, a person able to read and comprehend primary-grade materials is considered literate in English. Ultimately, one's ability to read and write English is intimately tied with one's ability to speak and comprehend that language. As the children of Lynx Lake are in an environment where English is a second language, literacy and comprehension skills are taught simultaneously in the classroom, with English as both subject and medium of instruction. An attempt to increase English literacy skills assumes an increase in English grammatical skills. Therefore, using Euro-Canadian standards, one who speaks minimal English may become at best minimally literate as literacy assumes a prior knowledge of the language.[3]

However, once a person's familiarity with English reaches a certain level (by approximately the fifth or sixth grade), literacy skills often outstrip oral skills. In fact, there are several women in the Lynx Lake community who rarely or never use English orally, but who will buy English reading materials. I worked with one such young woman who was an outstanding syllabic transcriptionist. She was able to listen to any Native-language tape collected in Lynx Lake and, regardless of external noise or voice overlaps, could decipher what was said and write it down in fully phonemic syllabic form. While we worked almost exclusively in Severn Ojibwe, she would on occasion offer me English translations of words. Usually she would whisper a word in English, then write it down in the margin of my data book to show me. When I had read the word, she would erase it and we would go on with the transcription. This example fits Heath's definition of a literacy event: "A literacy event is any occasion in which a piece of writing is integral to the nature of participants' interactions and their interpretive processes" (Heath 1978, as cited in Heath 1982: 93).

The primary English literacy events in Lynx Lake focus around the following situations: business in the Band office and store, which involve dealings with the English-speaking matrix society; reading of English materials, including especially comic books, romance magazines, *Wawatay News*, record album notes, some religious books, and, on occasion, instruction manuals; formal education settings at the request of English-speaking teachers; ordering goods from English-language catalogues; symbolic uses of the roman orthography by a minority of elders who have learned to print their names; and the practice common among young people of writing words, especially names, on their arms, hands, and clothing. The words 'Angels in Satanastic Service,' written on the back of a teenager's Levi jacket, were made particularly memorable by the irony of reading them for the first time as the teenager knelt at the front of the church to receive communion. These uses of English and, as we will see later, syllabic materials, certainly fit the following statement by Heath: "examination of the contexts and uses of literacy [in] communities today may show that *there are more literacy events which call for appropriate knowledge of forms and uses of speech events than there are actual occasions for extended reading or writing*" (ibid: 94, italics are Heath's).

SYLLABIC LITERACY: INTRODUCTION

The older literacy tradition in Lynx Lake is the use of 'Cree syllabics' (*anihshiniiwipiihikewin* or ◁ᓄᠪᠥ·△∧△ᑫ·△ᵃ), an orthographic system created in the 1800s by the Wesleyan missionary James Evans. At that period, shorthand systems were the vogue in England, with some three hundred to four hundred varieties in use. Evans experimented with various non-roman scripts, ultimately settling on a syllabic system, based upon syllables rather than on an alphabet, perhaps influenced by the Cherokee syllabary, which had been written up widely as an effective literacy device. However, the actual characters appear to have been influenced by current shorthand practices. (See the syllabic chart below [table 1] for evidences of this, especially found in the final character set of the Western variety.) Evans began his mission work and work on non-roman scripts with the Ojibwe, which included a sophisticated phonemic analysis of Ojibwe, prior to his work with the Cree of Manitoba. It was while he worked with the Cree that he published his syllabic materials, hymns in pamphlet form; hence the system is now known as the 'Cree syllabary' (John Nichols, personal communication).

The current syllabic orthography is very easy to learn as the combinations of consonant and vowel which form the basis of the system are very predictable. Each consonant provides the unique shape of the syllabic character, and the vowel provides the orientation. Thus, all the syllables beginning with the /p/ sound have the same basic angular shape: ᐯᐱᐳᐸ. The direction the ᐯ is pointed determines with which vowel it is associated. Thus, the downward-pointing /p/ syllable is /pe/, the one pointing upward /pi/, the one pointing to the right /po/, and the one pointing leftward /pa/. This orientation is the same for the t-series: ᑌᑎᑐᑕ (/te/, /ti/, /to/, and /ta/, respectively), and the vowel series: ᐁᐃᐅᐊ (/e/, /i/, /o/, and /a/, respectively). The other syllabic characters are similarly related to each other in shape and orientation, but the orientation for the vowels is somewhat different from the t, p, and vowel series. For example, the c- and k-series are very close to each other in basic shape. The k-series is ᑫᑭᑯᑲ (/ke/, /ki/, /ko/, and /ka/), and the c-series is ᒉᒋᒍᒐ (/ce/, /ci/, /co/, and /ca/). The position of the protruding area determines the vowel. Thus, ᑫ and ᒉ are /ke/ and /ce/, respectively. The s-series (ᓭᓯᓱᓴ [/se/, /si/, /so/, and /sa/]), m-series (ᒣᒥᒧᒪ [/me/, /mi/, /mo/, and /ma/]), and y-series [ᔦᔨᔪᔭ (/ye/, /yi/, /yo/, and /ya/]) work in exactly the same way. The n-series (ᓀᓂᓄᓇ [/ne/, /ni/, /no/, and /na/]) and l-series (ᓓᓕᓗᓚ [/le/, /li/, /lo/, and /la/]) have the same basic shapes as the k- and c-series, but these are 'lying down.' The eastern sh-series (ᔐᔑᔓᔕ [/she/, /shi/, /sho/, and /sha/]) and r-series (ᕃᕆᕈᕋ [/re/, /ri/, /ro/, and /ra/]) are the only characters which do not immediately fit the patterns set by the other characters, but each series does have one basic shape which provides the consonant value. Figure 2 further displays the simplicity of the system. Note that each of the standard syllabic characters (except

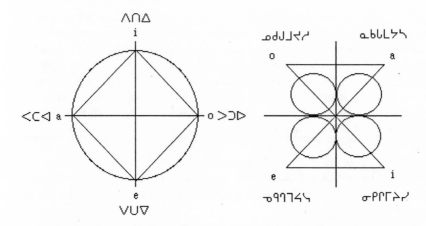

FIGURE 2 Basic Syllabic Shapes

for the sh-series and eastern r-series) may be placed upon one of the two figures and, depending upon the orientation, the vowels easily remembered. This system is indeed simple.

SYLLABIC STANDARDS

Since its inception, the syllabary has undergone many changes. Ultimately, three variations of the system have become accepted as regional standards: eastern syllabics, western syllabics, and the so-called Catholic western. The choice of standard indexes both geography and religious affiliation. Table 1 shows the basic syllabics system, with both eastern and western finals indicated.

Other syllabic characters[4] include ✕, which stands for Christ, and ₓ, which is the symbol equivalent to a period, signalling the end of a sentence. Long vowels are optionally marked by a raised dot over the syllabic character, as in ∫∫ˁ /shiihshiip/ ('duck'). The vowel ▽ /e/ is always long but left unmarked (undotted) in all syllabic characters. While the /l/ and /r/ sounds are not part of the Severn sound system, they are used in many personal names; as the /l/ is common in the Moose Cree literature used in Lynx Lake, these symbols have been included in the orthography.

Because the symbol for /h/, which occurs preconsonantally or intervocalically, is rarely represented in writing, and because vowel length is rarely indicated, a single syllabic character may represent up to four dis-

Table 1: The Basic Syllabics System

Consonants	e		i		o		a		Eastern Finals	Western Finals
	▽	(e)	△	(i)	▷	(o)	◁	(a)		
w (East)	·▽	(we)	·△	(wi)	·▷	(wo)	·◁	(wa)	°	
w (West)	▽·	(we)	△·	(wi)	⊃·	(wo)	◁·	(wa)		°
p	V	(pe)	∧	(pi)	>	(po)	<	(pa)	‹	'
t	U	(te)	∩	(ti)	⊃	(to)	C	(ta)	c	∫
k	٩	(ke)	P	(ki)	d	(ko)	b	(ka)	b	‹
c	٦	(ce)	٢	(ci)	J	(co)	L	(ca)	u	–
m	٦	(me)	Γ	(mi)	⌐	(mo)	L	(ma)	L	‹
n	⊃	(ne)	σ	(ni)	⊃	(no)	⊾	(na)	ɑ	›
s	٢	(se)	٢	(si)	٢	(so)	٢	(sa)	˥	∩
sh	٢	(she)	ʃ	(shi)	⊃	(sho)	⊃	(sha)	∾	∪
y	∠	(ye)	ʎ	(yi)	⊻	(yo)	˥	(ya)	ˀ,°	·
r (West)	³▽	(re)	³△	(ri)	³▷	(ro)	³◁	(ra)		³
r (East)	⊃	(re)	∩	(ri)	٩	(ro)	٩	(ra)	٩	
l (West)	³▽	(le)	³△	(li)	³▷	(lo)	³◁	(la)		³
l (East)	⊃	(le)	⊂	(li)	⊃	(lo)	⊂	(la)	⊂	
h									"	"
hk										×

crete syllables. For example, ∧ may indicate any of /pi/, /pii/, /hpi/, or /hpii/. The potential for ambiguity makes the process of reading syllabic materials very different from that of reading English written materials. Even the best readers typically read through a syllabic text once to disambiguate the words, and then a second time for comprehension. Because of the ambiguities inherent in the normal syllabic writing practices (which, incidentally, cause surprisingly few problems for the Native speaker) and the need to disambiguate the written code, one would never expect syllabics users to approximate the previously cited (Euro-Canadian) literacy standard expressed by Mailhot as "being able to decode a message at approximately the same rate at which one speaks (if not more rapidly) ..."

DIFFERENCES BETWEEN STANDARDS

Each syllabic character is made up of a consonant and a vowel (except for the vowel series, which has no associated consonant). However, as many syllables end with a consonant as well, these extra characters must be represented uniquely. This need for single-consonant characters gives rise to finals (*cahkipiihikanak*), the small, raised characters seen most commonly at the end of syllabic words. The consonant /w/ is treated uniquely as a separate character, represented by a dot, called appropriately the 'w-dot,' located mid-height next to the syllable with which it is associated. The primary differences between the standards are based upon the orientation of w-dots to syllabic characters and the shapes of the finals (see discussion below).

Below, the sentence *Ekwa wiin nistam kaa-takokosiyaank peshikopipoon kaawin ishkoonoowin onci-takwahsinoon* ('And when we first arrived here, there was no school for the first year'), is rendered in each of the three main, book standards used by the Ojibwe of Northern Ontario. This sentence, taken from a discussion about the move from Mihshamihkowiihsh to Lynx Lake, was chosen for the number of finals and w-dots exhibited:

Eastern Syllabics (a-finals):
ᐁᐧᑲ ᐧᐃᓐ ᓂᔥᑕᒻ ᑲᑕᑯᑯᓯᔭᓐᒃ ᐯᔑᑯᐱᐳᓐ ᑲᐧᐃᓐ ᐃᔥᑯᓄᐧᐃᓐ
ᐅᓐᒋᑕᐧᑲᓯᓄᓐ᙮

Western Syllabics:
ᐁᑲᐧ ᐃᐧᐣ ᓂᐢᑕᑦ ᑲᑕᑯᑯᓯᔭᐣᐠ ᐯᓯᑯᐱᐳᐣ ᑲᐃᐧᐣ ᐃᐡᑯᓄᐃᐧᐣ ᐅᐣᒋᑕᑲᐧᓯᓄᐣ᙮

Catholic Western Syllabics:
ᐁᐧᑲ ᐧᐃᐣ ᓂᐢᑕᑦ ᑲᑕᑯᑯᓯᔭᐣᐠ ᐯᓯᑯᐱᐳᐣ ᑲᐧᐃᐣ ᐃᐡᑯᓄᐧᐃᐣ ᐅᐣᒋᑕᐧᑲᓯᓄᐣ᙮

Notice that the eastern and western Catholic standards have the w-dots to the left of the associated syllabic character (i.e., *ekwa* is divided into the following syllabic order: e-w-ka, or ᐁ−ᐧ−ᑲ in eastern) and the western standard has them to the right of the character (e.g., e-ka-w, or ᐁ−ᑲ−ᐧ). The eastern finals are essentially miniaturized versions of the a-series syllabic character. Thus the symbol for the final /-k/, ᒃ, is a small, raised version of the symbol for the syllable /ka/, ᑲ. The a-finals are the eastern book standard, but normally the i-series finals (based upon the i-series syllabic set, ᐱ, ᑎ, ᑭ, etc.) are used in handwritten texts. In the western and Catholic western standards, the finals are completely different from the other syllabic characters (see table 1 above): these were based on English shorthand symbols. The other difference between the eastern and western standards is the orthographic neutralization of the /s/ and /sh/ distinctions in the western syllabic set. Thus, the /sh/ series is written in the western standards using the /s/ series, ᓭᓯᓱᓴ, rather with the separate sh-series, ᔐᔑᔓᔕ,

found in the eastern standard. This orthographic neutralization has been influenced by Plains Cree, where the orthography follows a phonological neutralization of these phonemes. Except for the sh-series, the eastern syllabics set is subsumed within the western, making it very easy for western-syllabics writers to read and use eastern syllabics. This is not the case with eastern-syllabics readers as the western syllabic finals are unique to that system.   .

As its name suggests, the Catholic western standard is used in northern Cree and Ontario communities where Catholic missionization was strongest. There is only one Ojibwe community in Northern Ontario which uses Catholic western as a community standard. The western (Anglican) standard is used in most communities in the Winisk subdialect of Severn Ojibwe but also in Lynx Lake, and the eastern standard is used in most Severn communities with nasal-clusters, the eastern subdialect. Another interesting convention involves the elimination of internal nasal finals (as found in the word *maank,* which would normally be represented as $\mathsf{L}^{a\cdot b}$ in the eastern system, but is realized as L^{b}). This convention minimizes the Severn subdialect differences, allowing for easy access to materials across the dialect.

Another variation on syllabic writing is the 'fully pointed' type rarely used by anyone outside a school setting. In this variety, length dots and /h/s are used in appropriate places, producing a fully phonemic orthography. This may be done using any of the standards as a base.

SYLLABIC LITERACY IN LYNX LAKE

The Ojibwe words used for 'someone reads' (displayed on map 4) exhibit interesting regional variation, which provides evidence of very different contact situations and of very different introductions to literacy. Notice that in southeastern Ontario (not including Golden Lake [GL] and North Bay [NB]) and in a large portion of southwest Ontario, the term *agindaaso* is used: in the area north of Lake Superior as far as Summer Beaver (SB), one finds the related form, *akinjige.*[5] These forms come from the word 'someone counts, reckons,' suggesting that reading in these areas was first associated with the fur trade. As the furs were brought in by the Native hunters and trappers, they were counted by traders, and the tallies written in a book, creating a relationship between counting and reading. By contrast, at Lynx Lake (LX) and Deer Lake (DL), the term used is *ayamichige* and among all Saulteaux communities the term is the closely related *anamichige,* in both cases apparent Cree loans for the word 'someone prays'

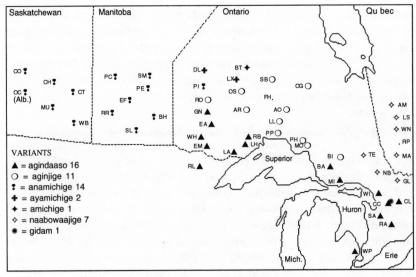

Someone reads (VAI)

MAP 4
Source: R. Valentine 1994

(cf. Fort Severn [Cree] *ayamihtaw*). In the church liturgy, many prayers are read from the prayer-book, giving rise to the intimate association of reading and praying. Literacy and missions entered Lynx Lake together, a fact which correlates well with the general principle espoused by Diringer (1962) that 'alphabets have followed religion. That is, the movements of religious conversion have often introduced scripts into a vast geographical area' (cited in Stubb 1980: 91).

DOMAINS OF USE IN LYNX LAKE

Every Sunday morning the church bell resonates from atop the esker in the centre of the community and is answered below by the sounds of snowmobiles and all-terrain vehicles as the people of Lynx Lake begin to make their way to the top of the hill to attend the worship service. The lay readers and women of the choir are among the first to arrive; they set down their plastic bags filled with books to don their robes, surplices, and ribbons in the arrangement and colour appropriate to the Anglican liturgical calendar, creating a flurry of activity in the two small rooms at the rear of the church. Soon, the elders and younger families join the trek up the hill, some riding in trucks or on snowmobiles, weather permitting, or on foot, also carrying the familiar plastic bags. The ubiquitous bags are filled with an array of liturgical books usually including *Horden's Book of Common Prayer* and *A Collection of Psalms and Hymns* in Moose Cree, and Faries's *Collection of Hymns* in Plains Cree. In addition to these books, which are used throughout the service, some elders also bring their large, black tome, the *Kihci-masinahikan* (Bible, or literally, 'Big Book'), a Plains Cree translation available since the turn of the century, and a few younger people bring one of various English translations, usually *The Good News Bible.* Readings from the *Book of Common Prayer* and songs from the hymn-books comprise approximately two-thirds of the two-hour Sunday-morning service, making the church setting the one most associated with syllabic literacy events.

However, the use of religious books is not limited to a church setting; in particular, the hymn-books are used for weekly choir practices held in individual homes and for the Sunday-evening hymn singing at the radio station. The prayer-books are used in some homes each morning and evening, used most mornings during the first hour of radio broadcasting, carried to the homes of those who cannot attend church because of infirmity, and used by visitation teams in the Advent season, during which time a team of two church leaders (male and female, lay and clergy) visit each home to talk, pray, and sing with the occupants. An Ojibwe (primarily in the Berens and Severn dialects), biscript (syllabic and roman Ojibwe) translation of the New Testament was recently published and is apparently being read in homes.

Most other syllabic materials used in Lynx Lake, known throughout Northern Ontario as the most (syllabic) literate community in the north, are produced within the community, the main exception being the *Wawatay News* (see chapter 3 for details of its use). The other materials represent the other side of literacy, writing. Examples of common uses of syllabic writing include announcements (see example below) and schedules to be read over the radio; translations of reports from various institutions, such as health bulletins and notes from the Anglican bishop; yearly reports from the SocioEconomic Development Corporation, the community-run organization which owns the store and other businesses in the village; the sporadically published local newspaper; minutes of meetings held in the community; and as a school subject. The frontages of most public buildings in Lynx Lake have syllabic and English signs attached to them, which allow for fleeting, symbolic displays of literacy.

NOTICE

Omahamo Store will be closed on Wednesday, Nov. 11, 1987 for

Remembrance Day.

ᐊᐧᐃᐧ·ᑊᐧᕽ ᑕ᙮Ꮲ<ᑯᒧᐤ ᐊᐱ᙭ᐊᐧ· ᕋᐧᐁ<ᔅ 11, 1987
·ᐃᓇᕈᑌ ᑊᐧᒡᐅᓂᓇ᙮ᐧ·ᕠᐧᐊᐧ· ᕝᕈᑊ ᕍᔆᕠ

Notice at Lynx Lake Radio Station, 11 November 1987

The announcement shown here provides an excellent example of the combination of English and Ojibwe literacy commonly found in the community. The syllabics, which were handwritten in the original note on lined, notebook paper, show an interesting mixture of standards, with several eastern i-finals, one eastern a-final, and one western final. The w-dots are predominantly western, as is the the use of the s-series syllabic i for the syllable /shi/. While this mixture of standards may appear to the reader to be an indication of poor literacy skills, this is not the case. Many Cree and Ojibwe elders who write syllabics do so with no finals or w-dots, and with no spaces between words or sentences. While this causes the reader a bit more trouble in reading, the basic skills are clearly in evidence. In this sample, the expected western w-dots and presence of finals attests to a writer with good literacy skills, learned locally, possibly self-taught.

TEACHING AND LEARNING SYLLABICS

In Lynx Lake, syllabic literacy is taught formally in the school by local experts. The selection of the syllabic teacher has been a politically charged issue, at least in the eyes of the Euro-Canadian principals in residence, as this skill has been associated with the village religious hierarchy. The Venerable William Pipoon is known throughout the Severn area for his outstanding syllabic literacy skills: he controls both eastern and western syllabics, is able to mark both vowel length and aspiration consistently and accurately, and has an excellent command of spelling in general. He has created many of the syllabic standards, and thus has been in the position to teach syllabics in the local school, which he did for several years. His teaching style was quite traditional: he taught the sounds of the characters from the syllabic chart that has been a symbol of syllabic literacy since Evans first produced one, and he also provided example after example of writing on the blackboard for the students, often writing out entire conversations about current events. Thus, he taught by example rather than by Euro-Canadian design, which tends to focus on keeping the interest of the student at all cost. This caused the Euro-Canadian teachers some concern as they saw only unruly students in the classroom rather than a renowned expert teaching a traditional skill[6] in a traditional fashion, albeit in a non-traditional setting. In 1987, his eldest daughter took over this job, teaching in much the same manner as did the The Venerable William Pipoon.

One of the most interesting aspect of learning syllabics is that, despite being taught in grade school, syllabic literacy is not actively acquired there. In the community, almost every adult over the age of twenty-five is literate in syllabics, although the definition of syllabic literacy, as noted earlier, is quite minimal, implying only that one is able to decipher the code. Thus, if one is presented with a Cree hymn-book, the literate person would be able to sing the syllables even if the words, being Cree, were not understood. This is considered the minimal definition of syllabic literacy in Lynx Lake. When younger people in Lynx Lake reach their early twenties, they usually marry, get permanent jobs within the community, and become involved in church activities, such as joining the women's (junior) choir or becoming an organist if one is male. It is at this point in village social life that syllabic literacy becomes important.

For example, most jobs in the Band office, and there are quite a few, involve the use of syllabics, in both reading and writing. In order to get such a job, one must suddenly become literate, which is precisely what is done. I was told by one young man that he literally learned how to read 'overnight.' This is not far from the truth, as one realizes that syllabic literacy skills, such as how to read the syllabic chart, and hence the symbols, are constantly available, particularly in the church. Many songs, such as 'The Doxology,' are sung at almost every public gathering, and regardless of how well one knows a song, the songbooks are used. Thus, young people are exposed to repeated correlations of memorized oral material with syllabic characters, providing an environment in which the basics of reading are well covered; that is, even outside of a Euro-Canadian school setting (which is, after all, a *very* recent addition to this society), these young people learn to correlate unique sounds and symbols. Thus, passive literacy can become active literacy overnight as the foundation has been set and only the particulars need be learned. As there are very few syllabic characters to learn, this takes little time.[7] Most of the people that I have asked about learning syllabic skills say either that they learned them by themselves, using the syllabic chart, or that they learned from either The Venerable William Pipoon or his brother, the Reverend Simon Pipoon.

Clearly, the people of Lynx Lake hold literacy as an ideal which virtually all adults achieve; but conversely, they fit the traditional profile of an 'oral' society, where face-to-face interaction is primary and where myths and history are part of a spoken discourse. At the same time that these people lived on traplines, hunting and gathering, they were also reading and writing letters.

ROMAN OJIBWE ORTHOGRAPHY

In the 1960s, a standardized phonemic roman writing system began to be used for Minnesota and western Ontario Ojibwe. There are two versions, southern and northern, which differ primarily in the representation of fortis and lenis consonants, each representing the phonetic facts of the dialect in which it is used. The primary orthography system used in this book is the northern roman system. This system is rarely utilized outside educational settings in Northern Ontario, but.it is mentioned here because the newly translated Ojibwe New Testament uses a format of facing pages of roman and syllabic texts. Given the high use of such materials in Lynx Lake, it is not unreasonable to expect younger people literate in English to gravitate towards the roman writing system. Whether this happens remains to be seen.

CONCLUSIONS

Associated with the changes in the second language from Cree to English are changes from Cree to English as the primary language of literacy. English literacy is an integral part of grade school, as both medium and target of instruction; syllabic literacy is taught a few hours each week in the grade school, but usually not learned until needed as a young adult. However, as syllabic literacy is tied closely to the church in Lynx Lake, the importance of the religious structure in the community ensures that syllabic literacy will continue for quite some time. This division of domains in literacy allows for a stable biliteracy situation to continue. The presence of the newly translated Ojibwe New Testament may indicate a further move from the Cree liturgy and Cree as a second language, but the use of syllabics in that document will probably reinforce syllabic literacy.

Chapter Six

Intersection of Language and Music

To fill in the mosaic of discourse types in Lynx Lake, especially the genres and channels of language use, the intersection of language and music must be explored. This chapter provides an ethnographic overview of the types of music found in the community, along with social constraints on participation, and a description of the continuum between language and music which is found in the context of religious discourse. Echoing the literary situation described in chapter 5, Cree and English are the predominant languages used in the musical expression of the people of Lynx Lake, and, once again, the greatest generic variations are found in the context of the church. In addition, this chapter extends the investigation of literacy in community life by exploring the little-studied, oral aspects of reading, which are manifest through the lyrical content of the formal readings, chants, and music performed from books.

To the outsider not used to winter in the remote northern expanses of Canada, the overwhelming impression is that of silence. The myriad lakes stand paralysed with ice crusts well over three feet deep; the muskeg silenced by layers of wind-packed snow. However, to the Severn Ojibwe people who call the northern wilderness of Ontario their home multitudes of voices cry out from both the earth and the sky. When the lakes begin freezing in the long, clear autumn nights, the expansion and contraction of the vast ice sheets reverberate in eerie wails. People talking quietly to each other of this rare event speak of *e-mawikawacic mihkwam,* 'ice that cries with the cold.' Another clear winter night brings the *waawaahte,* the northern lights, which whistle from the netherworld.[1] I am warned in semi-jest not to whistle during the borealis display, lest I be called from earth to join the heavenly activities.

The school janitor leaning over his mop in the hallway listens intently to the far-off thunder, trying to understand. The voices of *pinehsiwak*, 'the Thunderers, thunderbirds,' who live farther south in Thunder Bay, are speaking, their words just beyond the ken of understanding, but with a message that should be understood. The four winds, traditionally known as *manitook*, 'spirits,' also cry out as they make their way across the vast northlands. Sounds are voices; voices denote life. The sound of a voice is extremely important, so important that in stories of the dreaded *Wiintikook*, the ice-hearted cannibals ubiquitous to the Algonquian northland, a *Wiintikoo* need merely to shout in order to kill its victim.

In the midst of these earthly and unearthly sounds, the voices of the Severn people themselves can be heard. The sun rises late, around 8:30 a.m., during the short winter days of Northern Ontario. Walking through the snow at sunrise, carrying empty containers to be filled at the school water faucet, one of only two in the community, one can hear the faint voices of elders singing morning hymns, the tunes echoing in the frigid gusts of wind. At a birthday party, after the feast of fried smoked fish, bannock, fish gut soup, and cookies has been prepared, the uncle of the honoured hostess leads the group in several readings and prayers, and finally in the singing of 'The Doxology' before the guests pull their plates and utensils out of their plastic shopping bags and line up for their share of the delicacies. Turning on the radio to catch the early morning 'show' by an elder and his wife, one is startled by the volume of the song led by the man, which is often overwhelming as the sound had been turned up earlier to hear their otherwise quiet voices.

Music is a central part of life in the Severn Ojibwe community of Lynx Lake, with few restrictions as to when and where it will be found. Along other parameters such as lyrical content, gender and age of the performer, and style, however, music, and especially singing, are tightly constrained. The interplay of these constraints provides interesting insights into aspects of social structure within the community.

LYRICAL CONTENT OF MUSIC

With rare exceptions, the music of Lynx Lake is the music of the Cree Anglican church. But for 'The Doxology,' singing is performed from songbooks, all written in the Native syllabic script, not from memory even if the song is well known. In this way, among others, literacy comes into play; the songbooks, and the prayer-book containing many sections that are sung, are essential to the singing event. Notably, the songbooks and prayer-books are all in languages other than Severn Ojibwe.

Most hymn singing is from either the Moose or the Plains Cree hymn-books called, respectively, *waapi-nikamowimasinahikan,* 'white songbook,' and *oshaawashko-nikamowimasinahikan,* 'green songbook.' The white songbook is used most widely in church, with a ratio of about five songs from the white book sung to every one from the green songbook. All songs sung in the morning services at the church are either from one of these hymn-books or from the Moose Cree prayer-book. Each adult carries his own set of books, often complete with the 'Western' or Plains Cree Bible, in a handbag or the ubiquitous shopping bag to any meeting at St Paul's Anglican Church. As expected, these books are carried to Sunday services, but they are also carried along to weddings, christenings, funerals, and, by certain people, to feasts, opening ceremonies, and even to friends' and relatives' houses when visiting.

There are typically two or more services each Sunday at St Paul's Anglican Church. The morning service is at least two hours long, with the liturgy read and sung in Moose or Plains Cree (often with the unmistakable accent of Severn Ojibwe) and the sermon given in a stylized form of Severn, which reflects its origin in the study of the Cree Bible. The church services, while High Anglican in form, are viewed as thoroughly local and hence indigenous. An adult is missed if he or she does not attend this service, and failing to attend two or more Sundays in a row will generate indirect but pointed inquiries as to the reason for the absence. Even the itinerant ethnographer and linguist were included in this system of spiritual concern and social control, but complaints about plywood benches, hours of listening to archaic Cree, and the difficulty in following all but the sermon were never appropriate and would have been ignored even had they been so. The Euro-Canadian teachers, monolingual English speakers, were never aware of the expectations that extended even to them.

In the afternoon or early evening, the church bell rings, calling the young adults to the *wemihtikooshiwipiintikaaniwan* (literally, 'Whiteman in-gathering,' in English, 'the English service'). As it is recognized that the Cree liturgy is difficult to understand, especially for the younger members of the community, an English service is held in which the traditional Anglican liturgy is read in English, with English songs. However, it is often the case that one or more lay reader[2] involved in this service does not read or speak English, so that, not infrequently, parts or all of the liturgy is read in Cree and the songs sung in Cree and English simultaneously. Outnumbering the congregation about two to one, the junior-choir members sit in their robes and surplices in facing pews located behind the lectern and in front of the altar. The members of this choir, the younger counterparts of the morning choir, all read English and practise and sing the songs in that language. Typically, the sermon is in Severn Ojibwe: the 'Englishness' of the English service is defined by the language in which the choir members read and sing. The hymns sung in English are performed in precisely the same musical style as they are in the Native language (discussed below under 'Style').

As stated earlier, the performance of these religious songs is not bound to certain times and places, despite their original contexts. The songs that are sung in church are also sung at home, on the radio every morning and all day Sunday, at feasts, at birthday parties, at the opening of new buildings in the community such as the store, the laundromat, and the beadwork shop, and at school concerts. Hymns are heard throughout the week, all through the day and into the night. Other songs are rarely sung – the most frequently encountered musical tradition not associated with the church is contemporary rock. Walking through the village during the evening, one can often hear popular tunes played and sung by one of the two or three bands who practise most evenings in one of the community's empty buildings. These bands are usually made up of about five young men, most of whom are employed in permanent positions in the Band office and store during the day. The best of the bands, the one that has played gigs outside the community, practises in the Band hall. The teen and pre-teen audience for these band practises gathers outside the hall, occasionally peering through the windows into the dim interior, where several coloured lights shoot their reflections off the centred spinning mirrored ball. The observers are quiet; walking by, one hears the band playing the old Beatles song 'Can't Buy Me Love.'

GENDER AND AGE IN MUSIC PERFORMANCE

There is a brief pause in the evening church service. A couple of members of the choir whisper together behind songbooks, the lay reader looks around, first into audience of about ten people, then behind him, towards the choir. One of the women from the choir steps down to play the organ, and the service continues. Later, a discussion ensues about the propriety of the situation.

One of the most immediate differences between Lynx Lake men and women in the domain of music is that in most public situations the men play the music and the women sing it. This division is very apparent in the formal structure of the choir and organists in the church. The 'senior choir' (*nikamohkwek*, 'song women') is made up of women from the age range of about thirty-five to sixty-five; approximately fifteen women comprise the core of this choir. A second choir, the 'junior choir' (*kaa-wemihtikooshiiwi-ayamihcikewaac*, literally 'those who are Whiteperson pray-ers,' also called *wemihtikooshiiwi-nikamohkwek*, 'Whiteperson song women'), consists of about fifteen of the younger women, ranging in age from twenty to thirty-five.

Men do not join the choir; rather, they become organists. In 1988 there were approximately twenty-eight organists, all male, who took turns playing the organ for church services. Often, two organists would switch places between songs during a service, each having a particular corpus of songs with which he was most familiar, and hence, most accomplished. The organists range in age from twenty to forty-five, with the majority being in their late twenties to early thirties. A couple of the organists also doubled as 'choir masters' (*nikamowikimaak*), those who play the guitar along with the choir during choir practice and other choir sessions outside of the church. The population of the community was just under three hundred, at least half of whom were under age twenty. Thus, we can see that the total number of choir members and organists was significant, comprising around 40 per cent of the adult population.

We can see that the structure within the church almost guarantees that the men play the instruments and the women sing. The scenario of the choir member leaving her seat to fill in as an organist was considered remarkable. In the discussion after the event, it became clear that the junior choir in attendance felt they were not being given the respect that was their due; no organist had been assigned to play in the service that evening, despite an earlier request for one. Although the situation was marked by social problems, I found it interesting that the choir member played the organ with a proficiency equalling that of a regular organist.

At least half the community is crammed into the Band hall, many of the elder women and young families sitting on benches backed up against the side walls. Men of all ages, interspersed with more families, sit on benches in the rear of the hall, behind the single, tiny, barrel-shaped woodstove, its walls glowing red with heat. A horde of young people stand huddled together near these rear benches, making entry into the hall through the two doors a feat of determination and daring. They move for no one, but neither will they venture farther into the room. The band on the raised platform at the front of the room plays 'Oh, Dem Golden Slippers,' beckoning would-be dancers onto the floor, but despite all the playful shoving of people towards the centre, no one will begin the dance. At last, a group of men break from the ranks as a single unit and literally pull partners from the watching crowd. After a half-hour of instrumental beckoning, the square dance has finally begun; the pace will not abate for another four or more hours.

The public preference for a male instrumentalist extends to those who play for square dances (*niiminaaniwank*) as well. The ability to play a musical instrument is highly valued, so that many men play several instruments, allowing for a rather fluid membership in a band. As one performer tires, or decides to take a turn on the floor, others easily move into the vacant position. A band for a square dance usually consists of a lead, rhythm, and bass guitar player, a drummer (standard kit), and a fiddler. There is little or no group practice outside the dance itself, reminiscent of the organists, who often practise with the volume off, or with headphones on, during the church service. Many of the songs played have historical precedents in the music of the Orkneys, which was brought to the Hudson Bay area by 'Company' men (cf. Lutz's [1978] discussion of contemporary fiddle music found in Eskimo communities, originally introduced by White whalers, now termed 'Eskimo music').

All instrumentalists are male, as is expected, but there are no vocalists in this kind of a band. The square dances are not 'called,' but rather are similar to the old Virginia reels in that the dancers know the steps, or follow their partner or the next couple while learning the steps. In 1981, the men were the 'fancy steppers,' using a semi-clogging step, while the women 'walked' through the dances, making a studious effort to avoid swinging or bouncing to the music. However, in 1987 a group of women was attending weekly sessions to learn how to 'clog' from another local woman who had learned the style of dance in a neighbouring community. Indeed, new dances and songs came into the community in 1981 in a similar way, but almost exclusively through the men. Once the dancing gets started, everyone, from young adults to elders, joins in.

In situations where group singing is called for, as in church services, at feasts, and on the radio, men and women sing together. For the most part, even in these less formal group situations, men are the instrumentalists, as they are in any public situation in which a portable instrument is played. Where otherwise very rare, solo and duet singing is commonly heard on the radio. As noted in chapter 3, the first person to 'sit' at the radio station in the morning usually reads sections from the prayer-book and sings a hymn or two during the hour. This early-morning time slot is filled by one or two of a very small group of elders, and most often at least one of those scheduled to sit is male, so that a man is usually the one to initiate the singing. A woman sitting in this time period will not sing solo, but men sitting alone are often heard singing hymns by themselves.

On Sundays, the radio station is run almost exclusively by those heavily involved with the formal church structure, that is, by priests, lay readers, choir members, and organists. The Sunday radio shows (*apinaaniwank*) are much like the first-hour shows of the rest of the week, including many songs, some teaching, and some preaching and prayers. On Sundays, however, both young (early twenties and up) and old people sing, with one to two hours in the evening set aside for ensemble hymn singing by a group which includes most of the senior-choir members, the priests, the lay readers (men and women), and some of the elder men. Whereas elders sitting singly or in pairs invariably sing *a capella*, when younger people and groups sing on the radio, singing is accompanied by a guitar or two, played, as expected, by a male, unless one is not available.

In the beadwork shop, a not-too-elderly woman sits hunched over her emerging moccasin, humming quietly; her neighbour, with similar posture, stops in mid stitch, peers over her glasses at another worker across the table, and enters into an animated discussion about a skunk that has been wandering through the community. When the discussion ends, the humming, which had continued throughout the discussion, once again is heard.

While women are less involved with the public performance of music than are men, they sing in more contexts than men do, and indeed participate in one genre of music exclusive to them. The situation in the beadwork shop is very common, especially among women of senior-choir age. When not directly involved in verbal interchange, women frequently hum the tunes of hymns. This may take place as they are walking outside, either alone or with someone else, when beading or sewing, when sitting at the radio station with another person who is talking to the radio audience, and so on, in any situation where they are not immediately involved in verbal interchange. Humming may span an entire song, or be as brief as two or three notes, depending on the interchange 'gap' that is being filled.

The only pre-contact song type that remains in current usage is the lullaby, which is sung while rocking children to sleep in swinging hammocks (*memepison*) or as they rock in their cradle boards (*tihkinaakan*). The lullabies used consist of a single repeated syllable (*me*) sung softly in time with the pushes of the swing. Men do not sing lullabies, and they hum far less frequently than women.

STYLE IN SINGING

The pace of the songs sung and played in Lynx Lake is quite slow by White American/Canadian standards. (See timing of the sample below.) People prefer two-part harmonies over unison singing, and a soprano descant is greatly admired, although most women in the community have voices in the alto range. A complaint heard several times from members of the young women's choir was that because no one in the choir sang soprano, they had a hard time harmonizing.

Vibrato is considered undesirable, a sign of excess emotion. This stands in stark contrast to Densmore's (1910: 4) observations of Chippewa singing in Minnesota: "One of the characteristics of Chippewa singing observed during this study is that a vibrato, or wavering tone, is especially pleasing to the singers. This is difficult for them to acquire and is considered a sign of musical proficiency. The vibrato may seem to indicate an uncertain sense of tone, but the singer who uses it is ready to approve the song when sung with correct intonation. He declares, however, that this is not 'good singing.'"

A woman once asked me why "White ladies all have shaky voices," incredulous that an entire population would be thus afflicted. A good woman's voice by community standards is one that is true to pitch, displaying no vibrato; loud with no breathiness; and suited to singing in both alto and soprano ranges. Music is typically sung by all members of the community in a slow pace with minimally variable timbre.

It is interesting to note that, in normal speaking, there is minimal variation in intonation, aside from a very brisk drop at the end of a sentence or phrase. It is even more notable that normally expected downdrift does not occur – the intonational contours remain virtually straight until the final drop, which indicates that these people are compensating to maintain such an even intonation. In the same vein, speakers of the nearby Berens dialect were said by some community members to 'sing' their words. The intonation of Berens Ojibwe is substantially more variable than that of Severn Ojibwe, which again ties into the question of vocal fluctuation.

On the radio, the elder men who sing morning hymns perform the songs *a cappella* at an extremely loud volume, to the point where the radio signal is distorted. The senior choir members sing considerably louder than do their junior-choir counterparts. Thus, the few men who sing publicly, often solo, sing louder than the elder-choir women, who in turn sing louder than the junior-choir women, who are in turn louder than their non–choir member counterparts. The relative ranking of volume at which songs are sung seems to be associated with respect given to personal roles in a broader social context.

As soon as they have finished singing their last song, 'Jingle Bells,' written in English on huge pieces of pasteboard, the children in their crepe-paper angel and shepherd costumes fly off the stage, tearing their and their neighbours' costumes off before they hit the ground. The principal announces the next number: the junior choir is going to sing some songs. The adults' eyes swivel to the rear of the Band hall, where a group of young women are standing, eyes downcast to the plywood floor, fiddling with their plastic shopping bags which hold their songbooks. After about a minute of whispering together, heads still bent, eyes intent on the ground, the group troops single file to the front of the hall and up the steps to the stage, and arranges itself in a single line against the back wall of the stage, which becomes a support for most of the women. The postmaster stands slightly forward of the group, on the far left side, already strumming a hymn on his guitar. Heads still pointed downward, the women pull out their hymn-books, words in English, no musical scores, which they then hold at chin height or higher. They are ready to begin their section of the school Christmas concert, which will take almost a half-hour, as they sing five Christmas hymns. Throughout their songs, the children tear the decorations from the hall, throwing the debris at any likely target, while the parents and teachers sit, each group wondering why the other doesn't take charge of the kids. After the junior-choir songs are through, eyes still studiously avoiding any other, the choir vacates the stage, making room for seven of the senior-choir members. The women, each carrying her own songbook, line up on the stage like their younger counterparts, standing only slightly closer to the audience, to sing another four or five Advent hymns, this time in Cree.

In all cases of organized singing, people use hymn-books. When singing publicly outside the church building, as in the school concert described above, the choir members line up in a row across the extreme rear of the stage, each member holding her own hymn-book. The elder women hold their books at about waist level, and the younger women at chest or even chin level. If someone makes an error, she lifts the book to cover her face. Teenagers singing in public, which happens only in school concerts, will stand in the same configuration, but facing the wall, with the songsheets or books covering their faces the entire time.

At the radio station and in homes, people sit around the perimeter of the room and sing from their books. In all situations, the eyes remain almost exclusively on the book, except for brief glances around to see what is going on. When performing before an audience, singers have virtually no eye contact with the listeners, and they in turn rarely look at the singers. In everyday conversation, eye contact is fleeting and rare. In public performance, the non-performance standards of (non-)contact are exaggerated. A person who holds direct eye contact with another is considered to be bold, to the point of challenging another. Young people, whose heads are usually bowed when talking with elders, extend this behaviour to covering their faces with their books, or by turning their backs, which is not considered to be rude, but a posture of modesty. Among the women singing, the younger adults have their books closer to their eyes, ready to shield them if they make an error, ready to show humility. The older women hold their books at waist level: they have earned the right to be front and centre publicly, regardless of the quality of the performance.

OTHER MUSICAL EXPRESSIONS

The local radio station, in use daily from 8:00 a.m. to 9:00 p.m., is the outlet for much music in the village. Whereas the elders who 'sit' earlier in the day fill their scheduled hour with stories, new and old, occasionally interspersed with a song or two that they sing themselves, many of the middle-aged, and most of the younger participants, play tapes and records. In general, the younger the scheduled 'sitter,' the more music is played and the less spontaneous talk is heard throughout the hour.

Middle-aged men play far more music on the radio than do their female counterparts. In order of preference, the records and tapes that are played range from 'old time' fiddle music with no vocals to 'old time' gospel, similar musically to the first type, with four-part vocal harmonies and gospel lyrics, to country and western music, heavily represented by Waylon Jennings and Willie Nelson. Middle-aged women who play music on the radio tend to prefer the gospel songs – both Anglo and Native sung.

Younger people play a variety of songs. Among those of the youngest age group scheduled to sit at the radio station, heavy metal music was the current favourite in 1988. However, since few members of this group are ever scheduled to sit at the station, this music is not generally heard. These heavy metal aficionados were easy to spot as they wore studded, black leather jackets often accented with heavy chains, and, in the late 1980s, favoured razor-cut hairdos.

Native-authored and -performed music is most often heard on Sundays, the day on which religious programming is expected. The Native-authored songs are usually written in English, with a typical gospel musical structure. Such songs are usually sung by more than one person, usually a mixed duet, often a husband and wife. That the songs are sung and authored by Amerindians is apparent, in the first case, by the English pronunciation and the characteristic voice timbre and, in the second instance, by the structure of the lyrics. A predominant feature of gospel songs created by those whose first language is English is line final rhyming. Songs authored by Native speakers of Severn Ojibwe tend to ignore this convention entirely, reflecting the total indifference to rhyme in the Native language. The polysynthetic nature of Algonquian languages leades to the creation of rhyming as a by-product of parallelism of syntactic form, with the result that rhyming often occurs. Perhaps, however, its ubiquity means that rhyme is not manipulated for its own sake. The syntactic and semantic parallelism itself is poetic, and the resulting phonological rhyme essentially ignored.

Few people in Lynx Lake create songs which are publicly aired. During my time of fieldwork, I heard only one person, a young man accompanied only by his guitar, sing a song of his own creation. On that Sunday-afternoon radio show, he made up the lyrics as he sang, making no attempt to rhyme. The lyrics focused on his commitment to God, detailing both his own failings and his intentions to improve his life, both tune and lyrics very much in keeping with the Native-authored recordings under discussion. Recently, another young man, affected by the suicide of his brother, created a 'gospel band,' performing songs written in a country-western style with Severn Ojibwe lyrics focused on a religious message of hope. The band played in Lynx Lake and neighbouring communities in an attempt to influence and encourage other Severn youths who might be struggling with the tide of suicide that has swept through Native communities across North America.

Yet another group of songs is sung privately by the junior-choir members in their weekly practices. These are contemporary religious songs, which are sung from songsheets that are typed, copied, and bound by the group itself. These young women learned these songs while attending religious conferences outside the community, conferences heavily attended by Euro-Canadian Anglicans, or through the yearly week-long 'vacation Bible schools' staffed by White Anglican youth from as far south as London, Ontario. These songs are sung at a considerably faster pace than are the standard hymns, although still somewhat slower in tempo than they would be sung by the typical singer in the matrix society.

SPEECH VERSUS SONG

> Standing in his black robe topped by a white surplice, the ribbon hanging down around his neck – on this Sunday, a deep purple to commemorate the Advent season – one of the lay readers begins to read from the small, red prayer-book, its edges characteristically frayed by years of use. The liturgy is long; it continues for over an hour and a quarter, the rapid pace of the reading contrasting with the slow tempo of the songs interspersed throughout the service.

Listening closely to the two lay readers, ones hears several subtle variations in their voices as different sections are read from the prayer-book; the difference between reading and song is the least subtle of the vocal variations occurring throughout the liturgy. There appears to be a continuum from speech to song which occurs only in the context of the church liturgy. This continuum, or perhaps even full circle, from speech to song, is examined here.

Reading quickly or evenly is a sign of competence in the church hierarchy, whether the readings are prayers, prose, or songs. In looking at speech genres of the church, we find that literacy skills are essential to competent performance of the religious liturgy, and religious discourse in general. Outside the church there is no chanting, little oral reading, and, as seen earlier, little singing other than of hymns. Thus, those genres which are most marked and distinguishable by variation in pitch, tempo, volume, and density of syllables to silence are intricately interwoven with literacy skills, and occur within the context of the church. As the church itself represents a post-contact innovation, we may assume that many of these genres are quite new. While it is possible that the Anglican forms are overlays over older Ojibwe genres, there is no direct evidence for this in the synchronic data, nor is there evidence for this in reports of the area through the last century.[3] Synchronic separation of Native and outside musical traditions is well attested in Native North American ethnomusicology (see Nettl 1989, Lutz 1978, Merriam 1967, and List 1964, among others).

Below, I explore some of the prosodic phenomena associated with, and unique to, singing, sing-chanting, reading-chant, read prayers, spoken prayers, religious oratory, formal public announcements (in Severn), and animated narrative. Except for the singing and narrative, all examples were collected in St Paul's Anglican Church in Lynx Lake, on the morning of 25 October 1987. The services in Lynx Lake follow the Anglican church schedule. Thus, in this case, the songs and readings are those appropriate to the nineteenth Sunday after Trinity. There were two lay readers this day, Kerena Pipoon and Isreal Kookii, and the sermon was given by the Reverend Simon Pipoon. (This sermon is presented in chapter 7.) I chose to use data from a single church service, in part because several of the prosodic styles were provided by a single speaker, allowing for controlled cross-generic comparison.

Linguistic genre is usually determined by examining a combination of thematic elements and stylistic, textual features. However, even those not trained in linguistics are capable of naming genres in their own speech community – and often without even being close enough to make out the words being spoken. For example, one only need hear the intonation contours to tell a sermon from a conversation, a rap song from an oratoria, a lecture from a nursery rhyme. The intonation of oral discourse is perhaps the most important feature for marking and keying genre. All of the following genres, from song, to chant, to conversation, do have attendant linguistic features that could be studied and, in many cases, are within this volume. To a certain degree, functional features are encapsulated by the headings used. While these genres are not locally named, the attendant performative features are explicitly learned and used by both clergy and laity. These features are recognized and used across the Severn region and are shared also by many of the Anglican Cree communities. I have chosen to study here the prosodic distinctives of genres, in part because these are often the features most definitive of genre, but least often addresssed by researchers. The following analysis of prosodic features is unique for cross-genre comparisons, but one that I feel is long overdue.

Singing

'Singing,' as used here, refers to syllabic song where, generally, each note has no more than one syllable associated with it. The example illustrated below is a single melodic phrase, part of a song sung on the Lynx Lake radio station one Sunday afternoon in November 1987 by a married couple in their early forties. The song was from one of the Cree hymn-book, so the language is Cree. The husband played a guitar accompaniment, strumming down and up with a flat pick on each beat: the two sang the melody in unison. One stylistic device consistently used by singers in Lynx Lake is moving from one pitch to another just prior to changing syllables. This device, which creates a tight cohesion within the phrase, is difficult to capture in a transcription, as in doing so the basic tune tends to be obscured.

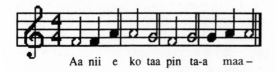

Aa nii e ko taa pin ta-a maa –

This eight-syllable phrase[4] took 10.3 seconds to sing, giving a ratio of 0.77 syllables per second. This parameter is used here as a convenient measure for distinguishing genres. It is more interesting in the less musical genres as it highlights an emic category associated with good oral-reading skills, skills which are evident also in the most musical categories.

Sing-chanting (Musical Reading from the Cree Book of Common Prayer)

Anglican chants are used in a few places in the Cree liturgy in the Lynx Lake church. The very typical chant presented below is characterized by a simple five-note melody in A-flat major. As is characteristic of chants, a number of syllables are sung on a single note. In my recording of this song, the voices of the senior-choir women and The Venerable William Pipoon are the only ones to be heard. The example given here is presented in the Cree *Book of Common Prayer* in the following format:

ᑭᓵᑕᒍᑊ ᑌᐯᕆᖅᖃᕝ ᐁᑭᒪᓂᐧᐊᑦᒎ ᐧᐃᓓ ᐁᐧᐊᐧᐸᓇ ᑿᐱ ᐅᔭᕓᐊᑕᑊ, ᐊᒪᑭᐅᕆ ᐅᔭᐃᓂᕐᐃᐊᓇᐤᒎ ᑭᑊ ᐅᑦ ᐃᑦᑎᕐᕆᑕᓇᐤ ᐁᔪᑕ ᑭᑊ ᐅ ᒪᓂᔑᕐᕆᑕᓇᐤ ᑿ ᐸᓇᐧᐁᑦᑎᑕᑊₓ   (Horden 1970: 13)

In this transcription, the reader is given only minimal cues to guide the timing of the music. Colons mark the end of melodic phrases, although in this performance, only the first colon is heeded. The paragraph indentation marks the beginning of the verse, and a period (the small ₓ found at the end of the sentence) marks the end. There are sixty-eight syllables in this verse, which took twenty-three seconds to sing. The following is a somewhat idealized score of the verse:

The numbers above the notes correspond to the numbers above the corresponding syllables, which can be found in the second rendition of the musical structure below. In the following transcription, in the line directly beneath the syllabic representation, a series of bullets appear, each bullet corresponding to a single syllable. This line is offered as an aid to a quick reading of the syllabic structure for those who do not read Cree syllabics. The time notations found the line with the Cree syllabics provides the real time elapsed from the beginning of the verse to that point. Thus we find that between 1 and 4 on the score, we have fourteen syllables, which take 4.5 seconds to sing.

1   (Slowly)   4   5   6
ᑭᕁᒡᒋᒢ   ᑌᐯᒡᕆᖅᖅᓯ   ᐁᑭᒥ (4.5 sec)   ᓂᒍᐧᐃᕠ: (8.65 sec)
•   •   ••   •• ••••   ••••   •   •   •

7 (Very quickly —)
ᐧᐃᓭ   ᐁᐧᐊᐧᐸ   ᑿ   ᑭ   ᑐᗩᐊᒃ,   ᐊᒪᑭᐳᕆ   ᑐᗩᐊᐣᕑᐊᓇᐤ   ᑭᕀ   ᐳᕀ
•• • • • ••   •   •   •• • •   ••••• •••••••   •   •
         (Slowly) 8-9 10 11 12 13
ᐃᒡᒡᑎᑎᑕᓇᐤ ᐁᐧᐁᐨ ᑭᕀ ᐳ ᘗᓸᑎᑎᑕᓇᐤ ᑿ (15.5 sec) ᐸᐧᐁᒡᑎᒃᐻ (23 sec)
••••••   •   •   •   •••••••   •   •   •• ••••

Note that syllabic characters which touch the baseline represent single syllables. Those characters which reach only mid-line (called 'finals') represent syllable coda consonants, except for the w-dots, which represent syllable onset ws. Thus, by counting syllabic characters, one quickly arrives at the number of syllables read. Dots directly above syllabic characters mark vowel length.

There are six paragraphs, or melodic verses, in this section of the readings. The verses are all sung with the same melodic structure, averaging from twenty to twenty-five seconds to perform. The number of syllables does not account for the variation in time in a straightforward manner, however. One would expect that those verses with the greatest number of syllables (the verses have fifty-two, sixty-eight, fifty-one, fifty-five, twenty-nine, and thirty-nine syllables, respectively) to be the longest in absolute time, but indeed, the final two verses, which have the fewest syllables, are sung most slowly. Another interesting performance feature is that the melodic structure is imposed upon the boundary syllables of the phrase: the final three syllables in the first line of the verse have a one-to-one correspondence to notes, as do the final four syllables of the second line. Thus, the chant is most musical at what in speech would be considered intonational boundaries, and least melodic inside the phrasal unit.

As was noted above, this verse is sixty-eight syllables in length and was performed in twenty-three seconds, giving an average ratio of just under three syllables per second. During the interval between the marks 7 and 8, a 6.85-second span, there are forty-five syllables, giving a tempo of 6.57 syllables per second, a remarkably quick pace. Remember that these syllables are read from the hymn-book: to be a active participant in the church service as member of the choir or laity, one must have excellent literacy skills.

Reading-chant (Public Reading from the Cree Book of Common Prayer)

This is essentially an oral version of the previous genre. Here intonational contours associated with everyday speech are minimized and stylized: the aural impression is almost that of a song being sung in a monotone. The reader, Kerena Pipoon, intones loudly (at about the same level as an average university lecture, which, within the Severn speech community, would be considered quite loud) and the pitch of her voice is unusually high. Individual syllables are not stressed; rather, the pacing of syllables is markedly even. This combination of vocal qualities is used only in oral reading of scriptures and other publicly read portions of the liturgy.

The reading is from Revelation, chapter four. Once again I offer two different transcriptions in an attempt to illustrate some of the more important prosodic features of this genre. In the first transcription I began with the syllabic characters as they are found in the prayer-book. Below this, bullets once again provide the syllabic structure. On the fourth line of the transcription is a roman rendition of the syllabic characters, with vowel length marked where it is in the syllabics. On the top line, a note is given which represents the pitch of the voice over the intonational phrase, here a single sentence. Thus, the first syllable is intoned on a B, the following eighteen syllables are given at a higher pitch, on a D, and the final three syllables drop again at the intonational boundary to a B.

B D .... B ....
∇∧ᒉᓇ·ᐃᓇᐤ∪ᔑ·◁ᵇ ∇ᖀ᠊ᒉᑄ Γᓇ ∇∩∧ᵔᑄₓ
● ● ● ● ● ● ● ● ● ●   ● ● ● ● ●   ● ●   ● ● ●   ● ●

E-pisiinamowinaashteyaawak   e-kiisikaanik miina e-tipishkaanik.

The second transcription brings the musical nature of the reading to the fore: here, using a musical staff, I have marked each syllable at its approximate pitch. The advantage of this presentation is that minor variation in pitch, such as the downdrift which begins on the final word, *e-tipiskaanik*, may be indicated, as they are here, by the slightly lowered x which appears above the syllable *-tip-*.

E-pisiinamowinaasteyaawak e-kiisikaanik miina e-tipiskaanik

This sentence of twenty-two syllables took 5.2 seconds to read. At about 4.25 syllables per second, the pace of this reading is somewhat slower than that of the internal portions of the sing-chanting, which was 6.57 syllables per second.

Read Prayer (Reading from the Book of Common Prayer*)*

The next genre under investigation is the public reading of a prayer from page three of the Cree *Book of Common Prayer*. This example came from a reading by the lay reader,[5] Isreal Kookii. In many ways, this genre is very similar to the reading-chant. I have included it here primarily as a basis of comparison with the next genre, personal prayer. However, in analysing this sample, I was amazed to find that Kerena and Isreal read at virtually the same pitch (although Isreal's voice was an octave lower than Kerena's). The similarities between the reading styles, as brought out in the transcriptions, are remarkable, with the beginning and ending boundary tones lower than the central portions by one step, and so on. The prosodic similarities which are shared in these formal public readings are clearly markers of genre.

The two transcriptions of Isreal's reading of the Cree prayer have precisely the same structure as the reading-chant in the previous section. Note once again that the roman transcription is based upon the written syllabic code, not upon spoken Cree.

A   B   .A- - - -

ᒥᓯᐌ ᓯᐅᑲᓂᓯᔭᐣ ᑏᐢᑕ ᒥᔭᐃᐧᒋᑫᔭᐣ ᔕᐌᓂᒋᑫᔭᐣ ᐅᑖᐃᐧᒪᐤ

Misiwe   siyokaatisiyan   nesta   miyawacikeyan   shawenicikeyan   otaawimaw

D   (Begins downdrift)

ᓯᑊ ᐸᒡᑫᐊᑫ ᐅᑊᒡ ᓯᑊ ᐸᑲᐅᑫᐸᑲᐊᓀᐸᑉᑕᐸᓀᑊ ᐅᒡ ᒡᐱᐱᒡᑯᑫ

•• • ••• •   •   •• •••   ••   •• ••

nikii paskenan   nesta   nikii   pakaanishkaanaankimekanaak   oci   taapishkooc

                        B------
ᐁ ·ᐊᓯᒡᑊᑊ ᒪᓯᓀᓯᓀᓯᑊ×
• • •• ••   ••   •• •

e-   wanishkik   maanishcaanishik.

For ease of transcription, I have raised the pitch in the following 'musical' representation one octave.

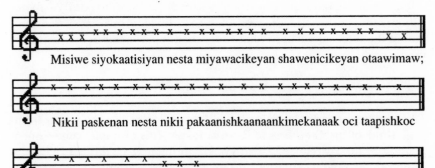

Misiwe siyokaatisiyan nesta miyawacikeyan shawenicikeyan otaawimaw;

Nikii paskenan nesta nikii pakaanishkaanaankimekanaak oci taapishkoc

e wanishkik maanishcaanishak.

There are two intonational units, sentences, in this portion of the prayer. The first is marked by a semi-colon in the prayer-book; the end of the second is marked by a period. The first sentence of thirty-two syllables was read in 3.3 seconds, giving a syllable-per-second pace of 9.7, twice as fast as Kerena's reading, and faster even than the middle portions of the sing-chanting. The ability to read this quickly is the mark of a good lay reader. It is important to note that this prayer is one that is used constantly in the liturgy, so that this material is quite familiar. To my knowledge, no one in Lynx would be able to read new materials this quickly. The reading of prayers in the Cree prayer-book is, for the general Severn population, rote, as Moose Cree (the language of the *Book of Common Prayer* used in Lynx Lake) is not mutually intelligible with Severn Ojibwe. Cree is closely enough related, however, to show many cognates, which make reading somewhat easier than it might be otherwise.

Personal Prayer (Spontaneous, Oral Severn Ojibwe)

In the liturgical progression, there are places where individuals are instructed to provide prayers for local communities and people. The prayer from which the next sample was taken was given as a response to the prayer-book's written cue. It comes directly on the heels of a prayer read in Cree and is followed immediately by another read prayer. The read prayer and personal prayer differ in many ways: whereas the Cree prayer (given in part above) was read by Isreal Kookii, this prayer was spoken by him, using Severn Ojibwe; the personal prayer (provided in full in chapter 7) is syntactically highly structured and repetitive: most of the prayer consists of parallel dependent clauses beginning with the particle *miina*, 'and, also,' and the prosodic features associated with the read prayer are entirely different from those of the personal prayer. The personal prayer was spoken very quietly: Isreal began each intonational phrase in a quiet voice, which became a whisper phrase finally. This is true of all personal prayers heard in the community, whether in the church service or from someone sitting at the radio station.

The tempo of this personal prayer was also notably different from the read prayer as, after each intonational phrase in the personal prayer, Isreal paused for a second or more. Below I present two adjacent intonational phrases. The tempo was 5.5 syllables per second in the first example, and 7.08 syllables per second in the second (pauses were not included in the calculation), which is a little faster than Kerena Pipoon's reading style. However, the long pauses within the prayer are not found in any of the other styles presented to this point. These text internal pauses are associated with spontaneous speech in Lynx Lake but not with reading or singing stylistics.

The first transcription of the personal prayer simply gives a phonemic Severn rendition with the syllables marked below; the final line is an English translation. The translation was given in these cases because, when Severn is used within a church service, content, more than form, is important.

Miina, miina aanimaahpinewin kaa-ayaawaac.
• •　• • • • •　• • •　• • •　　•
And, and those who have a terminal illness.

Miina ekaa kaa-kihkentamowaac ci-kii-mino-ayaawaac.
• • ••　• • • • • •　• • • ••　• 　•
And those who don't know if they will get well.

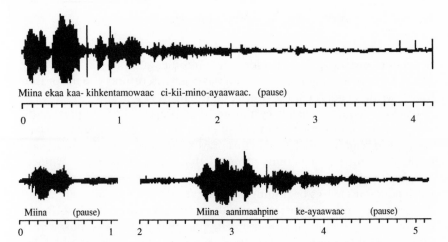

I have also included graphic representation of a digitized verson of the two phrases.[6] In the illustration, the dark area represents relative energy: the farther the black extends from the midline, the more energy is expended, and thus, the louder the sound. The numbers on the grid beneath the transcription mark real time in seconds. The transcribed words (or pauses) sit roughly below their corresponding waveforms. The most outstanding feature of the digitized form of this speech sample was the consistency of movement from relative loudness to quietness in each phrase. Thus we see that the output appears as a string of arrows pointing to the right.

Religious Oratory (Oral Severn Ojibwe Sermons)

This stylized oration is quite similar to the reading intonation (especially as represented in the sample by Kerena Pipoon) although considerably slower in tempo, and is used in formal, especially religious, settings. As described in chapter 4, this genre is often marked by a symbolic phonological movement towards Cree through the denasalization of nasal clusters. (There are two cases of denasalization in this sentence: they are marked by an underlined blank where the nasal would be in standard Eastern Severn Ojibwe.) The sample of the genre given here is the first sentence of the sermon found in chapter 7. The Reverend Simon Pipoon was the speaker on this Sunday morning. His sermon was unusually short, but he spoke in his usual public manner: incredibly slowly (2.8 syllables per second in this sample), in a clear, loud voice.

Noonkom kaa-kishepaayaak "waaciye" kahkina kitininaawaa.

This morning I say greetings to you all.

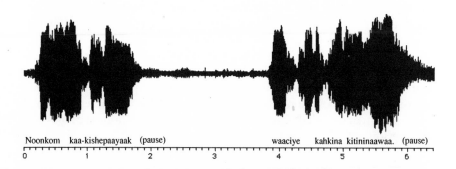

Note the differences between this sample and the personal prayer (both having been recorded through the loudspeaker attached to a microphone used by each of the major participants involved in the church service: this is quite a bit louder than the personal prayer, and the sentence does not show a fade in energy near the end, as did the prayer. Again we find a pause in this sample of spontaneous speech: here it is sentence internal. Pause, then, appears to be associated with spontaneous speech: in public, oral reading, pause does not appear to be used as a rhetorical device, as it is in English. In English, 'good readers' are those who 'put feeling into the reading,' essentially by introducing prosodic elements associated with oral speech (pause, variations in loudness and pitch, and the like) into the reading. In Lynx Lake, the mark of a good reader appears to be the ability to read passages quickly and fluidly. Pauses are thus not consistent with a good public-reading style. They are, however, consistent with good spontaneous oratory.

Formal Public Announcement (Severn Ojibwe)

Announcements were the least formal, public speech style heard during a church service. On this occasion, The Venerable William Pipoon gave the announcements: the important news of the day was that the service would be somewhat shorter so that people could see off a group of Native priests and lay readers who had come from other Severn communities to attend a series of meetings in Lynx Lake held in the previous week. Other announcements, including the example analysed here, gave the time and place of church meetings in the community; these are entirely representative of the type of announcements presented during Sunday-morning services.

This genre was included as an intermediate step between the more heavily structured sermons and the animated narrative provided next. This announcement is marked as religious speech (given by a member of the religious hierarchy) by the presence of denasalization (shown again as underlined blanks). The Venerable Pipoon's voice was loud and clear, like the Reverend Pipoon's was in the sermon, but his pacing was decidedly 'freer'; that is, it approximated normal speaking pace, with just over 5.5 syllables per second (cf. Isreal Kookii's personal prayer where the first sample was spoken right at 5.5 syllables per second). The transcriptions are similar to the previous speech sample.

Ekwaa miinawaa tahsh kaye ta-onaakoshi-ayamihcikaaniwan
● ● ● ● ● ● ● ● ● ● ● ● ● ● ● ● ● ● ●
And so also there will be evening prayers

ahii_k wemihtikooshiwi-ayamihcikewini_k.
● ● ● ● ● ● ● ● ● ● ● ● ● ●
there at the English service.

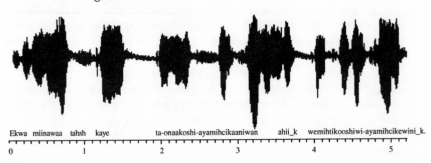

| Ekwa miinawaa tahsh kaye | ta-onaakoshi-ayamihcikaaniwan | ahii_k | wemihtikooshiwi-ayamihcikewini_k. |

0   1   2   3   4   5

Animated Speech (Severn Ojibwe)

At the far end of the song-speech continuum is non-ritual narrative. The sentence presented here comes at a peak point in a narrative about the legendary Wemishoohsh ('The Father-in-law'), which was told in the spring of 1983 by Swanson Turtle. I chose this particular sentence because its prosodic features are precisely the same as those which characterize animated conversation: the speech is relatively loud, marked by wide variation in intonational contours and syllable stress.

In especially the initial portions of monologic narrative performance, intonation contours tend to be minimized so that there is little variation in pitch. Indeed, this is a mark that a performance has begun. This flattening of intonational contours, as we have seen in some of the earlier, more ritualized speech samples, is characteristic of public speaking. However, in peak sections of a narrative, as in conversation, the content often overrides the solemnity of the performance, so that the narrative becomes like a dialogue in that the audience is expected to react and interact (at least emotionally) with the storyteller in these sections. In this case, I have given transcriptions of two types: the first minimally provides a roman transcription, with a line for noting syllables, and a line for the English translation. This is a case where a traditional linear transcription and translation completely hides the prosodic characteristics which mark this sentence as part of the peak:

Wiih-kii-wanishkaa piko.

•   •   ••   •   •   •

He had planned to wake up.

In the digitized version of the sentence, we find that each syllable is spoken with essentially equal intensity. There is little or no diminution of loudness over the intonational unit. In this representation, we can see that the initial syllable, *wiih-*, is longer in duration than any other syllable by almost

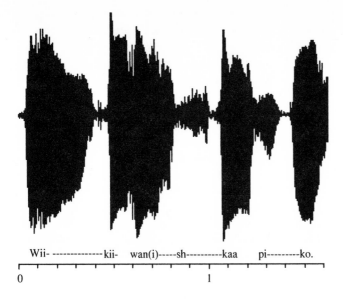

Wii- --------------kii-   wan(i)-----sh----------kaa   pi--------ko.

0   1

twice. Thus, stress and length appear to correlate in Severn Ojibwe, and loudness appears to be less a marker of stress than either length and pitch height. Overall, the pace is relatively slow, at just over 4.33 syllables per second.

The final transcription focuses on the variations in pitch and length heard in the sentence. In the reading-chant and read prayer, where a similar transcription was used, we saw that the intonational contours associated with the two styles were highly constrained. Each sentence in those styles was marked by extremely even pitch, especially through the central portions of the sentence. In the narrative-peak transcription below, we find considerable variation in the relative pitch. Of all contiguous syllables in the sentence, only the first two have the same pitch. Unlike the reading examples, the boundary tones in the narrative are higher than the sentence internal tones. Also represented in this transcription is the aural impression of length of syllables.

Wiih- kiih- wan i shkaa pi ko.

In many ways, animated speech moves us back to the beginning of our speech–song continuum. In song, syllables have a roughly one-to-one correspondence to notes: such a correspondence is suggested in this sentence. Song has variable pitch; so does animated speech. In song, syllable length is variable; so it is in animated speech. As mentioned previously, the Severn impression of the Berens Ojibwe dialect (spoken in the area of Red Lake in northwestern Ontario) is that speakers 'sound like they are singing.' Berens intonational patterns are much different from those of Severn, particularly as they display considerable pitch variation associated, in Severn, with emotional outbursts and singing.

Table 2 shows the presence (and absence) of many of the parameters discussed here. Included in the table are only the samples discussed here, so the parameters do not necessarily hold for every example of the genre. For example, as noted earlier the chapter, not all songs in Lynx Lake are Cree. Even so, as most religious singing is done using a Cree hymn-book, the Cree language and reading parameters are important. Although the table covers only one sample in each genre, even in this initial investigation, such prosodic elements as pitch variation, the ratio of syllables to

TABLE 2 Variables in the Song-Speech Continuum

	Cree	Read	Level pitch	Variable length of long syllables	Pauses: unit internal	Fast: above 6.5 syll/sec	Slow: below 4 syll/sec	Louder than average
Singing	*	*		*			*	*
Sing-chanting	*	*				*		
Reading-chant	*	*	*					*
Read prayer	*	*	*			*		*
Personal prayer			*	*	*	*		
Religious oratory			*	*	*		*	*
Public announcement			*	*	*			*
Animated speech				*	*			*

seconds, and the use of pause within a given syntactic unit appear relevant generally.

The following is a linear representation of the song–speech continuum based on prosodic elements in Lynx Lake:

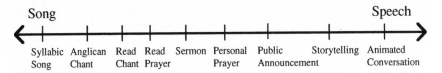

This exploration of relationships between language and music was conducted using primarily linguistic factors, and does not pretend to be comprehensive.[7] As better resources for analysing a variety of prosodic features become available, prosody will undoubtedly be recognized as a major mark of genre which correlates with other formal linguistic features of morphology and syntax. In discussions of genre, this area has been too long ignored.

Chapter Seven

Church, Discourse, Church Discourse, and Discourse about the Church

In previous chapters we looked at some of the formal phonological features of religious discourse and at some of the genres introduced within a religious setting. This chapter focuses on the content and social context of naturally occurring, spontaneous discourse directed at other members of the speech community.

An enormous cross, carved out of the forest even before people moved to Lynx Lake, cuts through the centre of the community. In the centre of the intersection of the two arms of the cross, located at the highest point of the Lynx Lake village, stand the old and the new church building. Among the three hundred Band members in the Lynx Lake community are twenty-eight male church organists, twenty-six female choir members, eight lay readers, one priest, and one archdeacon. The only store in Lynx Lake, purchased by the community from the Hudson Bay's Company in 1980, adds a two-cent surcharge per dollar to each price, which is then channelled into the church coffers. Community-wide rummage sales are organized and run by church members, raising several thousand dollars a sale for the benefit of some church need. The local radio broadcasting day is opened and closed seven days a week with Anglican prayers and hymn singing. The Sunday radio schedule is completely dedicated to religious broadcasting. Political decisions which affect Native rights are protested by holding special prayer meetings in the church at the top of the hill. Birthday parties, feasts, and Band meetings are begun with prayer. Lynx Lake is the site of numerous meetings of Native Cree and Ojibwe clergy, and the site of a yearly, week-long Bible camp for adults to study the Cree Bible together.

The actions and voices of the people of Lynx Lake attest to a long-standing, community-wide commitment to maintaining a strong, unified Christian profile. The symbolism of the cross-shaped clearing overlooking and running through the community reflects a commitment to a Christian identity that had begun by the turn of the century, encouraged by the charismatic Anglican religious leader William Dick, a Native from York Factory (a Cree settlement in the far northeast of Manitoba, on Hudson Bay) who settled at Big Trout Lake, the largest of the Severn Ojibwe communities, around 1900 (Rogers 1962: A28). He travelled much of the eastern Severn area during the winter, training local catechists, among them Judas Pipoon, a Native Severn Ojibwe whose trapline was north-northwest of Lynx Lake. In the days before the families of Mihshamihkowiihsh, and later Lynx Lake, settled into community life, while they still lived on widely separated traplines for most of the year, Judas Pipoon functioned as an itinerant preacher, travelling from campsite to campsite, preaching and teaching from the Cree Bible. It is only within this historic framework that the role of Christianity and the Anglican church can be understood in contemporary Lynx Lake.

This religious tradition has been continued by Judas Pipoon's eldest son, The Venerable William Pipoon.[1] In large part through the efforts of Judas Pipoon's offspring, Lynx Lake became the centre of activity for the 'Anglican north,' a term used to designate most of the Severn area. The community of Lynx Lake has been unique for its isolationist position towards outside, non-Anglican religious activities; no religious representative, individual or group, is welcome in Lynx Lake without official approval from the local clergy. Those who are allowed to work in the community, either for an hour or for a period of months, do so only with the understanding that their concerns are secondary to that of St Paul's Anglican Church in Lynx Lake. This aggressively self-deterministic attitude is reflected in social, political, and economic realms as well. Indeed, as indicated earlier, these institutions are intimately connected with the Anglican church in Lynx Lake, rendering a division between sacred and secular institutions insignificant.

Contact between indigenous and outside religions has been studied extensively, especially in Mesoamerica and the U.S. southwest, where Spanish Catholicism was actively introduced to a variety of Native populations with unique results in every situation. These studies have often focused on 'syncretism,' a term which has almost as many definitions as there are scholars studying religions in contact. Vogt's (1988) useful typology of scholarly treatments of Mesoamerican syncretism distills the various treatments into five basic camps.

The first looks to the end result of syncretism, labelling as 'Christo-paganism' (the term is from Madsen) the process whereby "Indian and Spanish culture are combined, mixed, fused or hybridized ... in both form and meaning" (Vogt 1988: 42). Here the two systems are amalgamated in such a way that there is no way to determine which elements came from which original system.

The second analysis presents an oil-and-water scenario: here the researcher is concerned with "Spanish elements 'encapsulated into the pre-existing cultural patterns'" (ibid). The aboriginal system is the matrix into which Catholic elements are inserted. Presumably, the Spanish elements are maintained in essentially their original forms so that they are easily recognizable as later additions to an earlier system.

The third type outlined by Vogt appears to be a subset of the first. Vogt's summation of this view is that "syncretism is the process in which the forms and meanings of the Indian and the Spanish Catholic religions had so many similarities that the Indians basically became Hispanicized Catholics" (ibid). As in the first, there is a combination of two systems, but the end result here appears to be more like the introduced religion than like the original indigenous religion.

The fourth category is different from the others in that the focus is on Native resistance to imported religious institutions, and the attempts by Native populations to divorce themselves from the non-Native populations espousing the new religion. This has become the norm for most contemporary studies in Native North American anthropology outside the American southwest.

The final type of syncretism, the one adopted by Vogt, involves "a creative and highly selective recombination of symbolic forms and meanings" (p. 43). This view of syncretism differs from the first (where elements are "fused, mixed, combined, or hybridized") in that only certain elements are combined, elements which vary from culture to culture. Thus, some elements of both religious systems may be left intact, some may be entirely missing, and others may be purposefully combined and transformed. While Vogt's divisions between the types of syncretism are oversimplified, they do illustrate a broad spectrum of concerns included in studies of syncretism, many of which will be addressed in this chapter.

In most contemporary anthropological studies of Native North American communities outside of the American southwest, only those aspects of Native American religion considered aboriginal ('traditional') were considered legitimate foci of study.[2] As Gill (1987) points out, anthropologists and researchers in religious studies have until recently rigidly divided the study of religions of non-Western peoples: anthropologists study native, local religion, and researchers in religious studies focus on the major world religions. Gill's (1987: 8) observation that "even today very few students of religion acknowledge anything in Native American cultures as religion except Christianity" is precisely the converse of the situation for anthropologists.

The Severn religious situation is unique among the Ojibwe in large part as a result of the indigenous (Cree) missionization efforts. In more southern areas, where wild rice and sugar maple trees abound, Ojibwe bands formed seasonal aggregations and, in fact, in many places, could live in relatively large numbers for at least half the year. Such aggregration allowed for more complex social organization, including, at least in post-contact times, the creation of the multilevelled Midewiwin religious societies. The Severn situation was very different historically because the resources in the Severn area allowed little aggregration: the major food sources seasonally available were animals and fish, which, except for about a month during the yearly fish runs, could support only a small family group within a very large area. Thus, the Severn people were semi-nomadic within their own trapping areas and, until recently, overwhelmingly non-aggregating. Traditional religious specialization was minimal: the occasional shaman was necessarily also a full-time hunter and trapper.

Most southern Ojibwe groups have been encompassed by a White cultural matrix at least since the turn of the century. Missionization was accomplished by White religious leaders, by the school system, and even, in some cases, by the government (Vecsey 1983: 6). The creation of the Midewiwin society may have been in part a reaction to the White encroachment. Whether or not this is the case, it is true that many southern Ojibwe people have maintained an antagonism towards certain Euro-Canadian/American institutions as at least potentially threatening to Native culture. The Severn Ojibwe people, on the other hand, remain insulated from extensive White contact, although Euro-Canadian policies and programs beginning with the Hudson's Bay Company have caused many social and economic changes. Despite such changes, most of which are considered by the Native population to have improved the quality of life in the Severn area, Severn Ojibwe people have not yet felt the physical threat of an overwhelming White population. When these people were missionized, the discourse came from the mouths of fellow Natives. Because Christianity was brought into the Severn area initially by Cree people living along Hudson Bay and James Bay, the Christian discourse had already undergone transformation from a Euro-Canadian Anglicanism to a more indigenous Anglicanism before it reached the Severn people. The actual form of the initial transformation has been lost in memory, but the broad acceptance of this more or less indigenized Christianity attests to a more compelling mission effort in Northern Ontario than was evident in Southern Ontario and Minnesota. The historical differences in contact and missionization between the Severn Ojibwe and more southerly Ojibwe groups remain critical.

Rogers (1962) takes a compartmentalized view of the contact between Christianity and the Native religion in his writing on the Weagamow Ojibwe. In the final chapter of his monograph *The Round Lake Ojibwa*, Rogers concludes that "the most evident, if not the most profound, changes have taken place in the economic life of the people. Social organization has undergone certain changes, perhaps fewer in number, but no less important. *Religion has been perhaps least affected except from a superficial point of view*" (p. E2, emphasis added). While it is true that the economic life of the people was profoundly changed – these people, like the people of Lynx Lake, moved from an economy based primarily on hunting and trapping to a cash economy within a span of some fifteen to thirty years – just such changes allowed for a strengthening of Christianity through the extended social contact allowed by village life.

However, Rogers's summation of how superficial the religious changes were in Weagamow was followed four pages later by a different picture: "The Round Lake Ojibwa have come to accept Christianity and in most cases are firmly convinced that they are true Christian, in the sense that they adhere to the doctrines of the church. They have abandoned their former religious practices and attend church faithfully, even conducting services at home. Yet, for all this, the people are not Christians in the Euro-Canadian meaning of the word" (p. E6).

In this portion of his statement, Rogers reveals a major problem faced by outsiders studying Severn Ojibwe religious practices: Christianity is defined as Euro-Canadian, and as such, its influence must necessarily be superficial in this area, where direct Euro-Canadian religious modelling is so minimal. However, according to Rogers, and consistent with the Lynx Lake data, the people define themselves as Christian, conduct Christian rituals, and have abandoned earlier religious activities. Later in this chapter several religious discourses from Lynx Lake will provide some insights into the forms of Christian beliefs these people hold.

As discussed in chapter 5, the Bible was translated into Cree in the 1860s and has been used by Severn Ojibwe people since the end of the 1800s. This document has remained the major resource for Christian teaching and understanding among both the Cree and the Severn peoples. As Rogers reports, the Anglican church structure came in with the initial missionization through William Dick, and it is this structure that Rogers equates with Euro-

Canadian Christianity. However, in May 1988, an active church worker in Lynx Lake, a young Native woman, pointed out that the Euro-Canadian bishop of the Anglican Keewatin Diocese, to which the churches in Weagamow and Lynx Lake belong, changed his style of worship when travelling in the Severn Ojibwe communities to a much more restrained and conservative one, which reflects the Severn mode. Thus, even within the Anglican religious tradition and hierarchy, Severn Ojibwe forms are acknowledged as uniquely Native and different from the matrix Euro-Canadian religious expression.

Rogers continues: "In large measure [the Round Lake Ojibwe] have retained their former beliefs and have interpreted Christianity in terms of these. Nevertheless, the ability to secure religious power has been weakened, and an individual can no longer effectively protect himself from the harm directed against him by those in other communities. Only the native preachers have, in general, acquired sufficient power to protect themselves. The result is that individuals still believe in and fear witchcraft but can no longer effectively retaliate. Furthermore, where Christianity comes into conflict with their old beliefs, the people are thrown into a state of confusion, and find it difficult if not impossible to resolve the conflict" (p. E6).

In Lynx Lake, in the 1980s, there was little evidence of the conflicts and confusion reported by Rogers. Indeed, as we will see in the following explanation of the state of cosmology spontaneously provided by an elder during a two-hour storytelling session in his home, Christianity has provided a paradigm shift which has not forced a repudiation of a traditional world-view.

The storytelling session from which the following excerpt is taken was held in the home of the late Anapat Memekwe in December 1987. Anapat was considered the best storyteller in the community, and it was to him that I was constantly guided to collect the old stories, the ones which could be told only on winter nights when the lakes had frozen over solidly and the land lay under a mantle of snow. This was one of three, two-hour storytelling sessions that Anapat graciously allowed that December: he died the following spring. The text presented here is a metanarrative statement about cosmology which was interwoven within a story about an ancient *wiintikoo*. Anapat explained a bit later in the session that there were three very different types of *wiintikoo*, and that this was the oldest and probably most dangerous type.

The selection begins with an explanation that *long ago* young children by the age of three or four were placed upon an island with no provisions for several days so that they might be approached by a guardian spirit which would protect them from the myriad 'evil beings' which were on the earth. Anapat contrasts this state with the present where 'as far back as we can remember ... there were none of [the evil beings] around.' He credits the change to 'the Saviour' [Jesus] who 'killed them off when he came ...' Nearer the end of this section, Anapat explains that these creatures will return ('come out') during the 'difficult times' (at the end of the world), but that people who are religious and pray will not be bothered by them. Note both the predominant theme of how difficult life was prior to the religious changes and the perception that these changes had occurred prior to Anapat's lifetime – hence, prior to 1913.

While the selection presented was an uninterrupted stretch of discourse, it was taken from its two-hour-long storytelling context here because of space considerations. The side-by-side Ojibwe and English paragraph format was chosen to underscore that this is prosaic Ojibwe discourse. For the same reason, the translation is quite literal, reminding the reader that the speaker is Severn Ojibwe. The paragraphs were divided at junctures marked either by the discourse particle *(a)mii* ('That's it ...') or by a temporal particle. On the few occasions when these particles do not mark a new paragraph, topical cohesion takes precedence over the presence of the particle.

Pimaatisi piko. Iniweniwan tahsh mihshiin kekoon, okii— okii-kitimaakenimikon aha awaashihsh, eh-kohpaatisic. Ekaa onci kekoon eh-tapinawihshiink kekonenini miina ke— ke-onci-akwaniic kaawin kekoonini. Okiih-kitimaakinaakon kekoonini. Mistahi kekoonini okiih-kitimaakinaakon, mistahi kekoon okiih-pawaataan. Okii-kihkentaan kahki... kekoonini ke-ishi— ke-ishi— ke-ishi-pamihoc. Miina ke-ishi— ke-kanawenimikoc. Okii-naasihkaakon kekoonini. Okiih-kanawenimikon kekoonini, ci-kihkentank ahaweti awaashihsh kaa-kii— kaa-nanaantawi-kihkentank kekoonini.

Mii hi kaa-kiih-tootawaakaniwic weshkac anihshini. Ikiweniwak kaa—

[The child] was alive. Then he[3] was empowered by many things, because he was pitiful. He was empowered by something. He was blessed by many things, and he had visions of many things. He knew how to look after himself. And what will look after him. He was approached by something. He was taken care of by something (as a guardian), so that [the child] would know what he was seeking to know.

That's what was done to children of long ago. Those evil beings

*kaa-ayaawaac maci-ayahaak. Kaawin
kiinawint kikii— kikii— kaawin
kiinawint noonkom isihsehsinoon.
Weshkac kii-miihshiinwaa awiya okii-
pi-okii-nihshiwanaacihikowin kiishpin
ekaa kihkenimaac naanta e-maacaac,
pane eh-kihkenimocin. Eh— okii—
okii-otihsikoon, okii-nawihanikoon.
Kaawin okiih-kihkenimaahsiin. Mii
tahsh iko tepwe e-kii-nihshowin-
aacihikoc inweniwan awiyan, kaa-
kiih— kaa-kii-naasihkaakoc
iniweniwan. Mii hi kaa-ishi-ayaac.*

*Ahawe tahshiin mihtahi kekoon kaa-
kiih-kihkentank, kaawiniin okii-
tootaakohsiin, okihkenimaan iko,
aasha pehshonhc kaa-pi-naasihkaakoc
kaa-wii-otihsikoc. Kiishpin hiwe e-ishi-
ayaac, hiwe kaa-kiih— kaa-kiih-
tootawaakaniwic weshkac awaashihsh,
wiipac ci-peshiko-ayaac wiinehta.
Wiinehta piko kiyaam ci— ci-antawi-
ayaac mihshiino-tipihkaa niikate.
Naanta, naanta ci-maaciwin-
aakaniwic. Naanta ci-maacihon-
aakaniwic minihtikonk. Minihtikonk
ci-ishi-nakatahwaakaniwic. Kekoon ci-
nanaantawi-kihkentank. Kekoon ci-
kitimaakenimikoc. Mii kaah-
toocikaatek weshkac.*

*Mii tahsh kaa-kii-onci— mii tahsh
kaa-kii-onci-kihkentamowaac anihshaa
hiweni, awanenan kaa-wii— kaa-wii-
naasihkaakowaac, e-maci— ci-maci-
tootaakowaac ci-nihsikowaac, okiih-
kihkenimaawaan piko. Ekwa wiin
haweti kaa-ishi-ayaac, kaawiniin, mii
piko tepwe e-nihsikoc, kaa-otihsikoc,*

were there. That's not how it is with us now. Often, long ago, [a person] was destroyed by [it], if he were not aware of [an evil being], maybe when he went out [to look for food, etc.], and [the evil ones] knew of him. [The human] was encountered by them, he was tracked by them. He wasn't aware of them. Oh, indeed, that person was destroyed by them, when he was encountered by them. That's the way it was.

And to the one who knew a lot [i.e., to the one who had a lot of power], they couldn't do anything to him, he was aware of [the evil ones], when they were close to encountering him, when they wanted to come upon him. If he were [vulnerable] like that, what was done to the child of long ago [was] that he should be alone by himself early on, that he should go and be alone in the wilderness for many nights. To be taken away, perhaps to be left alone on an island. To be left on an island. In order to come to know something. To be empowered/blessed by something. That's what was done long ago.

And that's how they knew, if someone were approaching them, [if they were going] to be done harm by [the evil ones], to be killed by them, they were aware of them. And someone who's not [aware] like that, he was indeed killed by them, when he was come

*kaawiniin iko eh-kiishikaanik
otootihsikohsiin, paanimaa kaa-
nipaaniwank, paanimaa ekaa ci-
kihkenimaac. Mii hi kaah-tootam-
owaac. Kaawiniin eh-kiishikaanik
otoonci-naasihkaakohsiin iniweniwan
maci-ayahaan kaa-wii-nihsikoc.
Paanimaa eh-tipihkaanik, paanimaa
e-nipaac, ekaa ci-kihkenimikoc.*

*Mii kaa-ishiwepahk weshkac. Mitoni
kii-aaniman, mitoni kiih-aaniman
ihiwe. Noonkom itahshiin kiinawint
kaa-pi-ahko-kihkentamank kaawin
wiihkaa awiya onci-nihshowinaac,
kaawin awiya onci-ayaahsiiwan,
ikiweniwak, kaawin awiya onci-
ayaahsiiwak. Kekonen tahsh onci-
ishiwepahk. Ahaweti opimaacihiwe
kaa-tipaacimaakaniwac, ahpin kaa-
kii-piishaac, amii ahpan kaa-kii—
kaa-kii-nahinintwaa, ekaa omaa ci-
ayaawaac iki maci-ayahaak.
Ikiweniwak kaa-mihkoshkaacihaawaac
anihshininiwan kaa-wii-nihsaawaac,
kaawin ahpin kaa-ayaahsiiwak imaa
wakitahkamik. Naanta kiih-
tootawaawak. Mii hi kaa-ishwepahk.*

*Mii tahsh hi kaa-kii— kaa-kii—
kwayahk kaa-kii-pa-pimaatisic awiya,
kwayahk kiih-pa-pimaatisi awiya.
Kaawin kekoon otoonci-mikoshkaa-
cihikohsiin, kaawin kekoon otoonci-
wanaahikohsiin. Kaawin kekoon
otoonci-nanihtentamihikohsiin, kekoon
kekoon otoonci-wanaahikon eh-
papaami-ayaac, naanta e-ishaac, eh-*

upon by them. He wasn't come
upon by them during the day, but
later, when everybody was sleeping, later, when he wouldn't
apprehend them. That's what they
did. He wasn't approached by
these evil spirits during the day,
when they wanted to kill him.
Later, at night, later, when he
asleep, [they would approach him]
so that he wouldn't apprehend
them.

That's what happened long ago.
It was really hard, that was really
hard. But now, as far back as we
can remember, nobody was around
who destroyed [people], there
were none of them around. So why
this [change] has happened: the
Saviour, who is told about, who
came, that's when those evil beings
were killed off, so that they won't
be here. Those evil beings who
troubled and killed people, they
were not around anymore there
on the face of the earth. Perhaps
something was done to them.
That's what happened.

So then that's when people lived
peacefully, people lived peacefully.
Nothing troubled them, nothing
distracted them. Nothing both-
ered/troubled him, nothing
distracted him as he went around,
even when he was away for long
periods of time, nothing happened
to him. Because there was no one

*papaamohsec, miina kinwesh e-inentic,
kaawin naanta ishi-ayaahsiin. Anihsh
kaawin awiyan ayaahsiiwan iniweniwan kaa-pi— kaa-kakwe-mikoshkaa-
cihikowaac.*

*Howe tahshiin hiwe eh-pi-aanimahk
weshkac, kaawin iko ahpin awiya,
eshkam iko ahpin kii-onci-nehpitenti
awiya, ahpin kaa-mihkaakoc
iniweniwan kaa-wii-nihsikoc amii piko
e-kii-nihsikoc. Ohowe kaa-papaami-
ayaac waahsa kaa-papaami-ayaac
awiya kaa-pa-peshikoc, mii hiwe kaa-
ishi-ayaa— kaa-ishiwepahk. Kaawin
kii-wentahsinoon weshkac weti eh-pi-
oshki-ayaak, naahpic kii-mihshiinowak
awiyak kaa-wii-nihsaawaac anihshininiwan. Kaa-wiih-amwaawaac hsa
piko, otamwaawaan hsa piko anihshininiwan. Anihshininiwan hsa piko
otamwaawaan. Maawac kii-
mihshiinowak.*

*Kaawin tahshiin noonkom ahpan
kii-ishiwepan keniin kaa-pi-ahko-
kihkentamaan. Kaawin ahpin aashay
ishiwepahsinoon. Kaawin awiya
ikiweniwak, maci-ayahaak. Kaawin
ahpin aasha awiyak. Noonkom—
weshkac, paanimaa tahs, mii tahsh
ahko eh-ihkitonaaniwank paanimaa
miinawaa ci-ani-moohkiiwaac
ikiweniwak. Ani-pehshinaakwahk
kekoon, kahkina kekoon ani-
aanimahk, ta-ni-mihshiinowak
ikiweniwak. Kii-ihkitonaaniwan.*

*Mii tahsh kaa-onci— hiwe tahsh kii-
ihkitowak ahaweti kaa-ayamihewaatisic kaawiniin iniweniwan oka-
pimenimaahsiin. Mii tahsh kakwe-*

around trying to trouble him.

But long ago, it was hard,
sometimes, [people] just never
returned. When one was found by
something who wanted to kill him,
he's gone for good. When someone was going around alone, long
ago [when] he was going around a
long distance, that's what happened. It wasn't easy long ago,
when the earth was new, there were
really many beings that wanted to
kill humans. When they wanted to
eat people, they ate people. They
ate people. Oh, they were incredibly numerous.

But today this doesn't happen, as
far back as I can remember. It
doesn't happen anymore. There
aren't any of them, of the evil
beings. There aren't any of them.
Now, it is said that later they'll
come out [again]. When it [the
end] is near, when everything
begin to be difficult, they will be
very numerous. That's what was
said.

And they said, that, as for the
one who's religious, they won't
bother him. So, try to be prayerful!
Try to pray!, that's why we are told

ayamihcikeyok, kakwe-ayamihaayok kaa-oncii-ikoyank. Kaawin iniweniwan oka-pimenimaahsiin iniweniwan kaa— ayamihaawin kaa-kiih-kishkaakonic, ahawe maci-ayahaa. Miinawaa ahpin ani-moohkiiwaac, kii-ihkitowak kihci-ayaahaak. Kaawin oka-kihkenim-aahsiin iniweniwan. Kaawin naanta oka-kiih-tootawaan iniweniwan. Iniweniwan kaa-kishkaakoc mino-kekoon. Miina kaa-kishkaakoc ayamihaawin. Kaawin iniweniwan oka— oka-pimenimaahsiin kii-ihkitowak weshkac kihci-ayahaak.

Mii maawiin tepwe ke-ishiwepahk. Hiwe kakwe — keniin, nikii-ikoo ci-kakwe— ci-kakwe-maamitonentamaan ayamihaawin. Keniin nikii-ikoo. Kahkina awiya inaakaniwi, "Kakwe-ayamihciken. Kakwe-ayamihciken. Kakwe-tootan ihiwe kaa-minwaa-hshink," miina, "Kakwe-saakihik kitootem," kitikoomin. "Kaawin maci-ishi kitootem," kitikoomin. "Kaawin maci-ishi piko awiya." Mihsawaac pahkaani-ayahaak, mihsawaac ekaa e-wiici-wiiyaahsemac, peshikwan kakwe-saakihik, kitikoomin.

this. He [the evil being] won't bother the one who has religion. When they come out again, that's what the elders of long ago said. He [the evil being] won't know him [the religious person]. He won't be able to do anything to him. The one who has good deeds. And who has religion. He won't bother this person, so said the elders of long ago.

Perhaps this will really happen. I was also told myself to try and remember religion/ have religion. I myself was told. Everyone is told, "Try to pray. Try to do what is right. And try to love your friend/ relative/neighbour." It is told to us. "Don't say bad things about your friend/neighbour," we are told. "Don't say bad things about anyone!" Even strangers, even the one who is not of your race, try to love them just the same.

Throughout this explanation, Anapat had no difficulty in reconciling Christianity and traditional Severn cosmology. The explanation was not provided by a member of the religious hierarchy; rather, it was volunteered by an elder whose expertise was in telling traditional stories and who was speaking in that capacity. An important factor in this revised world-view is that the traditional elements have been reconciled within Christian eschatology rather than the other way around. This is no thin veneer of Christianity laid over an older system: the changes represent a basic restructuring of an older world-view within a new framework.

This brings up the issue of alternative systems with the Lynx Lake community. The only person known to have direct contact with an older spirituality is one elderly woman who years ago married into the Lynx Lake group. This woman was a self-declared 'bear-walker,' a person who takes on the form of an animal, in this case a bear, and is able to travel great distances in that form. The woman had gotten the power, 'a thing that lives inside of her,' from her husband's father many years before.[4] This woman had considered it to be a positive force until recently, when her grandson, in his early twenties, became a habitual and serious solvent abuser, constantly threatening harm to himself through word and deed. The older woman attributed her grandson's problems directly to the presence of the power within her.

The community view of this power was overwhelmingly negative and fearful. Where in Lynx Lake grandparents are loved (if not revered) and seen as the containers of immense amounts of wisdom and knowledge, this woman's grandchildren were afraid to spend the night in her home. In some cases, the grandchildren actively avoided the woman and her home – considered by many in the community to be a very sad state of affairs, as these young adults would not have the advantages of their grandparents' knowledge. The members of that one family were instructed never to shoot a bear, because it was the bear which gave her its power. The woman herself faithfully attended the local church and participated in all the associated activities. Thus, while there is some evidence of pre-Christian beliefs, these are negatively evaluated by the community – to some degree even by the holder of the power herself. The negative evaluation is, however, not on the basis of its being un-Christian, but because that power is ruining one of the woman's kin.

It should be noted here that no anthropologist has previously reported women with power in the northern areas, nor has bear-walking been reported among the Severn Ojibwe. This may be an isolated incident, but it may also reflect problems in methodology. The reports about the bear-walking came from the woman herself over the community radio station, demonstrating once again that the Native-to-Native discourse is critical for discovering what is important to people.

The religious situation in Lynx Lake is different from many Native American situations of Mesoamerica in which Christianity (Catholicism) has been incorporated into the existing cosmology. The difference between the situation in Lynx Lake and that in southern Ojibwe communities, as in Mesoamerica, may in part be related to the comparative austerity of the traditional Severn religious system. There were few ritual elements in traditional Severn religious life, far fewer even than those reported for the

Cree populations located north and east of the Severn Ojibwe (Speck 1935). The sheer volume of ritual associated with Christianity, including the importance of the literary traditions which came into the Severn regions with Christianity which both reinforce and are reinforced by the Christian presence, seem to have been critical elements in the degree of acceptance of this new system.

One must not discount the many social and material benefits associated with Christianity in the Severn area. With Christianity came a new body of knowledge available to whomever would invest the energy to learn it. Among the Ojibwe, knowledge is power – one of the reasons that elders are considered authoratative is that with the years one accrues knowledge. Through knowledge, one obtains power over the spiritual and material world, as indicated in Anapat's discourse above. ('[The child] was empowered by many things, because he was pitiful ... he *had visions of many things.* He *knew* how to look after himself. And what will look after him.... He was taken care of by something [as a guardian], so *that [he] would know what he was seeking to know,*' and two paragraphs later: 'And *to the one who knew a lot* [i.e., had lots of power], they couldn't do anything to him, *he was aware of [them]* ...; emphasis added). In 1982, we were told by The Venerable William Pipoon's son, then a young man of twenty, that he had been offered a bag of cookies to pray to God for the successful hunt of a man twice his age. The son was approached because of the acknowledged spiritual power of the father; such power extends to the family members. Another sign of Christian power is dreaming about game prior to killing it. In one case, the same young man dreamed that several moose on a trail offered themselves to him. When he killed the moose, he took it as a sign from God that his impending marriage was sanctioned by God; the moose were used for his wedding feast.

Another less mystical but equally real way in which a powerful position in the church leads to material gain is in the amount of goods sent into the community from White churches in Southern Ontario which send literally hundreds of large garbage bags filled with clothes and linens into the community. These goods are addressed to one or another of the church leaders, all of whom are offspring of Judas Pipoon. These goods are ultimately sold at community-wide rummage sales, but prior to the community sales, private viewings and sales are held for close friends and family members – a situation similar to that in U.S. communities where an upper- or upper-middle-class Junior League rummage sale is held yearly, with exclusive, private pre-benefit sales held, ostensibly to get more money for the cause, but in actuality allowing a socially élite group pick of the goods.

Another benefit granted to the active Christian worker is extensive travel across Northern Ontario to attend clergy and lay meetings at the church's expense. The churches in the Severn area have promoted intercommunity networks, networks which are further reinforced by intercommunity marriages. These networks are maintained by phone calls and travel between communities. The travel is expensive, each trip to another Severn community costing a couple hundred dollars. However, when on church business, the cost of the airfare is minimized as mission planes are put at the disposal of the most active church clergy and laity. Thus, a close connection with the church allows for much more travel. The travel between communities confers prestige upon the traveller, and thus allows the travelling clergy to increase their power and prestige across the northern communities with each trip.

Another aspect of power which is facilitated by connection with the church is the respect conferred to good public speakers. The church provides many opportunities to demonstrate public oratory, both a symbol and a vehicle of power and prestige. This power is reinforced in multiple settings – at the radio station, at community feasts, in the church, indeed at almost every public gathering. Given the nature of the Anglican service, which centres around the written liturgy, priests, deacons, and lay readers are usually the literacy experts in the community as well, putting not just the spoken word but also the written word within the domain of the church. Very often, the literacy experts of the church are given positions teaching Native literacy in the schools, a prestigious position with good monetary benefits. As a young Native man from another Severn community recently told me, "You have to be good in language to have a place in the church." Conversely, you usually have to have a position in the church hierarchy to be considered 'good in language.'

A variety of benefits have been realized by a move to Christianity. But, while the institution of the Christian church facilitates the acquisition of power by individuals, the extent of the power is still a matter of individual initiative and is recognized as a gift from God.

The move towards a Native Christian lifestyle has not just been made on the community level: it is also considered a very personal decision, as the next two texts will attest. Both texts were testimonials given on 3 September 1987, the final day of the Anglican Bible camp held at Mihshamihkowiihsh, the third camp of its type held during that summer. The Bible camps are held each year in and around different northern communities and are run by Native church workers for Native people. Indeed, the only Euro-Canadian involvement was that of pilots who ferried

people from many of the seventeen northern communities into Lynx
Lake, where they were then transported to and across the northern part
of Mihshamihkowiihsh Lake. All teaching was in Ojibwe by Native
people, with syllabic notes taken on two-foot by three-foot pieces of
butcher paper. People had spent the last week camping together and attending Bible classes during much of the day. These camps were as much a
celebration of a traditional lifestyle associated with life in the bush as they
were a chance to learn. Throughout the large campsite of approximately
thirty tents were groups of women preparing *noohkahikan* (smoked and
dried fish shredded into a powder), *aanahkonaa* (bannock), and other
bush foods.

The meetings were held in a newly constructed plywood chapel at the
centre of the campsite. Inside the chapel were two rows of long benches
and tables: the ones speaking sat or stood at a head table facing the rest of
the group. The talks were amplified, so each speaker held the microphone
when on stage. On the table in front of many members of the Native audience, predominantly middle-aged and older, were battery-powered cassette
recorders used so that the lessons could be listened to repeatedly back
home. The note-takers, mentioned above, had papered the walls of the
chapel with outlines of the week's meetings. It was within this context that
the next two testimonials were given.

This first speech was given by Anitiya Kakwecim, a forty-year-old lay reader
in the Lynx Lake church and one of the designated note-takers for the
camp. An important feature of this discourse, and indeed of all the many
religious discourses recorded during my fieldwork, is that there is no
mention of discarding old beliefs, nor is there mention of adopting Euro-
Canadian (*wemihtikooshi*, 'Whiteman') religious practices. Rather, the focus is on personal commitment to service to *kaa-Tipencikec* (lit. 'the one
who owns,' the most commonly used term for God). Anitiya, an acknowledged lay leader in the local church, stood at the front chapel, holding the
microphone as she gave her address. Again, the text is presented in a prose
format, roughly divided into paragraphs at junctures marked by the discourse particles *(a)mii* ('That is …') and the particles *ekwa (ta)hsh(iin)* ('and
so').

Amii iwe. Pankii naanta keniin	That's it. Maybe I'll say a few
ninka-ihkit ohomaa kaa-isihsek ci-ka-	things here too, as it's my turn to
ihkitoyaan. E-minwentamaan kiyaapic	speak. I'm happy to have the
kaa-isihsek e-waapaminakok miina e-	opportunity to see you again and
wiiciiwinakok. E-kakwe-kashkihtoo-	to be with you. I'm trying to be

waan keniin kapeyahii omaa ci-ayaayaan, ohomaa kaa-kihkinooham-aatinaaniwank. Kaawiniin iko kapeyahii ohomaa e-nipaayaan kaa-itamaan.

Ekwa tahsh mii eshi-nanaah-komiyaan kaa-isihsek kiyaapic e-waapaminakok. Kaawiniin piko miina e-mino-ayaayaan, homaa kaa-ayaayaan.

Ekwa tahsh iko ninkakwe-tootaan ci-kakwe-naasihkamaan kihkinooham-aakewin, aasha kaa-noontamaan e-paahkitinikaatek. Ahpii keniin kaa-kii-paahkitinamaan nimpimaatisiwin, piko ci-kakwe-tootamaan aasha kaa-ishi-nantamikowaan kekoon ci-kakwe-tootamaan. Kaawin miina wiihkaa ninkaakwiinawi-ihkitohsiin kekoon eshi-anoonikowaan ci-tootamaan. Piko ninkakwe-tootaan. Cikemaa aasha ninkihkentaan e-kii-pakitinitisoyaan ihimaa keniin ayamihaawinink ci-ishi-anohkiiyaan.

Ekwa tahshiin iko kaawiniin piko ehta pi-tootamaan keniin nipimaa-tisiwin. Entahso-kiishikaak hsha wiin iko keniin nimpaa-pankihshin. Ekwa tahshiin iko kaawiniin iko eshi-pakiciiyaan. Nintishi-kakwe-anohkii hsa piko ihimaa keniin kaa-kii-ishi-kanoonikooyaan peshikwaa e-kiishikaak kici-anohkiiyaan.

*Mii hsha eshi-nanaahkomak kaa-Tipencikec peshikwaa e-kiishikaanik e-kii-kanoonihshic ohomaa ayamahaa-winink ci-anohkiiyaan.<Cough>
Ekwa tahsh ohowe kaa-wiih-animootamaan wahawe Coowiin. Mayaam piko mooshak nintoonci-*

here all the time myself, here at the studies. I don't mean to say that I have been sleeping over [= camping] here, though.

So it is that I'm thankful for the opportunity to see you again. Although I have not been really feeling well while I've been here.

And so I'm trying to go to the studies; I listened when [the teachings] are opened up. At that time I too laid down my life, trying to do something just when I am being asked to do it. And I try not to make excuses when I am asked to do something. I just try to do it. For sure I know that I, too, surrendered myself to do religious work there.

Even so, I'm not fulfilling what is expected of me. Every day I fall [short of this goal]. But I haven't given up yet. Regardless, I try to work where I was called one day to work.

So I thank the Lord for the day that he called me to work in religion. <Cough>

And I will discuss this man, Coowiin. I always work side-by-side with him during the teaching

wiitanohkiimaa ohowe kaa-kihkinoo-
hamaakaaniwahk. Ekwa tahshiin iko
nistam wiin iko keniin kaa-ni-maacii-
piintikeyaan kihkinoohamaakewinink,
mii wiin iko kaa-inapiyaan keniin e-
pimi-ishkoonoowiyaan e-nantoh-
tamaan miina e-kakwe-kaahcitini-
keyaan.
  Ekwa ahpin kaa-kii-ishkwaa-
onakamikooyaan miina masina-
hikanenhs kaa-kii-miinikoyaan. Amii
ahpin ekwa kaa-kii-maatanohkiiyaan.
Kaawin hshiin iko niin e-inentamaan
hiwe ci-tootamaan. Ekwa tahsh
okoweniwak tiihkans kaa-kii-
naakanowaac ayamihewiikimaa-
shihshak mooshak ninkii-nantomikook
ci-wiitanohkiimakwaa piko kekoon
ishi— ci-ishi-wiicihakwaa.
  Ekwa tahsh nistam naahpic ninkii-
aanimentaan ihiwe niin eh-kanoo-
nihshiwaac ci-wiitanohkiimakwaa.
Piko kekoon ci-ishi-waa-wiicihakwaa.
  Ekwa tahsh piinihsh kaawin
naanta nintoonci-inentansiin
niwiiciiwaakan howe ninkii-onapimin
e-kii-aani-mootamaank miina e-kii-
inak. "Aan enentaman owe okoweni-
wak kaa-wiitanohkiimakwaa
tiikanhs?" ninkii-inaapan.
  Ekwa tahsh ninkii-ikopan.
"Kaawiniin naanta nintinentahsiin.
Mii hsha piko eh-kohseyan miin ehko-
kashkitooyaan kekoon kici-kakwe-waa-
wiicihatwaa ikiweniwak kaa-
nantawenimihkwaa ci-wiitanoh-
kiimatwaa," ninkii-ikopan. "Cikemaa
aasha kikii-pakitinin ihimaa
ayamihaawinink ci-ishi-anokiiyan.
Niin ekaa e-kashkitooyaan kici-kiih-
tootaman kiin kaa-ishi-kashkihtooyan.

sessions. So when I first started
attending the studies, it [worked
out] that I sat there as I was
learning, listening, and trying to
catch on.

  And when I was appointed I was
given a little bible. That's when I
started working. I didn't *decide* to
do [the appointment]. And so the
deacons who were told, they also
called me over to work with them,
just to assist them in various ways.

  And at first I really found it
difficult when they called me to
work with them, just to help out
with various tasks.

  But at last, I didn't mind: my
husband and I sat down and
discussed it and I told him, "What
do you think about my working
with the deacons?" I said to him.

  So then he said to me, "I really
don't mind. So you try your
hardest and do whatever you can
to help those who want you to
work with them," he said to me. "I
certainly have surrendered you
there to work in church service. I
couldn't attempt to keep you from
doing what you are able to do.

*Ekwa tahsh mii hsha eshi-nanaah-
komak kaa-Tipencikec keniin ihimaa
kici-kii-onci-shawenimihshic ihiwe
nimpimaatisiwinink e-kii-pakitin-
amaan ci-wiitanohkiimatwaa
otayamihaak."
Amii ihiwe kaa-kii-inihshihpan. A
miihsh kaawin wiihkaa kaakwii-
nawentamowin nintayaahsiin ahpin
ihiwe ahkonaak kaa-kii-inihshihpan
eh-kohseyaan piko ninkakwe-
wiitanohkiimaak kekonini kaa-ishi-
kanoonihshiwaac ci-ishi-
wiitanohkiimakwaa.*

*Ekwa tahsh howe Coowiin kaa-apic
amii howe mayaam mooshak e-
wiitanohkiimak. Ekwa tahsh naahpic
aaniman ohowe anohkiiwin kaa-
tootamaank kaa-waapamihshiiyaank
onoweniwan masinahikanan kaa-
akootekin eh-akootooyaank.*

*Ekwa miina eshkam isihse niin eh-
tootamaan naanta piko mohsha e-
kakwe-naakahtooyaan iniweniwan ci-
masinaahtehsitooyaan kekonenan kaa-
kihkinoohamaakaaniwahk. Ekwa
tahsh wiin eh-ani-masinahankin.*

*Ekwa tahshiin niwiiciwaakan
kiishpin eh-piishaac ohomaa
kihkinoohamaatoowininik, a mii hsha
eshi-wiiciihikoyaank howe toohkaan
inanohkiiwin iniweniwan kekonan eh-
kakwe-payahtenaakohtooyaank
kekonenan kaa-kihkinoohamaakaa-
niwahk.*

*A mii tahsh esihseyaank ohowe kaa-
inanohkiiyaank. Kaawin wiihkaa
tipinawe ninkii-otaahpinansiimin
niinawint ci-kii-onasinahikehtama-
asiiyaank, miina ci-kii-kanawen-
tamaan ikweniwan ihkitowinan kaa-*

"And so I thank God that he will
bless me also in my life as I allow
you to work with the Christians."
That is what he told me.

And so it is that I haven't had a
worry since [my husband] told me
to try my best in trying to assist
with whatever they tell me to do
with them.

And Coowiin who is sitting there
is the one that I always work with.
This work that we are doing is
really hard; you see our sheets [of
notes] hung up.

And sometimes it happens that I
do them myself or I try to show
them in full view, to project the
things that are being taught. And
he writes them.

And whenever my husband
comes to the teaching sessions, he
helps us with this type of work,
trying to show clearly what is being
taught.

And that's how it goes in this
job. We couldn't ever presume to
write for ourselves. And for keeping those speeches that were
taught, we are truly trying to help
this study: when a person first

kihkinoohamaakaaniwahk. Cikemaa ninkakwe-wiicihtoomin owe ishkoonoowin miina oshkac awiya kaa-piishaac naahpic nanehsitaamii kici-kiih-ani-kaahcitinankin oniweniwan ihkitowinan. Mii hsh oniweniwan kaa-onci-kakwe-oshihtooyaank awiyak ci-kii-ani-onci-kakwe-kaahcitinamowaac iniweniwan kihkinoohamaakewinan kaa-pakitinikaatekin.

attends he is not used to it, to catch onto these words. That's why we try to make it so that the people can try to catch onto those lessons that are offered.

Mii hsha howe ekwa tahsh iko aaniman shiiniko owe kaa-ishi-waapamihshiyaank eh-tootamaank eh-ani-otaahpinamaank awiya kaa-kihkinoohamaakec otihkitowinan. Piko ehta miina ci-kii-isihsek pankii awiya ci-kii-nihsitohtank ihiwe kihci-masinahikan kaa-ihkitomakahk. A mii ehta ihimaa eshi-wenihsek oniweniwan mayaam kici-kii-ani-ishipiihikeyaan kaa-ishi-kihkinoohamaakaaniwahk.

And so it is that this is what you see us doing as we record the words of the one who is teaching. And so it just happens that one should understand what the Bible says. That is the place where it is easy to write down absolutely correctly these things that are being taught.

Ekwa hsh amii hi eshi-nanaa-hkomak kaa-Tipencikec kiyaapic payahtakenimowin kaa-miinikoyahk noonkom kaa-kiishikaak. Miina nintoonci-nanaahkomaa keniin tipinawe nimpimaatisiwinink kiyaapic e-miinihshic kici-nanaantanowak noonkom kaa-kiishikaanik.

And so it is that I thank God again for the peace of mind that he gives us today. And I also thank him that he has extended my life that I can search for him today.

Ekwa tahsh ami hiwe niin minikohk. Ekwa tahsh Coowiin kewiin ohomaa wii-ayamiipan, taapishkooc iko e-wii-aanimootamaankipan.

So that's enough for me. And Coowiin here wanted to speak, as has been discussed.

Mii hsha ihiwe niin minikohk. Ekwa tahsh kaana kiinihtam.

That's all for me. It's your turn.

The testimonial was followed by light applause, as were all that were given on this afternoon.

This talk was one of the longer of the closing testimonials, but despite its length was not atypical in content. A topical outline provides an overview of many themes covered in the afternoon session; topics which are repeated in many of the following religious discourses as well:

I.   Greeting
II. Problems
III. Call to religious work
     A. General call
     B. Confirmation from husband
     C. Confirmation of accepting call
IV. Job outline
V.   Thanks to God
     A. For peace of mind
     B. For health (extended life)
     C. For opportunity to increase knowledge of God
VI. Closure
VII. Coda

The greetings, closure, and coda are typical of all public discourses, but the structures found in II–V are associated with religious discourse almost exclusively. Note that the following discourse includes most of these categories.

The next speech presented here was given by Kerena Pipoon, the wife of the Lynx Lake priest. In this text she echoes several of the themes mentioned above, particularly that, in choosing the Christian life, one experiences many hardships ('much difficulty comes to Christians who work for the Lord') but that despite the 'unavoidable' problems, including severe physical ailments and even death of loved ones, such a choice is good. Indeed, the difficulties appear to validate the level of Christian commitment to this Native gathering by demonstrating the target of the hardships worthy of the attention of opposing spiritual forces. Again the format is prosaic, divided into paragraphs on the basis of the particles noted above.

"Waaciye," kitininaawaa ohomaa. Noonkom piko nimpi— noonkom piko nimpimii— nimpimishakaa. Inikohk esihsek ci-pi-maacaayaan kekishep piko nintanawi-pi-onci-maacaanaapan ahawe tahsh pinimaa e-kiih-

Greetings, I say to you all that are here. Just now by means of—, I just got in by means of— paddling here by canoe. Time has finally permitted me to come. I have been planning all morning to come but

*kanawaapancikehtamawankic ahaweti
kaa-kiih-kiiwec kihcii-ahaa, ihiweni
kaa-ishi-aw— kaa-ishi— e-waa-
wiicihankic oti piko. Paanima piko e-
maacaac e-wi-pooni-kanawaa-
pancikehtamawankic weti kaa-onci-
kanawaapancikehtamawankic weti
taawinink kaa-ayaac.*

    *Ekwa tahsh ahpan niinehta ahpan
nimpi-maacaa. Kaawin ahpan
Sayman kiih-pi-maacaahsii. Ekaa
tepwe e-mino-ayaac. Kaa-ishi-ayaac
tawiin iko.*

    Ekwa tahsh —<Pause> *Amii hi
keniin naahpic enanaahkomiyaan
ohowe ahpin kaa-ni-kii-isihsek
kimaawacihitiwiniwaa. Ekwa keniin
naahpic e-yaa— e-kii-ayihkameni-
moyaan e-kii-kakwe-wiicihtwaayaan
ohomaa howe mekwaac kaa-anohkaa-
cikaatek ohowe ohomaa ke-tashi-
maawacihitiyek. Mihshiinwaa
keniinawint ninkii-pi-ishaamin keniin
kiyaapic eh-ayaayaampaan, eh-
anohkiiyaampaan, ikweniwak
ihkwewak kaa-anohkiiwaac. Keniin e-
kiih-pi-waa-wiicihtwaayaan ohomaa.
Ekwa miina kaawin iko kekaat ninkii-
wiicihtwaahsiin nin— nint—
nintinentaan, hi haaweti noosihs kaa-
waapamaayek kaa-kanawenam-
aayaank. Ekaa waanihtak e-kii-maa-
maaciwinaayaank kaye ihiwe kaa-
ishinaakosic.*

    *Ekwa tahshiin iko shaakooc
noonkom nimpimaaciwinaah, ci-
waapankec ishkwaayaac e-inenimak.
Naahpic iko wiih-otootemimaan
awiyan. Kahkina piko awiyan*

someone intially delayed [it] as we were looking after the arrangements for an elder to go home— we were] just giving him assistance. Later when he left, we stopped attending to him there where we had been helping him there in the village where he was.

    And so it was only then that I left for here. Simon didn't come here because he is really not well — [it's] the same old thing.

    And so <Pause> it is that I am really thankful as this meeting is coming to an end. And I am really— I was persevering to try and help here during this time here, while it was being planned for you to get here. Many times we came here, me included, when I still had the ability to work along with those ladies that are working. I came to help here, also. But I couldn't help much, I think. We are taking care of my grandchild that you all see there. We can't take her as we wish because of her [medical] condition.

    Even so, I'm taking her now to witness the end [of this event], as I thought how she is very friendly with people. Just anyone. I think she loves about everybody.

*taapishkooc eh-saakihaac ahko
nintinenimaa.*
*Mohsha hi kaawin iko kekoon
nintayaahsiin. Kaawin iko ninihtaa-
ayamihsii naahpic, ohoweti wiiniko
kekoon kaa-ishpentaakwahk ci-
ihkitoyaan. Nintishi-ayaa piko.*
*Ekwa tahsh naahpic e-nanaah-
komiyaan ohomaa kaa-waapaminakok
nintootemak ohomaa miina kiihtwaam
kaa-pi-ishaayek. Mihshiinwaa kaa-
waapaminakok maawacihitiwinink.
Ekwa wiiniko eshkam e-ishi— eshi-
maamitenentamank. E— eshi-
noontamank naanta kitooteminaanak
mekwaac aanimisiw— aanimisiwin
kaa-ayaawaac. Miina eshkam mooshak
iko kitishi-mihkaamin mekwaac kaa-
maawacihitiyahk eshkam kitootem-
inaan eh-pi-wiintamawaakaniwic
naahpic ihiweni ahpin kaa-wanihaa-
waac otootemiwaan. Ekwa miina,
noonkom miina ahpin onaako kaa-kii-
maacaawaac ninkii-noontaan naahpic
eh-aanimisiwaac ohomaa kaa-kii-
tipihkaanik kaa-kii-ayaawaac. Ninkii-
mohci-maamitonentaan e-kiih-pi-wiin-
tamaakowaampaan keniin. <Pause>*
*Ekwa tahshiin iko oncita tahshiin
iko e-isihsek ihiwe kaa-pa-pimaa-
tisinaaniwank. Mistahi aanimisiwin
eh-ayaamakahk ihiwe mekwaac kaye
kaa-toocikaatek minwaacimowin kaa-
antohcikaatek. Oncita wiiniko hi
isihse. Naahpic aanimisiwin ci-
ayaawaac ikweniwak otayamihaak
kaa-anohkiihtawaawaac kaa-
Tipehcikenic.*
Mii keniin mooshak eshi-mihka-

I don't have anything else to say.
I'm not very good at talking about
something that is important. That
is how I am.

So, I am really thankful to see
you all, my friends, here once
again while you are gathered here.
Many times I've seen you at meetings, and sometimes— we all think
about it. When we hear our
friends, perhaps, during difficult—
their times of difficulties. [In
reference to some people having
to leave because of the death of a
relative.] And frequently we find
ourselves during the meeting
being informed that they have lost
a relative. And again, now again,
those that just left yesterday that
they were having trials last night,
those ones who were here. I, too,
[felt remorse] when I was told.
<Pause>

And so it is that this happens
during our lifetime. There is much
difficulty during times when the
gospel is being listened to [ac-
tively]. It is unavoidable that it
happens. Much difficulty comes to
Christians who work for the Lord.

That is how I always find it when

*maan owe kaa-inanohkiiyaank
ahaweti kaa-wiiciiyaamak. Naahpic
aanimisiwin eshkam e-mooshih-
tooyaank ihimaa nipimaatisiwinaank.
Shaakooc ninka-i— ninkakwe-tootaan
iwe ci-kakwe-niikaanentamaan
keniinawint kaa-inanohkiiyaank.
Mihshiin iko eshi— eshi-wiintamaw-
inakok. Naahpic e-minwentamaan
ohomaa kaa-pi-ishaayek kahkina piko
ohomaa kaa-pi-antohtamek
minwaacimowin.*

we are working, [me and] this
person that I am living with [= my
husband]. We have often experienced real hardships in our lives.
But we— we always try to make
first in our lives this work of ours.
There is a lot— I tell you. I am
really glad you all came here to
listen to the gospel.

*Ekwa miina keniinawint ohomaa
mooshak maawacihitinaaniwan kaa-
ishitaayaank. Weti wiiniko ninka-
pehshiwinaank kehciwaak.*

And then we are always meeting
here in our area. Right here in our
settlement.

*Ekwa miina naahpic e-ciihken-
tamowaac ohomaa kaa-ayaawaac
oshkaatihsak eh-paa-pi-ishaawaac
ohomaa. Miina kaa-pimoonaawaaci
iniweniwan kaa-paa-pi-ishaaninci
kaye. Ekwa miina ohomaa piko kaa-
ayaanici.*

And the very giving people that
are living here [at Lynx Lake] are
willing to come here [to the camp
at Mihshamihkowiihsh]. And they
have been transporting those who
have come here. And the locals,
too.

*Ekwa miina weti kaa-pimipisoh-
tamaakewaac naahpic e-ciihken-
tamowaac e-ishi-nawakwaa. Ohomaa
kaa-ayaawaac kaye. Mohsha ihi.*

And those drivers over there
[across the lake at Lynx Lake]
really appear to me to be willing to
[drive]. And those who are here as
well.

*Mii hsha hiwe minikohk ke-
ihkitoyaan, wahawe kaa-kii-kakitoc
tipinawe ahawe kekaat niwiiciniht-
aawikimaakan. Ekwa tahsh kekoon
kaa-inihshic wiipac ninkakwe-tootam-
(w)aan ohoweni otanohkiiwinink.
Mohsha hi minikohk kiwaaciyemin-
aawaa kahkina ohomaa kaa-ayaayek.
Miinawaa maawin ka-waapamin-
aawaa weti en-onaakohshink pi-taa-
takohshiniyek.*

That's it. That's all I'll say. The
person that spoke is almost my
own relative. And whenever she
tells me to do something, I try to
do it right away. That's it, I greet
all of you who are here. Maybe I'll
see you again in the evening when
you arrive [at Lynx Lake].

Mii iwe. Waaciye.

That's all. Greetings.

The humorous statements made at the beginning and ending of the discourse ('I just now got in by means of— paddling here by canoe' and 'The person that spoke is almost my own relative. And whenever she tells me to do something, I try to do it right away'), signs of a confident speaker, were greeted by laughter.

Vecsey's (1983) study of Ojibwe religion, which focused primarily on Southern Ojibwe communities, presents a view that is partially consistent with the 'Christo-pagan' fusion model of syncretism. In arguing that contemporary Ojibwe religious expressions are at best superficial, holding little meaning for Native people, he contends that only pre-contact religion is or ever has been truly efficacious and meaningful for Ojibwe people: "I discuss divergent religious activities in which Ojibwas have participated, movements which have incorporated some of the traditional religious aspects. I conclude that neither the Native religious movements nor Christianity has effectively replaced the traditional religion which has disintegrated through the past three centuries" (p. 6).

Vecsey's version of syncretism for the Ojibwe presents a two-step process: when the traditional Ojibwe religions came in contact with Christianity, the traditional religion was eradicated, and then a new system (either Christianity or another new religion, such as the Midewiwin) was put into place in the ensuing vacuum. Vecsey's extended discussion of how he views the results of religious contact in Southern Ojibwe communities serves as an excellent base for highlighting the uniqueness of the Lynx Lake community.

In [the place of traditional religion], some Ojibwas have turned to Christianity, Midewiwin, and other religious innovations in order to maintain their existence. But none of the religious movements has brought back abundant game; none has improved Ojibwa health. None has demonstrated the lasting strength of the traditional manitos or initiated a lasting interest in new objects of religion. Despite vestiges of their traditional religion, traces of recent religious developments, sporadic participation in Christianity and a recent renewal of interest in their past, most Ojibwas remain alienated from the traditional sources of their existence.

The loss has carried serious ramifications for the Ojibwas in their daily lives. Their religion was concerned with such vital issues as survival and ethics, and it provided them with a sense of coherency, meaning, and security. Now gone, it has taken with it the Ojibwas' firm grasp on life. Economic hardship, political impotence, environmental imbalances, and other tangible factors have helped produce the contemporary Ojibwa malaise, but in large part it also derives from their religious alienation.

Traditional Ojibwas viewed essential matters, those concerning health, subsistence, social organization and leadership, ultimately from a religious perspective. Today that perspective has been demolished, and the Ojibwas appear disoriented, having found no suitable replacement. (p. 6)

While this view may reflect the situation among some Ojibwe groups, its formulation appears to deny the groups studied any agency. In contemporary society, this is simply not the case. The study of naturally occurring discourses directed by the people of Lynx Lake to their peers in the community presents a decidedly different perspective on the efficacy and importance of the post-contact religious system from the one an outsider observer might take.[5] The next two exemplary texts, the first a prayer composed on the spot and the second an entire sermon, were directed to an entirely local audience. The themes presented are consistent with those already seen in the testimonials and with themes heard in virtually all religious discourse in Lynx Lake extending across the Severn Ojibwe community. Many of the 'vital issues' and 'essential matters' noted in Vecsey's discussion of religion are addressed in the discourses presented in this chapter. However, the discourses do not indicate malaise or disorientation; rather, the messages in these discourses reflect an overall picture of focus and agency of the community members. These are not discourses of desperation; they are the voices of people confident in their understanding of the world around them.

The following text is a prayer given during a Sunday-morning church service at St Paul's Anglican Church. This prayer, examined as an example of a spoken, not read, public prayer in the previous chapter, is typical of spontaneous prayers in both form and content. Again we find the predominant themes of hardship, illness and suffering, and requests for God's blessings for church workers – such blessings include comfort, happiness, health, safe travel, and strength of body and mind. As is true of most spontaneous prayers, this was performed in a markedly quieter voice than the surrounding discourse. The pitch is low, and at times the voice drops to a whisper. The prayer begins with the coordinating particle *miina*, 'and,' because it is inserted into a designated position within a liturgical prayer read from the prayer-book. All but two sentences of this prayer begin with *miina*, so typical paragraph structure is missing. For ease in reading this text, I divided it into paragraphs at roughly topical boundaries, or boundaries marked by extended pauses. The last two paragraphs are marked at the beginning by other particles (*ekwa miina,* 'and also,' and *mii tahsh* 'and so it is ...').

Miina e-mihkawinitawaankitwaa, piko aanti tashiikewinink kaa-ayaawaac ohomaa waahkaahi kaa-kayaakin tashiihkewininaank. Ikiweniwak aanimisiwin kaa-ayaawaac. Miina, miina aanimaahpinewin kaa-ayaawaac. Miina ekaa kaa-kihkentamowaac ci-kii-mino-ayaawaac. Miina, mii ikweniwak, piko aanti kaa-awaac miina ekaa kaa-kihkenimankitwaa, nitinowenimaakaninaanak, kaa-aanimisiwaac. Miina ci-wii-miinatwaa maskawisawin ihimaa opimaatisiwiniwaa miina omaamitonencikaniwaa. Miina ci-wii-otihsikowaac ihiweni kiin kikishewaatisiwin. Miina ohomaa tashiihkewinink kaa-ayaawaac ikweniwak kaa— kaa-aahkosiwaac miina aanimisiwin kaa-awaac. Miina, miina kanake pankii ci-wii-nakanik-owaac ihiwe otaanimiwiniwaa.

Miina aahkosiwikamikonk kaa-ayaawaac ihimaa shoo lookaawit miina wiinipek, miina tanta pe, miina wiyekamaank. <Pause, intake of breath>
Miina kikishewaatisiwin miina ihimaa ci-wii-pakintinaman ihimaa aahkosiwi—, ihimaa aahkos— aahkosiiwikamik miina ahii kima-skawisiiwin ihimaa ci-wiih-paki-tinaman, miina ci-wii-otihsikoowaac kikishewaatisiwin. Miina ci-wii-kaa-kii-ciihatwaa omaamitonencikaniwaa

And we are thinking about them, everywhere in the villages, the villages that are all around. [We think of] those in hardships. And, and those who have a terminal illness. And those who don't know if they will get well. And those that are (just anywhere) around there, and those that we don't know about, our relatives who are suffering. And for you to give them strength there in their lives and in their minds. And for them to receive your love. And for those that are sick and who have hard-ships here in the village. And, and even that [their hardships] leave them even just a little.

And for those that are there in the hospital in Sioux Lookout, Winnipeg, Thunder Bay, and Weagamow. *<Pause, intake of breath>*
And your kindness, will you provide [to them] there in the hospital, and your strength will you provide there, that they will receive your kindness and be comforted in their minds that they will have happiness in their minds. And that they would leave their

ikiweniwak, miina miwentamoowin ci-
wii-ayaawaac ihimaa omaamito-
nencikaniwaank, miina. Miina, ci-wii-
nakanakowaac ihiwe otaahkosi-
winiwaa miina ci- <Pause>
minoyaawan ci-wii-ayaawac.

sickness there and that *<Pause>*
they would be well.

   Ekwa miina, ikweniwak kii— kiin
kitanohkiinaakanak miina ci-wii-
wiiciwiikoowaac kikishewaatisiwin.
Miina payahtakenimoowin miina
minwayaawan ci-wii-ayaawaac miina
ci-wii— miina ci-wii-kiiwewaac miina
ci-wii-mino-takohshiniwaac weti kaa-
kiih-poonci-maacaawaac. <Extended
pause>

   And also, for these, too, who
have come here, those who are
your workers [priests], that your
kindness will be with them. And
for them to be well and for them
to go home [safely] to the places
where they came from. *<Extended
pause>*

   Mii tahsh keniinawint ohomaa
shawenimihshinaak maamaw ohomaa
keniinawint kaa-ayaayaank tashiih-
kewininaan. [Begins reading]

   And so to us here also, bless,
too, all of us here who are are in
our village. [*Begins reading*]

   The final sample of religious discourse included here is a sermon given by the Reverend Simon Pipoon on 22 November 1987 during the morning service at St Paul's Anglican Church in Lynx Lake. This sermon is uncharacteristically brief, truncated so that the church leaders could get out of church in time to bid farewell to the visiting (Anglican) Native priests and deacons from the Severn area who had convened for a meeting in Lynx Lake, as is mentioned within the text. Again, notice how consistently the theme of 'perseverance in the face of difficulties coming to those committed to God' is carried through yet another genre of religious discourse. This is the unifying theme of all the texts provided in this chapter, and indeed is a central theme of most public and much private religious discourse. The sermon is provided in its entirety.

   Again, I have used a prosaic format. In this discourse, the particles tend to be cohesive (*ekwa*, 'and,' and *miina*, 'and,' are the most common): there are many more changes in actors and events than in a typical discourse, and it is these changes that are reflected in the paragraph structure. The actors are juxtaposed because of shared experiences; these provide the topical cohesion found within the sermon, which is outlined following the text. The sermon was intoned; that is, it was spoken with a projecting voice as if the loudspeaker microphone perched on the pulpit in front of the Reverend Pipoon had not been present, and in an extremely slow and measured tempo. Indeed, while all Native Anglican preachers that I heard used a similar style, the Reverend Pipoon is remarkable for his clarity, attributable to his extremely slow tempo. The 'religious speech' phonological style shift described in chapter 4 is particularly evident in this text and has been noted in the Ojibwe column by underlined spaces where a nasal consonant would be expected.

Noonkom kaa-kishepaayaak waaciye kahkina kitininaawaa. Ohomaa kaa-pi— kaa-pi-wiici-piintikeminakok ohomaa ayamihewikamikonk. Ekwa noonkom kaa-kishepaayaak kaa-piintikeyank. Acina ehta isihse ci-naanoontakosiyaan. Ikweniwak ohomaa ayamihewikamaak kaa-pi-ishaawaac kaawin piintikehsiiwak. Ekwa aasha wiipac ta-maacaawak. Ekwa aatiht awiyak oka-wii-nohsa-waapmaawaan. Miina aasha ci-noocihicihsek tipahikan, ci-pi-naasihkawaakaniwaac okoweniwak ayamihewikamaak kaa-wiih-kiiwewaac. <Pause>

Kaa-kiih-amihtooyahk, kaa-kiih-kanawaapantamahk okiskentaakohkewin Sent Cwaan, kaa-ishinihkaatek niiwin maatinamaakan, kaa-kii-kanawaapantamahk. Pankii, pankii kanake naanta nika-ishikaataan. Ahawe Cwaan okiskentaakohkewin kaa-masinahahk.

Mekwaac ihiwe eh-ka-kiishikaak kiih-aaniman awiya kaa-ayami-hewaatisoc ci-kii-ayamihcikec.

Mekwaac ihiwe kaa-inaacimoc Cwaan, okiskentaakohkwin kaa-

This morning I say "Greetings [Waaciye]" to all of you here with whom I have come to church. And this morning as we are coming here to church, there is only a little time for me to talk. The priests that have come here are not coming to church, (as) they will be leaving very soon now. And some people will want to see them off. The hour is also coming for these priests who are going home to be picked up here. *<Pause>*

What we read, what we looked at, it is called the Revelation of Saint John, chapter four, that we looked at, I will say just a little bit about it. It was John who wrote the revelation.

During that day, it was hard for someone who was a Christian to pray.

During that time, as John told in the revelation, it was really difficult

masinahahk mitoni kiih-aaniman,
awiya kaa-ayamihewaatisic. Kii-isihse
hsa piko, kiishpin awiya waapamaa-
kaniwic ayamihcikec, naanta piko ci-
nihsaakaniwic. Ehpiihci noonkom
tahshiin, kii-aamentaakwahk e-wii-
ayamihcikewin kaye waahkaahik-
anink, kaye kitaaymihewikamikonk.
Kaawin kekoon, <Pause> *kaaw— ke-*
onci-aanimentaaman.

E-kii-inaatisic ahawe kihci-okimaa,
Siisan kihci-okimaa, rooman kaa-kii-
apic. E-kii-ishihcikec eh-aanimaninik
kekoon e-kii-ishi-pakitinahk okihci-
okimaawininink.

Ahawe Cwaan mekwaac e-kakiih-
kimiwec. <Pause> *Kiih-antawi-*
pakitinaakaniwi naawic kihcikamiik.
Minihtikwaapihkonk e-kii-antawi-
pakitnaakaniwic ahawe Cwaan. Ekwa
kiyaapic ci-isihsenik ci-kakiihkimiwec
piko ci-peshikoc minihtikwaapihkonk,
Paatimas kaa-ishinihkaatek minish-
tikwaapik. Mii himaa kaa-kii-
pakitinikoc kihci-okimaawan, ekaa
kiyaapic ci-aacimaac, <Pause>
Kraistan miina ominwaacimowin
Ciisahs.

Mintoni aanimentaakwanitok,
naawic kihcikamiik eh-tahkayaak,
kohtaatentaakwahk. Eh-pehsikoc
Cwaan minihtikwaapikok kii-
inentamotok kehcinaac nipeshik. Kii-
inentaakwan ihiwe minihtikwaapihk
taapiskooc kipahotoowikamik kaa-
inentaakwak. Taapiskooc eh-kipahonc
<Pause> *Peshikwaa isihsenik ihimaa*
mekwaac eh-ayaac minihtikwaapikonk,
mekwaac eh-ayamihewikiishikaanink

for someone who was a Christian.
It happened that if someone were
seen praying he might be killed.
(Right now, so far, things are
peaceful. When you want to pray,
in your home as well as in your
church, there is nothing <Pause>
for you to worry about.)

That was how that ruler, Caesar
who ruled over the Romans, was.
He was such that in his kingdom
he made it hard for [Christians] by
putting things in their way.

While John was preaching, he
was taken way out into the sea to a
rocky island. <Pause> That John
was taken out to be left there so
that it would no longer be possible
for him to preach — just for him
to be alone on that rocky island.
The rocky island was called
Patmos. That is where the king put
him so that he would not tell about
<Pause> Christ and the gospel of
Jesus.

It must feel difficult [to be] far
out in the sea, cold and dangerous.
All alone on the rocky island, John
must have thought "I am truly
alone." That rocky island must
have seemed just like a jail. That is
was it felt like, like he was jailed.
<Pause> Once it happened, while
he was there on that rocky island,
John saw an amazing vision. John
saw something supernatural. John

okii-waapantaan ahawe Cwaan. Kii-
ishi-ayaa ahawe Cwaan, taapiskooc e-
nipaac, taapiskooc awiya kaawin
entank. Mekwaac eh-aymihewikii-
shikaak. Mekwaac kaa-Tipencikec
okiishikaam, Ahcaahkonk ninkii-ayaa,
ihkito ahawe Cwaan. <Pause>
   Okii-waapantaan ishinamowinini
ihimaa minihtikwaapikonk mekwaac
eh-ayamihewikiishikaak. Eshkam kii-
ishi-ayaa ahkiink pimaatisic anih-
shinini, naanta eh-nipaac, naanta
kaye e-wanentak. Ahpii e-koshkoshkaac
owii_taan mamaahtawaapihshinowin
e-kii-waapanta_k ihiweni kaa-kii-ishi-
ayaac. Okii-wiintaan, owiintaan
anihshinini, e-waapantank kaa-
ahcaahkowank kihci-kiishikonk kaa-
onci-makahk. <Pause>
   A mii howe too? kaa-kii-ishi-ayaac
Cwaan, kaa-noontamahk noonkom
kaa-kishepaayaak. Ihkito Cwaan kaa-
ponihsek, Ninkii-waapantaan eh-
paahkintekootek ishkwaantem. Kihci-
kiishiko_k nkii-waapantaan, ihkito.
<Pause> *Ekwa ihiwe nistam*
ihkitowin kaa-noontamaan, taapiskooc
awiya eh-kanoonihshic taapiskooc
pootaacikan, eh-inihshic awiya ihiwe
kaa-kii-waapantamaan, ihkito
piishaan! Ka-waapantahin kehcinaac
ke-ni-ayinkihk, mwestahs inikohk.
<Pause> *Ekwa Cwaan ihkito,*
Shemaak ahcaahkonk ninkii-ayaa.
<Pause> *Apiwin, kihci-apiwin kii-*
onastew kihci-kiishiko_k.
   Ekota awiya kii-api kihci-apiwinink,
ihkito. Ahawe kaa-apic-kii-inaapam-
inaakosi taapiskooc caahs— caaspin

was just like he was sleeping, just
like someone unconscious. On
Sunday, on the day of the Lord. "I
was in the spirit," says John.
<Pause>

He saw a vision there on the
rocky island on a Sunday. Sometimes it happen(s) to a person
living on earth, perhaps while he's
sleeping, perhaps while he is
unconscious. When he awoke, he
told that he saw an amazing
revelation while he was in that
state. He told, he tells that he sees
something spiritual that came
from heaven. <Pause>

This is what happened to John,
what we heard this morning. John
says, when it was over, "I saw a door
that was left open. I saw heaven,"
he says. <Pause> "And that first
word that I heard was like someone was calling to me, just like a
trumpet. Someone that I saw said
to me, he says, 'Come here! I'll
show you what will certainly come
to be before (?it happens).'"
<Pause> And John says, "Right
away I was in the spirit. <Pause> A
chair, a throne was set up in
heaven." <Pause>

"Behold, someone was sitting on
the throne," he says. "That one
who was sitting appeared to be just

ahsinii miina sartiyis. Waaskaa maaka kihci-apiwinihk piihsimeyaapii kii-ayaaw eh-inaapaminaakwahk, taapiskooc emelaat. <Pause> *Mitoni maamaahkaac ninkii-ishinaan, ihkito Cwaan. Kihci-apiwin nkii-waapantaan e-onastek kihci-kiishiko_k. Ahawe kaa-apic mitoni maamahkaasonaakosi.* <Pause> *Taapiskooc caaspin ahsinii.* <Pause> *Mitoni maamahkaasinaakosi ahawe kaa-apic kihci-apiwinink.* <Pause>

Cwaan awanenan ini kaa-kii-waapamaac, awanenan ini kaa-kii-waapamaac kihci-apiwinink. Mitoni kaa-kii-maamahkaasinawaac, kihci-kiishiko_k. Amii hawe Kishe-manitoo, amii wanini Kishe-manitoo, kaa-kii-waapamaac kihci-kiishikonk kaa-apinic kihci-apiwinink, kaakike. Ekaa wiihkaa kaa-waapamaayahk wiiyaahsipimaatisiwin kaa-kikishkamahk noonkom kaa-kiishikaak. Mitoni maamahkaasinaakosi.

Aishaaya okiskwehikew, ninkotaahso-maatinamaakan kaa-ihkitoc. Eh-ihkitoc Aishaaya, ahpii kaa-kii-pooni-pimaatisic Aishaaya okiskwehikew, Ninkii-waapamaa kaa-Tipencikec eh-apic kihci-apiwinink kihci-kiishikonk, ihkito Aishaaya. Mitoni maamahkaac e-kii-ishinamaan, ihkito Aishaaya. Miina ninkii-waapamaaw kihci-okiishikowak, kihci-kiishiko_k kaa-atoshkawawaa. Kishe-manitoowa, kaakike miina kaakike. <Pause> *Eh-ihkitowaac, ihkito Aishaaya, ikiweniwak kihci-oskiishikowak, kaawin wiihkaa*

like Jasper stone and Sardis. Then around the throne was a rainbow that looked like an emerald. <*Pause*> What I saw was truly amazing," says John. "The throne I saw that was set up in heaven, the one sitting (in it) looked truly wonderful. <*Pause*> Like the gem Jasper. <*Pause*> The one sitting on the throne looks absolutely amazing."<*Pause*>

Who was it that John saw? Who was it that he saw on the throne? He was really amazing to him in heaven. It is God. It is he, God, that he saw who was sitting on the throne in heaven for ever and ever. The one we have never seen in the flesh[ly forms] that we are wearing today. He looks truly amazing.

In the sixth chapter of Isaiah the prophet, Isaiah [spoke, lit. 'said']. Isaiah says, "When the prophet Isaiah died, 'I saw the Lord sitting on a throne in heaven,' Isaiah says. 'What I saw is really amazing,' says Isaiah. 'And I saw angels in heaven serving God forever and ever. <*Pause*> They are saying,' says Isaiah, 'those angels, they never stop saying "Holy, holy, holy is the Lord almighty. The earth is full of his glory, (the glory) of the Lord,'" Isaiah says.<*Pause*>

opoonihtoonaawaa e-ihkitowaac,
Kanaatisiw, kanaatisiw, kanaatisiw
kaa-Tipencikec misiwesiwihkaatisic.
Misiwe ahkiink shaakishkine
okistentaakosiwin, ahawe kaa-
Tipencikec, ihkito Aishaaya. <Pause>
   Mitoni eh-kanaatisic ahawe kaa-
waapamak, ihkito Aishiaaya. <Pause>
Amii hi kaa-inenimitisowaan ihkito
Aishaaya, ahpii kaa-waapamak kaa-
Tipencikec, kihci-kiishikonk. Amii
ahpan e-nihshoowanaatisiyaan. Amii
ahpan e-nihshoowanaatisiyaan.
<Pause> *Aishaaya ihkito ohowe kaa-*
onci-nishoowanaatisiyaan cikemaa
ekaa eh-payehkiseyaan nitoonink.
Miina e-wiici-ayamiimakwaa, kaa-ishi-
ayamiimakanik otooniwaa ekaa eh-
payehkahk mitoon e-ishi-ayamiimakahk
miina e-otaawiniyaan ikiweniwak
anihshininiwak kaa-ishi-
pimaatisiwaac, ekaa pishihshik
kwanta kekoon. Kaa-ani-
mootamakaninik otooniwaa. Amii owe
ahpin kaa-nihshoowanaacihikowaan.
<Pause>
   Cwaan ihkito, Nkii-waapamaa kaa-
Tipencikec eh-apic kihci-apiwinink.
Ninkii-waapamaak ikiweniwak kihci-
kiishikonk, kaa-ayaawaac, e-waapis-
kohowaac, waapiski— waapiskikish-
kaacikanan e-kikishkamowaac. Miina
oshaawishooniyaan, oshaawishoo-
niyaaw̲ kihci-okimaawastotinan, e-
kikishkahke(waac) ikiweniwak kaa-
ayaawaac otiskawaayek okihci-
apiwinink Kishe-mantioo. <Long
pause>
   Pwaan ahpii ishkwaayaac kaa-

"That one I saw was truly holy,"
Isaiah says. *<Pause>*
"This is what I thought about
myself," says Isaiah, "when I saw
the Lord in Heaven. Surely I will
be destroyed. Surely I will be
destroyed." *<Pause>* Isaiah says,
"This is the reason I will be destroyed: indeed, my mouth is
unclean, for I talk with those
whose mouths are unclean, the
way the unclean mouth talks,
about my home, the way those
people live. And always their
mouths speak of nothing important. This is what is destroying
me." *<Pause>*

John says, "I saw the Lord sitting
on the throne. I saw those in
heaven who are there dressed in
white, who are wearing white
clothes. And they are wearing
golden crowns, those ones who are
there in front of the throne of
God." *<Long pause>*

When he talked for the last time

*ayamihaac otooskiniikiimo Timohtiiwa
ihkito ahawe Pwaal, ninkishipishkaan
nkakwe-cishkasiwewin, ninkii-noo-
tinike, mino-nootinikewin ayaank-
waamisin otinaan Timohtiiwan.
Aasha wiipac nka-pooni-pimaatis.
Niwaapantaan kihci-kiishiko_k ihkito
Pwaal. Nitahtamaakoo kihci-okimaa-
wastohtin ekaa ke-nihshoowanaatahk,
kaakike miina kaakike.* <Pause>

   *Mii tahsh ohowe toowihkaan Cwaan
kaa-kii-waapantank kihci-kiishiko_k.
Cwaan kaa-kii-waapamaac* <Pause>
*iniweniwan kaa-apinic kihci-apiwi-
nink. Ninkii-waapamaak, Cwaan
ihkito, kihci-okiishikoowak naanin-
kotaahso e-tahsininikin omiinkwan-
aawa miina oshkiinshikowa waaskaa,
e-o— kii-oshkii_shikowak waaskaa
miina piihcaayek. Kaawin aaste
ayaahsiiwak eh-kiishikaanik miina eh-
tipihkaanik eh-ihkitowaac,
Kanaatisiw, kanaatisiw, kanaatisiw
kaa-Tipencikec misiwe-siwikaatisic
kaa-ayaac miina ke-ayaac.* <Pause>

   *Mayaam peshikwan e-ihkitoc Cwaan
okiskentaakohkewin noonkom kaa-
kanawaapantamahk, taapiskooc
Aishaaya okiskiwehikew kaa-kii-ishi-
waapanta_k ishinamowin, kihci-
kiishiko_k. Mayaam peshikwan e-
ihkitoc Cwaan, Kihci-okiishikowak
ninkii-waapamaak, ihkito Cwaan.
Mooshak e-ihkitowaac ihimaa
otiskawaayek kihci-apiwinink,
Kanaatisiw, kanaatisiw, kanaatisiw
kaa-Tipencikec misiwe-siwikaatisic.
Oko kaa-waapamikwaa okiishikowak
kaawin wiihkaa ?aastene. Kaawin*

to his young man Timothy, Paul
says "I have come to an end. ?They
are trying to sacrifice me. I fought
the good fight. Be careful," he says
to Timothy. "Soon I will die. I saw
heaven," says Paul. "A crown has
been set aside for me that will
never perish, for ever and ever."
<Pause>

   This is just like what John saw in
heaven. John saw *<Pause>* that one
who is sitting on the throne. "I saw
angels," John says, "that had six
wings and eyes all around. They
had eyes around and within. Day
and night they never stop saying,
'Holy, holy, holy is the Lord
almighty who was and will [for-
ever] be.'" *<Pause>*

   John says exactly the same
(thing) in Revelation, where we
are looking now. [It was] just like
the vision the prophet Isaiah saw
in heaven. John says exactly the
same [thing]. "I saw angels," says
John. "As they are there in front of
the throne they are always saying,
'Holy, holy, holy is the Lord
almighty.' These angels that I saw
never rest; day and night they say
this phrase."

wiihkaa anwehshinook eh-kiishikaanik miina eh-tipahkanik e-ihkitowaac oho ihkitowin.

Mii himaa minikohk ke-ayamihtoowaan, noonkom kaa-kiishikaak, ayamihewikiishikaa. Okii-pahkaan ankitaan kaa-Tipencikec, ayamihe-kiishika. <Pause> *Tahsin kekoon, kaa-noohtamahk kihci-masinahikan, ayamihe-kiishikaak okii-ishi-pakitinaan kaa-Tipe_cikec. Mitaahso-onahshowewin kaa-kii-miinawaaniwank, e-ayamihekii-shikaak, kii-ocihcihse e-kii-miinaw-aaniwank. Kaa-kanaatisic ahcaahk e-kii-takohshink e-ayamihe-kiishikaanik. Cwaan e-kii-waapantank ishina-moowin, e-ayamihe-kiishikaa.* <Pause>

Kekiinawint kipakohsentaakosimin kaa-pimaatisiyahk miina ayamihe-kiishikaa kihci-nantonamahk kaa-ahcaahkowak, ci-nantawwapan-tamahk, miina ci-kakwe-mihkamahk. Ihiwe ahcaahk kaa-ahcaahkowak ekaa wiihkaac ke-nihshoowanaatahk, Kishe-manitoo otoo—otihkitowin.

Ekwa miina kaa-pimaatisiyahk ayamihewipimaatisiwin e-omaamin-tonentamahk, kaawin, kaawin kika-wencihsihsiin. Kii-ayamiwak kihci-ihkwek [unintelligible] e-kiih-aanimomaawaac kaa-oshki-maat-anohkiininc ayamihewikamiko_k oshkiniihkwewak. Kii-wiintamaa-konaanak eh-aanimak ayamihewi-anohkiiwin tepwe aaniman, (<Pause> kaawin wentahsinoon. <Pause>

Aanimisiwininink awiya oka-onci-

This is all I will read today, on Sunday. Today is Sunday. The Lord set aside Sunday. <Pause> All the thing(s) that we hear in the Bible. It was on a Sunday that the Lord gave out the ten commandments. Sunday was the time they were given out. The Holy Spirit arrived on a Sunday. John saw a vision on a Sunday. <Pause>

We, too, who are living, are wanted to listen for something spiritual on a Sunday, to hunt it down and to try to find that something that is spiritual, some-thing that will not be destroyed: God's word.

And also for us who are living, when we are thinking about Christian living, it will not, not be easy. The elder ladies [talked about] those who are just starting to work in the church, the young women. They told us that Christian work is hard, truly hard. <Pause> It is not easy. <Pause>

Through difficulty someone will

*waapantaan manitoo e-ishi-nanta-
wenimikoc, ahawe otayamihewi-
pimaatis, otayamihewiotanohkii.
Taapiskooc Cwaan ohoweni kaa-kii-
waapanta_k okiskentaakohkewin kaa-
masinaha_k, ka-kwaatakenimowinink,
okii-onci-waapantaan ishinamoowin
kaa-wiintamaakoyahk, ohomaa
omasinhikanink ahawe Cwaan.
    Manitoo kika-wii-shawenimikowaa
maamaw.*

see what God wants [from] him or
her, that Christian, that church
worker. Just like what John saw,
what he wrote in Revelation, [it
was] in suffering he saw the vision
that he tells us about here in this
book, that Joh

God bless you all.

The line 'the elder ladies [talked about] those who are just starting to work in the church, the young women,' referred to a couple of the elder members of the senior choir who addressed the difficulties and benefits of becoming junior choir members, a move which is interpreted in Lynx Lake as a commitment to a strong Christian life.[6] The content and rhetorical structuring of the sermon provides some interesting insights into current argumentation: what constitutes evidence?

I.   Greetings (announcement)
II.   Sermon introduction
III.   Intro to St John's life
IV.   St John's exile (includes heavy evaluation section)
V.   St John's vision
       A.   Rhetorical questions: Who was it that John saw? etc.[7]
       B.   St John's vision of God
VI.   The Prophet Isaiah's vision
       A.   Vision
       B.   Problem which caused vision: people speaking idly
VII.   St John's vision
VIII. St Paul's vision
IX.   Visions compared and equated
X.   Importance of Sundays (including evidence)
XI.   Admonition to audience
       'We, too, who are living, are wanted to listen for something spiritual on a Sunday, to hunt it down and to try to find that something that is spiritual, something that will not be destroyed: God's word.'

XII.   Warning of difficulties
XIII. Coda

Notice that this sermon pivots around the visions of three biblical characters. The visions were of God and of a heaven in which which the persecution and difficulty of the present world play no part. The emphasis on visions as compelling evidence is consistent with an older world-view in which visions were sought out to help humans deal with the physical and spiritual world. Visions are still a primary legitimating device to this day. Indeed, it was through a miraculous vision that the archdeacon first had his calling to the Christian ministry.

While these religious texts are but a subset of the religious discourses heard in Lynx Lake, these samples were chosen as representative. As such, the overwhelming evidence of the discourse is that the people of Lynx Lake have adopted a Native Christian world-view which has been used to re-evaluate and reinterpret an older cosmology.

Although Christianity has become firmly established in the Severn area in the last hundred years or so, some evidence of change is beginning to show up among some of the younger generations. In a *Wawatay News* article (16/5 [May 1989]) a young Native person from Webequie, Ontario, a dialectally transitional Severn community, called for a combination of Christian and Native religions. This request signals a change in the means of defining ethnicity: here a young man (or perhaps a group of young adults) is turning to sources outside the home community to define identity. The focus among anthropologists and others on studying the 'traditional' elements of Native religions has led to a situation in which 'Native' aspects of religion are defined as essentially, 'not White.' Using such an external standard which insists that 'Christianity cannot be Native,' those Natives who adopt Christianity as their primary religious affiliation are categorized as enculturated at best and deluded at worst. The external observers look to what they consider a more pristine religious state and declare that any memory of such activities indicates that this is the 'true religion' for the Native people. Now it may be true in many Ojibwe communities that Christianity is but a 'thin veneer' spread over an older system, but in Lynx Lake, and probably in many other Severn communities, Christianity is, and has been, considered an integral part of community life. Indeed, to be Anglican in Lynx Lake is to be a Native, and to be a Native is to be Anglican.

The young man's request for a new amalgam of Christianity and Native religion is a sign that the *folklorization of ethnicity* has just begun for the northern Ojibwe. In southern Ojibwe communities, where forced contact with the White matrix society has been long standing, Native people tend to define themselves *vis-à-vis* the 'other.' Thus, if something is 'White' then it is necessarily 'not-Indian' and vice versa. Vogt would align this reaction with his fourth category of syncretism. In the north, where there has been relatively little and generally recent contact with Whites, the Native peoples define themselves internally. In a situation such as that in Lynx Lake, it is moot to ask if one element or another is 'White' or even 'borrowed.' If the people are using it, the item is being used 'Natively.' The question asked by the people of Lynx Lake is 'Will X be useful to us?' not 'Will the use of X compromise our Nativeness?'

The folklorization of ethnicity is a process by which a group chooses a corpus of symbols with which and by which they define themselves. Language has typically held high symbolic value in the definition of ethnicity, but as many Native American languages slowly fade into memory, the symbols chosen are often in the area of religion. Some of the religious symbols which have been adopted, or perhaps reintroduced, by many Native groups include drums and drumming, peace pipes, sweetgrass, and certain dances. The fact that they have been introduced, in many cases very recently and from other, unrelated groups, seems to have bothered neither the academic nor the Native community, as indeed it should not.

However, in communities where there is no need for overt symbols, where ethnicity is doxa, the use, adaptation, and adoption of outside resources, including linguistic codes, religious systems, and material technology, are seen as no threat to group identity. This is the situation for most Severn people, or has been until the present inundation of outside influences, most important of which has been contact with other Native people who have had their ethnic identities threatened and who, in their understandable resistance against centuries-old policies of subjugation, have inadvertently begun to plant seeds of ethnic insecurity among younger, more mobile sectors of the Severn Ojibwe community. Thus, much concern with 'White' versus 'Native' religious styles is a recent development arising from the group of Native people who have had the most contact with the matrix societies that make such dichotomies. The layers of irony run deep here: a people who define themselves as Native have adopted as a central part of their social lives a religious system associated with White, Western society and have redefined the system as Native. However, the same White, Western society, particularly the academic community, in attempting to become 'more sensitive to Native needs,' has defined Nativeness on the basis of being 'not White' and have created often artificial boundaries between what is White and what is Native. These boundaries have in turn been taught to educated Natives, who are beginning to adopt this White viewpoint and now must redefine themselves on the basis of this new dogma taught from the outside. Furthermore, they feel that they must teach such a dogma to Native people who have as yet seen no threat to their aboriginal identities. For most people in Lynx Lake, to be Native is to be Anglican; but, suddenly, to be Anglican is to be not-Native. However, turning from the Church of England to a 'Native religion' would be denying a central focus of the Native identity in the community. This wind of change signals a broader trend towards external definitions of self, which indicates the insulation from the matrix society is quickly fading.

The tension between being Anglican and being Native seems to be a problem only for the youth. The wife of a past chief of Lynx Lake had travelled with him on several occasions to chiefs' meetings outside the Severn area. Most of these meetings are begun with sweetgrass and pipe ceremonies. Her daughter laughingly reported to me that her mother wondered why these people never 'thanked God' at the beginning of these meetings like the people from the Severn area did. All those people ever did, according to the mother, was 'smoke and beat on drums.' This woman, who spoke no English, who dressed in traditional garb of a brightly coloured skirt over pants and kept her head covered with a scarf, who had spent much of her life living and working on a trapline, who lived in one of the most remote Indian villages in Canada, understood the 'traditional religious observances' performed by predominantly English-speaking Natives at chiefs' meetings as mere displays of smoke and noise which ignored the spiritual importance of the gathering.

In conclusion, the Ojibwe are very spiritually attuned people – evidenced in many ethnographic descriptions (Casagrande 1952; Densmore 1929; Hallowell 1934, 1936, 1939 and 1942; Jenness 1935; Landes 1968[1937]; and E. Rogers 1962, among others). In Lynx Lake, Christianity has become the primary religious paradigm through which the spiritual world is addressed, owing in no small part to the efforts of two generations of strong, local leadership. Religious discourse in Lynx Lake is free from concerns about 'living like Whitemen,' 'turning from the old ways,' or any of the other reactionary themes that might be expected given the presentations of religion in the area by outside researchers. Lynx Lake has been designated by scholars and religious agencies in northwest Ontario as the heart of the 'Anglican North' and as is known as a community which allows only one church so that its spiritual and social unity might not be broken. Through representative discourses, we hear the voices of a people committed to a strong Christian world-view not expected of those whose Native identity is so unquestioned.

Chapter Eight

Telling Stories: First-Person Narrative in Severn Ojibwe

A major problem for those working with narratives in any language is separating out those features which are (a) language specific, (b) culture specific, (c) genre specific, and (d) narrator specific. 'Higher' forms of verbal art such as myths or legends are indexed by heavily marked performance features such as formulaic utterances, the use of direct discourse, form–content parallelism (see Hymes 1981 and Woodbury 1987), and the like. Because they are so well marked, these artistic forms are the most likely to be collected by folklorists and ethnographers.

This focus on the more highly marked genres has been extremely compelling to people studying the stories of others. Stories in these genres are viewed by both the storyteller and the audience as being in some way 'objectifiable.' Despite the inevitable indexation of the storyteller, audience, and context in the telling of these stories, the basic story is often separated from that context to stand on its own (cf. Bauman 1986a and 1986b; see also Basso 1983 and 1988 for arguments on the intrinsic placedness of text).

A problem arises, however, when these genres are privileged to the exclusion of all others in a society. Narrative, which is heavily marked, must be so in relation to other kinds of narrative. Only by a thorough study of all types of narrative can the art of the myth, legend, parable, and so on be delineated. In this chapter, I focus on a verbal genre often less highly valued than the myth – that of the personal narrative – as an initial step towards a fuller understanding of the broad range of narrative types in Severn Ojibwe.

TEXT AND GENRE

The narrative titled here 'The Airplane Crash' was chosen for analysis for several reasons. This story was the first one told by an elder, Swanson Turtle,[1] to Rand Valentine, a regular visitor in his home, during a storytelling session in the winter of 1982. This story was followed by several legend-myths, providing continuity of performer, audience, and context of the current analysis with analyses included elsewhere in this book. A second reason for selecting this text for analysis is that the narrator himself chose this particular story to perform. The self-selection of a text provides insights into the narrator's view of what is a worthy, even important, topic. In his studies of Black English Vernacular, Labov (1972b) proposed that the elicitation of narratives in which the narrator was faced with a life-threatening situation was probably the best way for the outside researcher to gain access to a "relatively unmonitored discourse style." I am sceptical that these stories are actually unmonitored, as such stories are often told and retold. However, such first-person narratives are excellent for cross-generic study as they *are* highly structured as a result of multiple airings. I found it interesting that this narrator (self-) selected a story which centres around a life-threatening situation, not only because it confirms the validity of choosing this narrative genre for elicitation, as Labov did, but also because it indicates that narratives with high information content are often chosen for multiple tellings. While Swanson's[2] life was not personally threatened in this narrative, the presence of imminent death and his proximity to the action work together to create a text with the emotive impact of a type sought by Labov.

Two important studies of first-person narratives are those of Labov (1972b, mentioned above) and Dolby-Stahl (1985). As indicated, Labov focuses on those narratives in which the narrator was in a situation of danger, in order to study the syntax of discourse. Dolby-Stahl's work focuses much more on the outcome of first-person narratives. She posits that such first-person narratives are presented as a means of establishing intimacy between a storyteller and a given audience, so that this relationship and its history is of primary importance.

Despite the apparent difference of focus between Labov's and Dolby-Stahl's work (the first study looks at form, and the second at content), they both reveal an important aspect of first-person narratives – namely, the intimacy which is engendered by such narratives. Labov treats intimacy in his discussion of the formal features of casual style which arise in first-person narratives. Dolby-Stahl teases out aspects of intimacy between speaker and audience, using referential content and contextual cues. In both studies casualness and intimacy are linked in this particular genre.

The present analysis will concentrate on aspects of both structure and function especially as they relate to higher (i.e., more marked and more formal) verbal art forms, specifically the legend-myth, classified in some instances as both *aatisoohkaan* and *tipaacimowin,* in Severn Ojibwe.

ANALYSIS

Telling the Text

The storytelling session which began with this narrative was held in Swanson's home, situated in the heart of the Lynx Lake community, near the main dock where most of the floatplane traffic clusters. Until the opening of the airport in the late 1980s, this dock was the gateway into the village, a place where the entire community would congregate to meet and greet incoming family, friends, and officials. The position of the Turtle home next to the dock meant that the Turtles were always among the first to see who was coming in or going out of Lynx Lake, information that was and continues to be of great interest to the entire community. The location of Swanson's house, *naasipiink* (at the shore), is an integral part of the story discussed in this chapter. Swanson and Rand were the only two people in the house at the beginning of this session, although Swanson's wife joined them in the middle of a later story.

The physical arrangement of the storytelling session was quite typical of most informal conversations: people sat on chairs placed at right angles to the ends of a table so that they do not directly face each other. A tape recorder was set up on the table, with a large microphone on a stand placed in front of Swanson. The microphone was virtually identical to the one in the radio station, where Swanson spent at least four or five hours weekly talking to the community, telling stories, and joking with different partners. When beginning a taped storytelling session with Rand, Swanson would move his chair to face the table, lean on his forearms over the microphone, and hold the upright bar of the microphone stand. The stories would begin quite soberly; his voice would be quite controlled, in a low register, with compressed intonational contours and a deliberate and slow tempo. However formally these sessions began, Swanson always got more animated as the stories progressed, sometimes to the point where he would jump out of his seat to portray some character or to act out some part of the action, often forgetting the microphone entirely.

Because of Swanson's familiarity with microphones and monologues at the radio station, he was quite comfortable telling stories in this context. Indeed, in most respects this storytelling session was quite natural: a younger person requested a story from an elder known for his storytelling; the storytelling session was held in a private home; the narrator and his audience had an informal teacher/student relationship built up through many conversations.

The Structure of the Text

In her paper on metanarration in folk narrative, Babcock (1977) demonstrated that metanarration found in all narrative is integral to a performance-centred approach in the analysis of such narratives. Metanarration is the means by which a narrative is 'framed' or 'keyed' (Bauman 1977: 15–24). Babcock (ibid: 66) described the metanarrative frame as "an interpretive context or alternative point of view within which the content of the story is to be understood and judged." On a more general level, metanarrative is just one kind of reflexivity found in cultural systems, and as such its function is to "render experience meaningful – the inevitable and necessary 'framing' that we all engage in" (Merleau-Ponty, as quoted in ibid: 5).

Metanarration is not simply 'narration about narration,' what Babcock termed explicit metanarration; it includes "any element of communication which calls attention to the speech event as a performance ..." (ibid). This second kind of metanarration, more pervasive and subtle than explicit metanarration, she called implicit metanarration.

In this study of Swanson's story, I will explore aspects of metanarration, the 'story within the story,' along with a Labovian narrative analysis. Swanson's narrative is offered as representative of a Severn first-person story and, as such, as an example of a tradition in which explicit as well as implicit metanarration are prominent and necessary to the interpretation of such narratives.

Labov defines the minimal narrative as a "sequence of two clauses which are temporally ordered" (1972b: 360). He further defines narrative as "one method of recapitulating past experience by matching a verbal sequence of clauses to the sequence of events which (it is inferred) actually occurred" (ibid). Swanson's story clearly fits these formal definitions, but the definitions certainly do not correspond to any Severn category.

Genre is particularly interesting in Ojibwe as it is indexed by the term for talk used to introduce most stories. This story begins with Swanson declaring that he is 'about to relate' *(ninka-tipaacim)*, where the root for 'relate' indicates the telling of an historical (non-mythological legend) story. This attention to genre is pretty much universal in Swanson's stories and is found in the initial frame of most Algonquian narratives. In Severn Ojibwe, there are two basic narrative categories: *tipaacimowinan*, 'stories,' and *aatisoohkaanan*, what I am somewhat awkwardly calling 'legend-myths.' The narrative under examination here is a *tipaacimowin*, a full-fledged story with an elaborated structure which clearly belongs in the historical category: it includes an event that happened within the lifetime of the storyteller or his ancestors. *Tipaacimowinan* may have religious or mystical significance, as in the *Wiintikoo* ('Windigo') stories, or they may involve telling about something as mundane as the price of food in 1936. These stories range from the profoundly serious to the profoundly hilarious, with the latter being the most common. (For more information on *aatisoohkaanan*, see chapter 9.)

THE PLANE CRASH
Narrative by Swanson Turtle

1 *Ninka-tipaacim eh-antawentaakosiyaan ci-tipaacimoyaan e-wii-kihkentank wahawe nimpi-kiwitamik ohomaa niwaahkaahikanink.*
2 *Peshik ohomaa wemihtikooshi e-wiiciiwaamaayaank Naanti Paanantahiin e-ishinihkaasoc.*
3 *Aasha niisho-pipoon niwiiciitaamaanaan*
4 *Pimihsewin kaa-wii-kihkentank kaa-kii-pankihsink niishiwii-ahki niisho-pipoon otaanaank.*
5 *Mayaam ninkii-waapantaan eh-pankihsink ohomaa piko kaa-ishitaayaan akaamink.*
6 *Ketahtawiin eh-poonic naawic ohomaa kaa-ishitaayaan.*
7 *Kaawin okashkihtoohsiin ci-kii-pi-naatakaamehs kaa-ciishinaakosi, aanti maa eshi-maashiskwen ihiwe pimihsewin.*
8 *Kayemaa piihshaakanaap tahkwahikan shahshaakootaahsin ishinaakwan aana-wii-pi-kakwe-naatakaamehoc.*
9 *Mii ahpin aana-wii-pimicitaacin ahpin eni-ishi-kiiwehsec.*
10 *Mii tahsh ntawaac kiyaam—*
11 *Maaskooc kaye kaawin mayaam okihkentaan kekonen kaa-isihsek.*
12 *Mii tahsh enaacimoc ihimaa anihshinini kaa-kii-poosic ahawe kaa-kii-pankihshink.*
13 *Peshik ninkiih-inaacimohtaak maahti ntawaac weti naatakaam tapinaawaank ninka-onci-pakiciimin ihkito, otinaan.*
14 *Mii ahpin kaa-ishi-kakwe-pasikwahoc.*
15 *Mayaam eh-oncishkawi-pasikwahoc.*
16 *Maawac eh-kihci-nootink.*

17 *Kekaat eh-ompipiiwank nipi.*

18 *Ahpii tahsh eni-ompahoc pankii, aapiskooc kaa-piihtaahkweyaak eh-piihtahank, ketahtawiin ahpin kaa-mate-onci-aapicikwaanakootek aashikici-aahpicikwaanakoote[k].*

19 *Kii-nawekoote piko pankii.*

20 *Ahpin ikoc kaa-mate-ishihsihpwaatikohsink.*

21 *Ahpin kaa-mihci-shashooshawaakamink.*

22 *Mii ahpin kaa-ishi-naasipiipanihoyaan ninciimaan eh-kii-wiihkopitoowaan eh-kwaayaantakohkekipan nimaacinikaahcikan niwaasakanaapihk ihimaa niciimaanink.*

23 *Peshik itahsh kiih-poosikwaashkoni ihiwe ninciimaan.*

24 *Kotakiyak kiih-pi-maamaaciipanihowak.*

25 *Mii tahsh ihiwe mekwaac e-niminaawepinamaan (eni-min.—[?]) ninciimaan, mate-onci-mooshkamoomakahk ihiwe pimihsewin.*

26 *Kaawin kekoon anihshinini niwaapamaa.*

27 *Wiipac nawac niwaapamaa kotak peshik anihshinini e-mate-onci-moohkiic.*

28 *Acina piko kii-naakosi.*

29 *Ahpin miina mate-ishi-kookiipanihoc ahaawe anihshinini.*

30 *Mii hawe pimihsewinini itok naake piko wiipac aasha miina kaa-mate-onci-mooshkamowaac niishin.*

31 *Mii ahpin eni-nihsiwaac hiwe.*

32 *Mete-ishi-waawenapiwaac ihimaa pimihsewinink wakic, wakic ihimaa.*

33 *Mii hiwe kaah-inaapihshinaan.*

34 *Mii tahsh eshinaakosic ahawe eni-takohshinaan ahaawe opimihse, pankii okanakaapink pankii sawiskosi, taapiskooc sakimen kaa-kii-maakwamikoc kekaat ishinaakosi.*

35 *Miinawaa onihkink ihimaa otooskwanink iko pankii miina saakiskwe.*

36 *Opakwaanakoot ehta napikopan.*

37 *M-ohsha hi niishwaayek ihiwe eshi-miskiiwic ahaawe opimihse.*

38 *Ikweniwak tahsh anihshininiwak peshik naape peshik ihkwe owiiciiwaak-anan iko, kaawin kekoon ishiwepisihsiwak, "Kaawin naanta niwiihsa-kihshinimin," ihkitowak.*

39 *Mitoni tahsh eh-kishiwishkaak oninkiinkan peshik nipiink eshiwepihsink.*

40 *Paanimaa tahsh ninkii-waapantaan ositink eshinaakwahk e-kiih-akwaahikaatek.*

41 *Mitoni e-kiih-?siwihsink peshik osit.*

42 *Aapihta miina mitoni kaawin kekoon kwehkihkaat ihiwe pimihsewin.*

43 *Oninkiinkwan tahsh kekaat kaawin kihkentaakwahsinoon.*

44 *Napane[?]inkiinkwan tahsh pankii wiin iko aapihta wiin misiweyaatok maawin.*

45 *Pimaatisiwin tahsh e-kiih-takakwak ihimaa anaamiintam.*

46 *Mitoni maamahkaac, ninkii-inentaan.*

47 *Pimaatisiwin ekaa e-piikoshkaak ekwa pimihsewin eh-aana-piiwaapihkowank e-kiih-piikoshkaak.*

48 *Misiwe e-kiih-piikoshkaak.*

49 *Mii piko kii-maaciisahoote ihiwe pimihsewin, kaawiniin kaa-kii-wawehsici-kaatek ishinaakwahsinoon.*

50 *Pankii maawin kii-onci-manaahonaaniwanitok aantahpin kaa-ishowitekopanen.*

51 *Wiiyaahs noohkan; ohkan kaye noohkan.*

52 *Kaawin piikoshkaahsinoon wiiyaahs.*

53 *Kaawin kaye piikoshkaahsinoon ohkan.*

54 *Piiwaapihk mashkawaa inentakwan, piiwaapihk tahsh takwac piikoshkaa.*

55 *Kaa-ishi-waapantamaan.*

56 *Ninkii-aacimotaw-aa ninkii-wiintamawaa wahawe naape ninkii-ayamihaa, pehshonhc nawac nintinawemaa, Mahkop ishinihkaaso.*

57 *Taklahs Mahkop maawin ishinihkaasotok.*

58 *Nahke piko.*

59 *Moosihs Mahkop ishinihkaaso ahaawe kaa-okosihsic.*

60 *Ahina Mahkop ishinihkaaso ahaawe kaa-okosihsic ihkwe.*

61 *Miina omaamaaman ahaawe kaa-kiih-pankihshink.*

62 *Mii-we ninkii-ayamihaa pankii ahaawe nintooshim nintinaankomaa, ci-maamaakaatentank ekaa kaa-piikohshkaak opimaatisiwin kaa-ishinaakwahk tahsh ihiwe pimihsewin kaa-ishi-poosic.*

63 *Mii-hi kaa-ishi-ayamihak.*

64 *M-ohsha hi.*[3]

1 Because I have been requested to tell a story by this one visiting me here in my house who wants to learn, I will tell a story.

2 This one Whiteman that we are living with is called Rand Valentine.

3 We have been living with him now for two years (winters).

4 He wants to know about an airplane that crashed two years, two winters ago.

5 I saw it exactly when it fell here, right across the lake from where I live.

6 [It was] all of a sudden that it landed way out in the lake here where I live.

7 He looks like he isn't able to make it to shore, "Where did that plane go wrong?"

8 It looked like maybe the rudder rope couldn't handle the wind although he wanted to come to shore.

9 So then, when he wanted to go sideways, he went backwards.

10 So then, he might as well even—

11 Maybe he doesn't know [either] what exactly it is that happened.

12 So that's what the one who crashed was telling a person there who was taking off [with him].

13 One [of them] "He told me, 'We might as well land [take off?] there towards the shore where there is no wind,'" he says, he said of him [he reported him saying].

14 So he tried to take off there.

15 He started to take off straight into the wind.

16 There was a really strong wind.

17 The waves were rising.

18 So then he is lifting up a bit, he was as high as the treetops, [when] all of a sudden then [the plane] flipped over and fell on its back.

19 It was on its back just a short time.

20 Then, somehow it plunged into the water there.

21 Then the water was completely smooth.

22 So then I hurried down there to the shore and my boat, where I pulled my motor, already in place there in my boat.

23 Then one of them jumped into my boat.

24 Others came quickly, one after another.

25 So then, during the time I was pushing my boat out, that airplane came up there from the water.

26 Not a person do I see.

27 In a little bit I see him, another person who appears there.

28 He appeared for just a short time.

29 Then that person dives in there again quickly.

30 So that pilot [perhaps] soon comes up [with another] from the water and there are two.

31 So then that [group] becomes three.

32 They try to make themselves comfortable there on top of the plane, there on top.

33 It is that that I saw.

34 So then when I arrive this pilot looks like he is bleeding a little bit on his forehead; he almost looks like a mosquito bit him.

35 There on his arm also, on his elbow, he is bleeding a bit.

36 He had been sitting in just his [light] shirt jacket.

37 That's it, that pilot was [only] bleeding in two places.

38 Then those people, one man and a woman, his wife, in fact, nothing happens to them, "We are not hurt at all," they say.

39 The wing in the water happens to be really crumpled.

40 Later then I saw how the float looked when it was dragged from the water.

41 The one float is completely crushed.

42 Half of that plane's other float is completely gone.

43 Its wing is almost not recognizable.

44 Indeed, the wing on one side [was] little, probably only a half [was] in one piece, then.

45 Life, then, was there deep in the water. [Those people's lives hung in the balance, deep under water.]

46 I really thought it was amazing.

47 Life is not destroyed and yet the plane was broken even though it's metal.

48 It was all broken up.

49 So it's just [when] that airplane was flown away, it doesn't look like it could be fixed.

50 They probably only took a little [of the plane] to where it was supposedly flown.

51 Flesh is fragile; bone is also fragile.

52 It wasn't flesh that was broken.

53 Neither was it bone that was broken.

54 Metal seems so strong, but it is metal that breaks instead.

55 That's what I saw.

56 I talked to him, I told this man, I entreated [?] him, (I am rather closely related to him, McKoop's his name).

57 His name must have been Douglas McKoop.

58 I don't know.

59 That guy called Moses McKoop has a son.

60 That woman named Ina McKoop has a son.

61 And she is the mother of the one that crashed.

62 So I talked to my [parallel] nephew a little bit, I'm related to him that way, to make him wonder [why] that his life was not broken, when that airplane he was in looked that way.

63 So that's what I talked to [entreated] him about.

64 That's all of it.

Returning to Labov's analysis of more elaborated English narratives, we find that they consistently display several features. Briefly, a fully formed narrative may show the following:

1. Abstract.
2. Orientation.
3. Complicating action.
4. Evaluation.
5. Result or resolution
6. Coda. (ibid: 363)

Many of these features are found in Swanson's story although not always in the same relative positions nor with the same prominence. The analysis below is guided by this organization, which seems to be quite appropriate for first-person narratives in Ojibwe; the organization of this text is different from that found in *aatisoohkaanan*, where Hymesian and Tedlockian analyses are more appropriate as they highlight the episodic nature of such discourse. Labov's analysis provides structure but also allows for the considerable variation found in first-person narratives where asides and tangential material abound. These same asides are exceedingly rare in the body of an *aatisoohkaan* and, if present, are highly marked to further bracket their intrusion. Below is a structural analysis of the text, using Labov's categories.

Structural Outline of 'The Plane Crash'
(First-person narrative)

	Sentence
0. Introduction	(1–6)
Metanarrative frame	(1)
Introduction of audience	(2–3)
Introduction of text	(4)
Personal connection with the text	(5)
Orientation – location	(5–6)
1. Narrative Action	(6–32)
Plane comes in for landing	(6)
Rhetorical question setting up evaluation*	(7)
Evaluation – possible reason for accident*	(8)
Plane turns around	(9)
Evaluation of pilot*	(11–13)
Plane tries to take off	(14–21)

* Evaluation within the text.

Swanson began this narrative with a classic metanarrative frame (sentences 1 through 6), introducing his story about a plane crash in Lynx Lake. In this initial section, he described the circumstances and outcome of the crash which occurred directly across the shore from his home.

1 *Ninka-tipaacim eh-antawentaakosiyaan ci-tipaacimoyaan e-wii-kihkentank wahawe nimpi-kiwitamik ohomaa niwaahkaahikanink.*
Because I have been requested to tell a story by the one visiting me here in my house who wants to learn, I will tell a story.
2 *Peshik ohomaa wemihtikooshi e-wiiciiwaamaayaank Naanti Paanantahiin e-ishinihkaasoc.*
This one Whiteman that we are living with is called Randy Valentine.
3 *Aasha niisho-pipoon niwiiciitaamaanaan.*
We have been living with him now for two years [winters].
4 *Pimihsewin kaa-wii-kihkentank kaa-kii-pankihsink niishiwii-ahki niisho-pipoon otaanaank.*
He wants to know about an airplane that crashed two years, two winters ago.

5 *Mayaam ninkii-waapantaan eh-pankihsink ohomaa piko kaa-ishitaayaan akaamink.*
I saw it extactly when it fell here, right across the lake from where I live.
6 *Ketahtawiin eh-poonic naawic ohomaa kaa-ishitaayaan.*
[It was] all of a sudden, that it landed way out in the lake here where I live.

Ojibwe narratives of all kinds are characteristically preceded by a frame which places them within their given social, temporal, and geographical matrix, usually within the first few sentences. Many features of this story's frame are similar to those introducing legend-myths; this frame provides an introduction of the genre and, typical of most of Swanson's introductions to his narratives, a synopsis of his own connection with the story being told. In most legend-myths collected from Swanson, he informs his audience how he learned these stories growing up; how he learned them by listening to repeated tellings. In this story, Swanson makes a point of connecting himself both to his audience – *wahawe nimpi-kiwitamik ohomaa niwaahkaahikanink* ('the one visiting me here in my home' – sentence 1); *Aasha niishio-pipoon niwiiciitaamaanaan* ('We have been living with him now for two years' – sentence 3); – and to the action of his story – *Mayaam ninkii-waapantaan eh-pankihsink ohomaa piko kaa-ishitaayaan akaamink* ('I saw it … right across the lake from where I live'— sentence 5); *ohomaa kaa-ishitaayaan* ('here where I live' – sentence 6).

After introducing, in his intial sentence, the genre of story he is about to tell, Swanson introduces his audience and his relationship to that audience in sentences 2 and 3. In sentences 4 and 5, Swanson introduces the particular story. This type of three-part narrative frame in the introduction is quite standard for Swanson.

In sentence 4 of the introduction to this narrative we find an abstract, a summary of action of the type outlined in Labov (ibid: 363), but in this case the abstract is embedded in the orientation to the broader narrative context: *Pimihsewin kaa-wii-kihkentank kaa-kii-pankihsink niishiwiiahki niisho-pipoon otaanaank* ('He wants to know about an airplane that crashed two years, two winters ago'). This form of abstract is not found in introductions to legend-myths. In its place would be an introduction to a story cycle, with perhaps the main character's major personality quirk highlighted.

The introduction to the storytelling session also introduces the relationship between the participants. Swanson's overt statement that he is telling the story 'because I have been requested to tell one,' to help this 'Whiteman that we are living with' to learn, attests to Swanson and Rand's long-standing relationship of teacher and student of Ojibwe language and culture. A degree of intimacy between the two is attested to by the use of the vérb *e-wiiciiwaamaayaank* ('that we are living with him'). The root is the same as in 'marry,' indicating that the interaction is inclusive and not merely a matter of co-presence in the same village.

While Swanson was requested to take on the storyteller role, he quickly accepted responsibility for his narrative as he frames the story in terms of his connection with the action of the narrative. (Sentences 5 and 6: 'I saw it exactly when it fell here, right across the lake from where I live … it landed way out in the lake here where I live.') He was considered a good storyteller within the village and was very comfortable in that role.[4] Here Swanson made it quite evident that the story is from his own personal experience which functions to invest him with the authority to tell this story and his legitimacy as a storyteller.

The last two sentences of this introduction provide the barest orientation to the narrative action; here Swanson provided the location of the events to follow ('here, right across the lake from where I live' in sentence 5, and repeated in sentence 6).

The narrative action is found in sentences 6 through 31, with sections of evaluation interspersed. The backbone of the action is found in sentences 6 (the plane comes in for a landing), 9 (the plane turns around), 14–20 (the plane tries to take off), 22–5 (Swanson gets into the action), 25 (the plane comes up out of the water), 27–31 (the people come up out of the water one by one), and 32 (the passengers sit on top of the plane). Further action occurs in sentences 34 (Swanson arrives to see the state of the pilot), 38 (the other passengers give a report of their well-being), 40 (Swanson looks at the float, out of sequential order), and 62 (Swanson talks to the pilot about the accident).

According to Labov's definition of narrative as "temporally ordered clauses" (ibid: 371), only the independent clauses of these particular sentences would fit into the category of narrative. In Ojibwe, there are three verb orders, independent, conjunct, and imperative, which have entirely different morphology. Independent and imperative verbs often stand alone as complete sentences, but generally, conjunct verbs are found in dependent structures. However, conjunct verbs are also often found in isolation or in a string within a sentence. The use of the particle *mii*, extremely important in the marking of the beginning of new sections in narrative, and other discourse particles cause a sentence to be realized in the conjunct. Thus, the use of independent clauses as the marker for narrative clauses as outlined by Labov is largely counterproductive in Ojibwe.

Throughout this section of narrative action Swanson provides several evaluations of different types. The first example is structurally interesting as he presents the gravity of the situation in the form of a rhetorical question: *Kaawin okashkihtoohsiin ci-kii-pi-naatakaamehs kaa-ishinaakosi, aanti maa eshi-maashiskwen ihiwe pimihsewin?* ('He looks like he isn't able to make it to shore, "Where did that plane go wrong?" – sentence 7). This question sets up his analysis of one possible reason for the plane crash which he gives in the following sentence: *Kayemaa piihshaakanaap ahkwahikan shahsha-akootaahsin ishinaakwan aana-wii-pi-kakwe-naatakaamehoc* ('It looked like maybe the rudder rope couldn't handle the wind although he wanted to come to shore' – sentence 8).

Swanson continues to give reasons for the accident, but in these later statements he embeds the evaluations further by attributing them to the pilot, in sentence 11; then attributing the pilot's thoughts to one of the passengers in sentence 12; and finally, Swanson 'quoting' the pilot's own evaluation through the 'quoted' words of the passenger, in sentence 13: *Maaskooc kaye kaawin mayaam okihkentaan kekonen kaa-isihsek* ('Maybe he doesn't know [either] what exactly it is that happened' – sentence 11); *Mii tahsh enaacimoc ihimaa anihshinini kaa-kii-poosic ahawe kaa-kii-pankihshink* ('So that's what the one who crashed was telling a person there who was taking off [with him]' – sentence 12); and *Peshik ninkiih-inaacimohtaak maahti ntawaac weti naatakaam tapinaawaank ninka-onci-pakiciimin ihkito, otinaan* ('One [of them] "He told me, 'We might as well land [take off?] there towards the shore where there is no wind,'" he says, he said of him [he reported him saying]' – sentence 13). In each of these cases, Swanson becomes more and more specific about what was going on, but also in each, the evaluation becomes more and more deeply embedded within the discourse.

The summary statement in sentence 33, 'That is what I saw' (lit. 'it is that that I saw'), concludes this section of narrative action and leads into the purely evaluative section of sentences 33–54. In this section Swanson's narrative is its most artistic, where he manipulated linguistic forms in the most highly structured ways. Swanson began in sentences 34–8 by giving an account of the minimal injuries suffered by the people in the airplane. He concluded this section with the quote by the passengers, 'We are not hurt at all.' He followed this with an account of the damage suffered by the plane in sentences 39–44.

Sentence 45, *Pimaatisiwin tahsh e-kiih-takakwak ihimaa anaamiintam* ('Life, then, was there deep in the water') is highly marked in structure. The unmarked word order in Severn Ojibwe is VSX (verb, subject, and everything else, where normally just one noun phrase is actualized). Here the sentence begins with the subject in initial position. Any noun in this position would be focused, but this noun is also unique in that it is derived from a verb, *pimaatisi* ('he lives'). Such nominalizations are rare in discourse[5] which marks this word and the sentence even further. In this sentence, Swanson gets to the essential drama of the narrative: life itself was hanging in the balance.

The parallels between the passengers' condition and that of the plane, which were explored in sentences 34–44 are drawn together and even redrawn in sentences 45–54, using variations of a comparative structure. Labov discusses the 'not X, but Y' format as a means of comparing potentialities. This structure is evident throughout this section of evaluation, beginning with the parallels just mentioned. The comparison which Swanson continued is brought together in sentences 46 and 47: *Mitoni maamahkaac, ninkii-inentaan* ('I really thought it was amazing' – sentence 46) and *Pimaatisiwin ekaa e-piikoshkaak ekwa pimihsewin eh-aana-piiwaapihkowank e-kiih-piikoshkaak* ('Life is not destroyed and yet the plane was broken even though it's metal' – sentence 47).

Swanson continued weaving this thread in even more artistic designs in sentences 51–4:

51 *Wiiyaahs noohkan; ohkan kaye noohkan.*
'Flesh is fragile; bone is also fragile.'
52 *Kaawin piikoshkaahsinoon wiiyaahs.*
'It wasn't flesh that was broken.'
53 *Kaawin kaye piikoshkaahsinoon ohkan.*
'Neither was it bone that was broken.'
54 *Piiwaapihk mashkwawaa inentakwan, piiwaapihk tahsh takwac piikoshkaa.*
'Metal seems so strong, but it is metal that breaks instead.'

In sentence 51, the two clauses are parallel in structure and meaning. This repetition is especially gratifying in the Ojibwe because of the unusual brevity and alliteration of the clauses. Again, the sentence is marked syntactically by fronted noun phrases and by the full repetition of the verb *noohkan* (is soft/fragile).

Sentences 52 and 53 parallel each other in precisely the same way as do the two clauses of sentence 51. In this case, Swanson alluded to the earlier report on the passengers' physical condition by a negative statement: 'It wasn't flesh that was broken. Neither was it bone that was broken,' the 'not

X' of the comparison. Sentence 52 presents the second half of the comparison, but in providing the 'but Y,' Swanson creates yet another unrealized probability. The metal seems strong in comparison with fragile flesh and bone, but the flesh and bone did not break; the metal airplane broke. The structure of this single sentence is 'Y is expected, but X,' giving yet another variation of the comparison. The formula

bone/flesh : metal
soft/fragile : strong
broken : whole

which Swanson so carefully crafted is violated by the actual crash, providing the paradox that is the essence of this narrative. As this evaluative section began, so it ends with 'That is what I saw' (sentences 33 and 55). The Ojibwe verb stems are semantically, not morphologically, related: *Mii hiwe kaah-inaapihshinaan* (sentence 33) and *Kaa-ishi-waapantamaan* (sentence 55).

Sentences 56–63 match Labov's 'result/resolution' category (ibid: 363) quite well. In this section, Swanson re-established his position within the narrative by recounting the gist of a conversation with the pilot (sentences 56, 62, and 63). He also made a point of establishing his kinship ties with the pilot involved in the accident (sentences 56–60), making his position even stronger within the narrative. The orientational material, defining the relationship of the narrator to the pilot, is left to the very end of the narrative. Intuitively, this seems quite different from the expected position for orientation in a first-person narrative in English. Finally, in sentence 62, Swanson repeated the paradox of the broken plane and untouched people.

The last sentence of this narrative is the coda, the formulaic *M-osha hi* ('That's all of it'). This closing is used with legend-myths, and in fact, with almost any closure of talk above the level of the conversational turn. Most sections of talk which are not purely conversational will be framed in some way. When reading a notice on the radio, Swanson will often begin with 'I am going to read what is written' and end with a parallel, 'That is what is written' followed by *M-ohsha hi*. Even a phone message delivered on the air at the radio station will often end with *M-ohsha hi*. This is a standard usage in the community, heard in all situations where talk is involved.

Artistic and Performance Features

Along with the use of parallel syntactic and semantic structures, as outlined in the formula (flesh/bone : metal, etc.) above, other kinds of parallelism are found in this text. In sentences 26 through 31, Swanson built up tension by individually numbering the people who appeared from under the water. First, there were no people; then, there was one person; then, two; and finally, all three appeared. By having the passengers appear in parallel fashion, one at a time, Swanson pulled the audience into participation in the tension and excitement he felt as he watched the event unfold.

The phonetic parallelism of sentence 51 was mentioned earlier. This is repeated in the parallel sentences 52 and, 53, with the words *wiiyaahs* and *ohkan* playing off each other both syntactically and phonetically (sentences 51, 52 and 53): *Wiiyaahs noohkan; ohkan kaye noohkan* ('Flesh is fragile; bone is also fragile' – sentence 51); *Kaawin piikoshkaahsinoon wiiyaahs* ('It wasn't flesh that was broken' – sentence 52); and *Kaawin kaye piikoshkaahshinoon ohkan* ('Neither was it bone that was broken' – sentence 53).

Some other features which are particular to narrative performance found in this text are: the metanarrative frame (sentences 1 through 4), the rhetorical question (sentence 7), direct discourse (sentences 13 and 38), and the historical present (sentences 7, 11, 13, 18, 26, 27, 29, 31–2, 34–5, 37–9, 41–4, 47, 52, and 53).

DIFFERENCES FROM AND SIMILARITIES TO LEGEND-MYTH GENRE

Differences

The focus of this section is to explore the differences between two narrative genres which are considered to display different degrees of artistry. One feature found in first-person narratives is the use of the first-person pronoun throughout the text. In legend-myths (*aatisoohkaanan*), the first-person pronoun referring to the storyteller is found in the metanarrative frame only in the introduction and in the coda. All other tokens of the first person in *aatisoohkaanan* are found within passages of direct discourse. Thus, use of the first person throughout the text is a distinctive of first-person narratives.

A second difference is in the time frame, which is spelled out within the introduction of these narratives. *Aatisoohkaanan* are introduced with a 'non-historic' time frame. In first-person narratives, the time frame stated in the introduction is well within the storyteller's memory, whereas in *aatisoohkaanan* the action occurs in another epoch, one prior to the time of the present world. Temporal orientation of a text seems to be quite significant to Swanson, as is seen in sentences 3 and 4, where he sets the time frame for his relationship both to his audience and to the events which occur within the story.

A third difference between the genres is the presence of overt evaluation throughout the first-person narrative. Evaluation in legend-myths is signalled more often through speaker laughter and non-verbal interjections, which often take the form of a brief exclamation. A final etiological section in many of the legend-myths is a type of evaluation, but most evaluation in those stories occurs after the coda. As seen above, it is within the sections of evaluation that the most verbal artistry is displayed in the first-person narrative. In *aatisoohkaanan*, verbal artistry, especially in terms of parallelism, is found in the overall structuring as well as in more localized sections of episodic set-ups.

Certain grammatical features also differ between the genres. In *aatisoohkaanan*, the dubitative is found in many verbs within the initial introduction sections, and to a lesser degree throughout the text. In this first-person narrative, all examples of dubitative found scattered in the body of the text refer to some specific fact in question. This can be illustrated by sentences 57 and 58: *Taklahs Mahkop maawin ishinihkaasotok. Nahke piko* ('His name must have been Douglas McKoop. I don't know'). In *aatisoohkaanan* the dubitative (usually associated with the preterite in these discourses) is global (cf. Valentine and Spielmann 1982), providing a key or frame for the text to follow. The scope of the modality in first-person narratives is clausal whereas in *aatisoohkaanan* it is on the discourse level.

The first-person narrative also shows a marked increase in the number of intensifiers used throughout. Swanson's use of such words as *mayaam* ('exactly'), *ketahtawiin* ('suddenly'), *kekaat* ('almost'), *mitoni* ('really'), and *misiwe* ('all over') create an overall intensity. These intensifiers are relatively rare in Severn conversation and also in legend-myths.

A final difference between legend-myths and first-person narrative outlined here is that of overall structuring. Legend-myths demonstrate a marked form–content parallelism (cf. Hymes 1981 and Woodbury 1987) based on numerical structuring not evident within this text. Parallelisms within this genre tend to be decidedly more local than those found in *aatisoohkaanan*, which encompass the entire story.

Similarities

As we have seen above, this first-person narrative exhibits many artistic and performance features, many of which are also found in legend-myths. Both begin with metanarrative frames and end with codas, typically the brief statement *amo-hsha hi.* Both genres freely use direct discourse, the historical present, and both syntactic and semantic parallelism. Evaluation is found in both types of narratives, but to different degrees and in different structural positions. Both genres also demonstrate similar usage of discourse particles such as *mii, tahsh,* and *ahpin.*

CONCLUSIONS

A storyteller begins with certain linguistic devices which may be manipulated within the narration. These devices do not necessarily differ in kind between one genre and another, but certain devices are highlighted within a given genre. This is what we find with Swanson's storytelling. Except for the difference in the overall structuring principles and the stated time frames of the narratives of *aatisoohkaanan* and first-person narrative genres, the differences between these genres appear to be a matter of degree. Legend-myths use somewhat more elaborate syntactic and semantic parallelism, but obviously such parallelism is also very important in the first-person narrative. The use of overt evaluation throughout a first-person narrative has its more subtle counterpart in the narrator's interjections and laughter in legend-myths. Comparators and intensifiers are also widely displayed in first-person narrative, but are not exclusive to that genre, as they are occasionally found in legend-myths as well. Clearly there can be art in any form of talk.

This study of the formal features of a first-person narrative was undertaken to discover the structure of these narratives, to demonstrate differences between narrative genres, and to established a ground against which the artistry of legend-myths can be made more evident. In the next chapter we look closely at form content parallelism in an *aatisoohkaan.*

Chapter Nine

When Humans Could Talk with Animals: Legend-Myth in Lynx Lake

Ojibwe legends have been the focus of interest since Schoolcraft first published a collection of Ojibwe stories in the 1800s. In the early 1900s, William Jones collected an excellent corpus of Ojibwe texts (1917), many dictated line by line by the storyteller, Pinesi, on the north shore of Lake Superior (in the Central Ojibwe dialect). These texts were transcribed in Jones's phonetic Ojibwe script, with a relatively literal English translation on the facing page. The best of the succeeding publications have used a similar format to Jones's, with the Ojibwe and English both represented (Bloomfield 1958; Quill 1965; Kaye, Piggott, and Tokaichi 1971; Kaye and Piggott 1973; Jones 1976; Kegg 1976, 1978, and 1983; and Nichols 1988). These collections of stories come from many of the Ojibwe dialects: Bloomfield's texts came from the Odawa dialect (Rhodes 1976); the stories told by Norman Quill (1965) are in the Berens River dialect; the stories edited by Kaye, Piggott, and Tokaichi are Odawa; the texts edited by Jones (1976) are from the Eastern Ojibwe dialect; and the stories told by Kegg (1976, 1978, 1983) are in the Minnesota Chippewa dialect.

With the exception of the texts edited by Jones (1976) and some texts in Nichols (1988), the more recent stories were collected in more or less 'natural' storytelling sessions, with the resultant Ojibwe transcripts based on tape-recorded sessions with Native storytellers. These texts came from live performances before an audience which minimally consisted of the collector or researcher with whom the storyteller interacted. The English translations, often quite literal, follow from the Ojibwe transcription.

The exceptional but increasingly popular method used in the volume edited by Jones (1976) was to use texts written in the Native language by storytellers. Written narratives differ, in some cases profoundly, from oral presentations traditional for Ojibwe stories. In writing what is normally spoken, the performance and the story are separated, leaving only the text. The limitations of writing and writing systems greatly restrict the use of extragrammatical information, including pauses, stress, changes in pitch or intonation, whispering, chanting, singing, laughing, and even acting-out of the storyline. In a performance the storyteller chooses from these and other devices to interact with a specific audience, in a specific time and place. Relating a story without the benefit of these extragrammatical options will change its tenor, as the writer will either minimize or ignore audience involvement or, at best, add grammatical cues in an attempt to include that information which would otherwise be lost. Both options will result in a text different from one that has been given orally. The written word allows for editing prior to presentation, whereas the performer edits on the spot. False starts, asides, errors in grammar (as perceived by the teller), and audience feedback are all part of an oral narration. While these 'lapses' are often edited out when a taped performances is transcribed, the editing tends to be as minimal as possible. In their preface to the Odawa texts told by Sam Osawamik, editors Kaye and Piggott express the prevailing attitude about the editing of oral texts: "We have avoided excessive editing for fear that we detract from the authenticity of the actual text" (1973: 111). This stands in direct opposition to written versions where editing is a major part of story production.

Most scholars who have published Ojibwe texts in the Native language have been linguists as opposed to anthropologists. The main exceptions to this rule have been anthropologists concerned with the music of the Ojibwe (Densmore 1910 and 1913; Josselin de Jong 1912). More recent texts collected by anthropologists interested in Ojibwe narratives have been published exclusively in English. However, these publications often lack information as basic as a notation of the source of the story, whether a story was translated from the Ojibwe or presented initially in English, or whether the story was presented orally or written, in either Ojibwe or English. Unpublished Native language text collections are known to exist, but are not currently available to the public (M. Black-Rogers, personal communication). There have been few references to the traditional occasions of the telling stories among the Ojibwe. No ethnographic study of Ojibwe storytelling has been attempted to date.

In this chapter, one episode of the Severn trickster series will be explored within the context of its performance. The text will be examined to reveal internal evidence of the storytellers' interaction with the story and his audience. The transcription of the oral text as well as the form of the English translation, utilize methods proposed by Tedlock (1977) and informed by work by Hymes (1985), which include the written presentation of some non-grammatical performance features.

GENRE

The question of genre among the Northern Ojibwe is crucial for this discussion, as the division between myth and non-myth has no discrete boundary. In this initial frame, a good storyteller will often discuss the 'story' to be told. As noted in the previous chapter, Ojibwe stories fall into two basic categories: *tipaacimowinan*, historical stories, and *aatisoohkaanan*, myths or legends. While certain series of stories are consistently placed into one or the other category (e.g., stories of the fur trade are always *tipaacimowinan*, and stories of *Wiihsahkecaahk*, the trickster, are always *aatisoohkaanan*), some stories defy categorization. In one story collected from an excellent storyteller with a good repertoire, the narrator explicitly states that he does not know whether it is a 'story' or a 'legend-myth.' The main character in this story was a trickster figure with magical powers similar to those of the prototypical trickster, *Wiihsahkecaahk*. Stories of the *Wiintikoo*, well documented by anthropologists in both Ojibwe and Cree traditions, are definitely in the category of contemporary history. This non-discrete categorization of myth and story forces a connection of the world of myth to the here and now. By naming the genre, the narrative is provided with an immediate dialogic relationship between the legend-myth and the present.

Assuming a non-ambiguous case in which a narrator is dealing with an *aatisoohkaan* (legend-myth), a narrative device of stepping out of the present time, through the recent past, to the time of myth is used to make the transition into the story. The intermediate step, to the recent past, comes in the form of attributing the story to some earlier storyteller. This may be done by naming the storyteller (normally a parent or grandparent) or by relating how the narrator heard and learned the story ('I heard this story many times as a child'). Thus, the legend-myth is not merely related to the here and now, but also to another generation of the here and now. Such references provide a degree of validity to both the storyteller and the story, interactively.

To this point, I have been using the rather awkward term 'legend-myth' to refer to *aatisoohkaanan* because, based on traditional folkloric definition, the *aatisoohkaanan* have elements of both myths and legends (Brunvand 1968: 79–99). They are like myths in that they are narratives "set in the remote past in the otherworld or an earlier world" (p. 79), having "as their principle characters ... animals" (ibid), and are generally etiological in nature. However, the *aatisoohkaanan* are more legend-like in that they are not considered sacred as such and do not function to explain rituals, religious or otherwise.

The *aatisoohkaan* appears to be equivalent to the *atayohkewin* reported by Darnell (1974) for the Plains Cree of Alberta. Darnell analyses these stories as originally religious but later secularized. She cites two Cree Natives, however, who both deny any religious content in these stories. Of the second she writes: "He believed it was important to transmit these stories to the younger generation, but they had become completely secular for him. The attitude is commonly expressed in this area that 'we didn't have any religion before the white man came'" (p. 319).

In contrast to Darnell's position, I believe that these stories have not had religious connotations for a very long time, if, indeed, they ever have had (an opinion shared by Vecsey [1983]), primarily because reports from Amerindian people that these stories are secular are found among the Ojibwe and the Cree peoples all the way from Quebec to Alberta – even in those areas where Native rituals are still practiced, such as in southwestern Ontario. However, the legends are, and traditionally were, shared at specific times and places, primarily in the winter in the evenings; a request for a story out of season evokes a recitation of consequences for such impropriety, but, despite their own warnings, most storytellers immediately and animatedly launch into narration.

In the storytelling tradition of the Northern Ojibwe, an *aatisoohkaan* is normally located both in time and in space. The location in myth time may be accomplished by the phrase 'when humans could understand the animals.' Interestingly enough, the communication between man and animals continues to this day, but it tends to be limited to the spiritual realm or dream world. Traditionally, people with power often had a particular spirit helper, normally an animal, with whom they communed (Hallowell 1971). While such spirit helpers appear to be rare today, premonitory dreams of animals offering themselves to a hunter may be a vestige of human–animal communication. Another type of spirit–animal communication still in evidence is that of the Thunder Birds, whose voices are heard as thunder. Incidentally, the Thunder Birds are located near Thunder Bay, Ontario, consistent with weather conditions in Lynx Lake – most thunder was heard only in the distant south. In Lynx Lake, I was often asked if I could make out what the thunder(birds) were saying, and what the message meant. I did not know, but neither did anyone else I asked. Thus, thunder was considered to be an animal language which, at least theoretically, could be understood.

The location of an *aatisoohkaan* in *contemporary* space is an important aspect of the narration. This connection of the *aatisoohkaan* to a known landmark is no mere setting of the stage; it is the land that validates the legend-myth. When asked whether a particular story about *Wiihsahkecaahk* and *Awanihshensh* (the Little Beaver) were true, an admittedly naïve and inappropriate question, a young friend responded that he had seen the red rocks where *Awanihshensh* had died, and so it *had* to be true. However, this validation goes both ways. The presence in the here and now of such landmarks proves that the *aatisoohkaanan* are true, which in turn legitimizes the message of the legend-myth for use in the present.

Among the Severn people, where until very recently settlements were transitory at best, where resources mitigated against aggregation, and where population density was somewhere around seven people per one hundred square miles, an intimate knowledge of a large area of land was crucial. The use of myths as mnemonic devices for mapping the land is unquestionable. When provided with a map of Ontario, a group of older men in the Severn area immediately began referring to stories which correlated with geographical locations, often several hundred miles away from the community. Many locations are known only by reference to such legend-myths, such as Thunder Bay, which is not only the home of the Thunder Birds, but 'as I have heard,' a Lynx Lake elder said with a sly grin, 'where *Wiihsahkecaahk* is sleeping.'

Another aspect of verbal art which connects the world of myth to the present is the judicious choice of which narrative to relate. A telling example of this emerged in the first *aatisoohkaan* collected in Lynx Lake by Rand Valentine, analysed in this chapter. The legend-myth narrated was a tale of the trickster *Wiihsahkecaahk*, who comes upon a nest of baby partridges. While this is an etiological story (on one level it explains why the partridge is brown), the intrinsic moral of this story was that the baby partridges erred by talking to a stranger and answering his questions. The potential connection of the moral of the myth to the situation of the here and now, where a White semi-stranger was asking a Native person to tell stories, is suspiciously appropriate.[1] Basso (1983) clearly demonstrates that Western Apache narratives are used to connect current situations with well-defined moral statements, without recourse to overt statements. Here we may be observing a playful variation on the same theme. Among those well versed in these narratives (most members of the Severn Ojibwe community), a metaphor is created between the world of myth and the current situation, with a moral force that can be understood fully *only* by those so versed in the old stories and familiar with the landscape.

The trickster legend series of the Ojibwe involve a central character who was the product of the union between a *manitoo* (spirit) and a woman. This character often takes on the characteristics of an animal, but, unlike most Amerindian tricksters, usually maintains the form of a (hu)man. The name of this character differs in each of the Ojibwe dialects. The more southern dialects use some variation of *Nanabushu* (Jones's [1917] rendition), but in the northernmost Ojibwe dialect, among the Severn Ojibwe people, he is called *Wiihsahkecaahk*.

As noted earlier, legends were traditionally told at specific times and places, primarily on winter evenings. These prohibitions against telling such stories in the summertime provide yet another connection between the world of myths to the present. A common statement is that if one tells or hears such myths in the summer, snakes and frogs will 'come and sleep with you' (*kika-wiihpemik*). This is, apparently, not considered an idle threat, despite the fact that many people, after making the statement will immediately begin telling a story. In this case, Swanson made no mention of such consequences, even though it was still daytime when this tale was told.

NARRATOR

The narrator, Swanson Turtle, introduced in the previous chapter, was a respected elder in Lynx Lake. In his youth, Swanson had travelled around Northern Ontario as far north as Hudson Bay, and worked for three months during the Second World War in a mine in the community of Pickle Crow, over one hundred miles south of Lynx Lake. During the time he worked in the mine, he picked up some English lexical items of which he was quite proud. His knowledge of English words is displayed on four occasions in this narrative.

As with the telling of the first-person narrative in the previous chapter, Swanson's audience for this narrative was initially limited to Rand Valentine, a daily visitor to his home from the fall of 1981 to the time of this telling, in the winter of 1982. Rand had gone to Swanson in order to learn and practise speaking Ojibwe and had established himself as being interested in the old stories, having heard them from several people in the community; at this point, he had demonstrated enough facility in Severn Ojibwe to be a proper audience for a performance of narratives, as seen in the previous chapter. This story was told during the same storytelling session as the first-person narrative about the plane crash. About halfway through this story, the narrator's wife entered the house, so that during the last half of the story the audience was both Native and non-Native. However, there is no evidence of a change in style or focus with her entry, and in fact there was no acknowledgement of her entry until after the story.

Evidence of a dynamic interaction between the narrator and his audience is seen throughout this text. As mentioned, Swanson and Rand had a mutual student/teacher relationship, often sharing information about their respective languages and cultures; these discussions were held primarily in Ojibwe. The important features of the relationship between the narrator and the audience pertinent to this text are:

1. The narrator was responding to a request to tell some stories. As stated in the introduction to the first-person narrative in the previous chapter, Swanson is responding to a 'Whiteman's' request for a story to be told. However distancing this may sound to the uninitiated, it is mitigated by Swanson's honouring Rand by naming the relationship of this Whiteman to the community as that of 'one who has lived with us for two years,' using the term *niwiiciihtaamaanaan*, which typically indicates a familial relationship.
2. The narrator wanted his audience to know of his travel outside the Lynx Lake area. This is seen in the statement about the location of the action of the legend, 'at Fort Severn River,' a Cree community located at the mouth of a river emptying into Hudson Bay.
3. The narrator related to his audience as a native English speaker functional in Ojibwe. His desire was to aid his audience in understanding the story as it was being told. On four different occasions, the narrator gives an aside in English. Because his facility in English was minimal, these explanations contain only an isolated word in English, usually embedded in an Ojibwe clause. In no case was the English word or phrase a substitution for the Ojibwe.
4. The narration is seen as entertainment by both the narrator and his audience. The subject of each of the stories told during the recording session was the choice of the narrator. The laughter through the final section of this particular legend is evidence that the narrator was emotionally involved with this text (finding it humorous) and that he expected a similar reaction from his audience.

The norms observed through this single storytelling session can be compared only to norms observed in other interactive sessions. New material of any kind, i.e., a story about an event which the audience has not previously heard, is given in a form very similar to the narrative, that is, as a monologue. However, with new material, listeners will punctuate the teller's story with exclamations such as *Mii na hi?* (lit. 'Is that all?'), *Ami icika hi* ('Is that right?'), *Kooshta!* (an exclamation of surprise), *Tepwe?* ('Really?'), or the colloquial *Kihci-akwenaak!* ('You're lying!' or 'No way!'). These back-channel cues give the go-ahead for the speaker to continue on with the story. Such a response might be expected from someone who has never heard these stories before, but, with legends, this is usually not the case. These stories are well known by the Native audience present during more typical storytelling sessions.

Aatisoohkaanan are told in Lynx Lake exclusively by men. This situation is in stark contrast to that described by Rogers in Weagamow, of which he wrote, "Grandmothers often play the leading role in storytelling" (1962: B39). In fact, the only woman reported to tell such stories had come from that community. However, in several cases that I observed, the wives of the storytellers acted as 'guardians of the tales' in that they provided pithy, one-word cues to episodes to their storytelling husbands if they felt the story was not progressing properly.

Promptings aside, legends tended to be surprisingly monovocal (as opposed to monologic). In a later episode, Swanson interrupted his own performance to ask Rand what the English word was for a certain term. This was pursued for about a full minute, with much give and take during that time. Such clarificational interactions between storytellers and younger members of the audience are not uncommon. Direct interaction, then, between the storyteller and his audience, seems to be accepted although not a requisite part of the storytelling session. When Swanson's wife entered the room, he did not stop his story, nor did she interrupt the telling, which might have been expected had she walked in during a casual conversation. Very shortly after finishing this legend, Swanson and his wife held a brief conversation, after which she immediately left.

This story was told by a specific person, at a specific time, in a specific place, to a specific audience. Hence, it is reasonable to find material within the text which is particular to that single telling. This text is not the generic 'Why the Partridge is Brown;'[2] rather, this is one version tailored to the given audience. Indeed, I would venture that a 'generic version' would only be found in written form as abstracted by someone outside the culture. However, the structuring and content are consistent with *aatisoohkaanan* collected at different times from other storytellers, indicating that this is a representative token of the genre.

STRUCTURE OF AN *Aatisoohkaan*

While some aspects of this telling are audience specific (e.g., the English lexical insertions), many of the features found in this legend-myth are standard for the genre. *Aatisoohkaanan* (and many *tipaacimowinan* as well) often begin with a general introduction to the story (and or genre) and to the qualifications of the one relating the story as a storyteller. In this initial metanarrative frame, the storyteller establishes: (1) the genre of the narrative, (2) a brief history of the narrative's transmission through earlier tellings, (3) location of the story in time, and (4) the location of the story in space.

In this narration, Swanson began by explaining that there are many *Wiihsahkecaahk* stories from which to choose, setting the stage for the presentation of a story from the trickster series. Swanson then presented his personal qualifications to tell a story from the series as 'one who had heard numerous accounts of *Wiihsahkecaahk* as a child.' In the appositive following this second mention of *Wiihsahkecaahk*, a verb with a dubitative ending (*ekii-ishinihkaasokwen* translated as 'someone supposedly called by that name') is found. Dubitative verbs (marked by *-kwen* in the conjunct and *-tok* in the independent), common in legends, carry the story into the realm of hearsay, liberating the story from contemporary life. The narrator using this form makes no statement about the absolute truth value of that story; he is free to report what he has heard without being held to its veracity.

After this initial stage setting for the telling of a legend comes the introduction to the time and location of the particular episode. The time is 'before man was here on the earth,' the time when animals could speak. Swanson located the action at a spot in Northern Ontario. This may be the traditional location of the story, or it could be an immediate variation inserted by the narrator. However, many of the communities in Northern Ontario have archaic names associated with legends that explain how the area got its unique features. The lakes both east and west of Lynx Lake were the sites of a battle between *Wiihsahkecaahk* and *Mihshamihk* (the Big Beaver). The lake to the west is called *Mihshamihkowiihsh* (Big Beaver Lodge) and the name of the community to the east is called 'Red Rocks,' red because of the blood of *Awanihshensh* (the Little Beaver) of the same legend. The reference to Fort Severn River is consistent with the tradition of locating legends in the physical sphere of the contemporary Ojibwe.

Next comes the body of the story. In most *Wiihsahkecaahk* stories dealing with animals, the main character plays a trick on some animal, gaining him an immediate victory. However, these tricks normally backfire, and *Wiihsahkecaahk* is eventually paid back for his mischief. Thus, although episodes are complete stories in themselves, they are usually a part of a larger series in which revenge is obtained.[3] The themes in *Wiihsahkecaahk* tales are recycled throughout the series. Some of the major themes which can be found in this version of 'Why the Partridge Is Brown' are: the risk of talking to strangers, the error in giving out information to strangers (a step beyond the first theme), insulting a member of a family in order to insult the head of that family, and explanation of the appearance of the natural world.

After the interaction between the characters, the action of the story is a formulaic exposition of how the preceding action explains some physical feature of the contemporary world. In this episode, the colour of the partridge is explained. This is followed by a coda, the simple *Mii iwe*, or 'That's all.' This etiological closing is formulaic, and as such, a comment on the genre.

Mii Tahsh Wenci-oshaawisic Pahpashki
As told by Swanson Turtle, Lynx Lake, Ontario

Pause in seconds

1 *Tepinaahk iko kekoon* (0.5)
   mihshiinoyek inaacimikosi Wiihsahkecaahk. (2)
2 *Kaawiniin mayaam tahshiin kaye kahkina ninkihkentahsiin kaa-kii-ishi-*
   noontamaan (2)
   enaacimaakaniwic, (1)
   kahkina. (0.5)
3 *Mooshak ohsha wiin eh-pi-awaashihshiiwiyaan, ninkii-noontaan,*
   ninkii-noontaan (0.5)
   eh-aacimaakaniwic ahaawe Wiihsahkecaahk, awiiya e-kii-
   ishinihkaasokwen. (3.5)
4 <Cough> *Niin tahshwiin kaa-kii-ishi-noontawakwaa* (1)
   cipwaa anihshinaape ohomaa eyaac ahkiink (1.5)
   awiyaashiihshak iko kiih-ayaawak (1.5)
   ninkii-tahtipaacim. (0.5)
5 *Taapishkooc tahsh e-kiih-kanoonikoc inweniwa* (1)
   entaso-ohkaanehsinici awiyaashiihshak, (1)
   'aanimo.' (2)
6 *Kahkina okii-nihsitohtawaan ahaawe Wiihsahkecaahk.* (3)
7 *Ekwa tahsh eshi-noontamaan weti peshik e-waapantamaan* (2.5)
   'Poot Seben' kaa-ishinihkaatek Waashahoowisiipi, (5)
   <Cough> *okii-mihkawaan pahpashkiinhsan.* (2)
8 *Mii tahsh – okiih-kanoonaan.* (2)
9 *"Aanti kimaamaamiwaa," okiih-inaan* (2)

eshi-pimihshinowaac ikiweniwak pahpashkiinhsak. (2.5)
10 *"Weti ahpin maacaapan,"* tahsh – okiih-ikoon ini pahpashkiinhsan. (5)
11 *Ahpii tahsh waa-ani-maacaac.*
12 *Mii hi eh-kii-ishi-pimoweshkitic ihimaa kaa-ishi-ohkohshinici* (1)
   'sehfer' (0.5)
   kaa-ishinihkaahtek, (1)
   owasihsoniwaank ikiweniwak pahpashkiinhsak. (0.5)
13 *Mii hi kaa-ishi-opihpimoweskitic.* (4)
14 <Cough> *Mii tahsh ahpii kaa-ishi-maacaac ahpin.* (2)
15 *Amii tahsh* – okii-waapamikoon tahsh ahpin eni-ishi-aninaakosic. (1)
16 *Wiihkaa tahsh naake kiih-takohshin ikiweniwak* (2)
   omaamaamiwaan ikweniwak pahpashkiinhsak. (3.5)
17 *"Kekonen wenci-ishinaakosiyek?"* (0.5)
18 *Misiwe e-moowiwaac kaa-inikiniwaac* <Laughter> *ikweniwak*
   pahpashkiinhsak. <Laughter> (3)
19 *"Wiihsahkecaahk ninkii-miicinikonaan,"* ihkitowak. <Laughter> (2.5)
20 *Mii hi kaa-ishkwaa-nooskwaatahwaac ahaawe pahpashki.* (.5)
21 *Mii tahsh wenci-osaawisic pahpashki,* (1.5)
   'paartric' *kaa-ishinihkaanaac wemihtikoosh.* (1)
22 *Mii hi kaa-onci-osaawisic.* (1.5)
23 *Moowini owenini kaa-kii-iniskaakowaac.* <Laughter> (4)
24 *Mii iwe.* (0.5)

'Why the Partridge Is Brown'

1 There are all kinds
   of stories one could tell about Wiihsahkecaahk.
2 I don't really know [how to tell] all the ones that I've heard,
   the ones that were told,
   all of them.
3 When I was a child, I often heard it, I heard it,
   when a story was told about Wiihsahkecaahk, as this person was supposedly named.
4 <Cough> Indeed, I heard them [say],
   that before man was here on the earth
   there were only animals,
   that's what I'm going to talk about.
5 Then it was like they talked to him
   every kind of animal,
   'animal.'

6 This Wiihsahkecaahk understood every one of them.

7 Anyway, so I heard it there [at that place] I once saw,
    it's called 'Fort Severn,' Fort Severn River,
    <Cough> that he found the little partridges.

8 So then – he spoke to them.

9 "Where your mother?" he said to them,
    to those little partridges that were lying down there.

10 "She went a long way away," – those little partridges said to him.

11 So then he got ready to leave.

12 That's when he defecated on them there where they were lying together,
    'together'
    it is called,
    those little partridges in their nest.

13 That's what he defecated beside.

14 <Cough> That's when he left from there.

15 So then – he was seen and then he [just] disappeared.

16 Some time later she arrived, their [mother]
    the mother of those little partridges.

17 "Why do you look like that?"

18 Those little partridges were totally covered with faeces. <Laughter>

19 "Wiihsahkecaahk defecated all over us," they say. <Laughter>

20 So then after this partridge licked them off.

21 So then that's why the partridge is brown
    it's called a 'partridge' in English.

22 So that's why it's brown.

23 Faeces made them look like that. <Laughter>

24 That's all.

TRANSCRIPTION CONVENTIONS

Some of the conventions used here for displaying the story were adapted from Tedlock (1977). The division of the text into lines is based on the oral delivery; where there is a pause in the exposition, it is shown in the text as a break between lines. The punctuation is standard, a period marks the end of a sentence, commas indicate doubled lexical items, explanatory clauses (on the order of an aside), or, along with quotation marks, set-off direct quotations. Commas do not indicate a pause. Parentheses surround parenthetical information; square brackets (used only in the English translation) indicate implied information. In this text em-dashes following a word represent a lengthening of the final phoneme. Angled brackets contain extragrammatical vocalizations within the text itself. The two types in this text are '<Cough>' and '<Laughter>'. The '<Laughter>' is a bit more complex as laughter often creates a filled pause in the storyline. The length of the laughter is marked similarly to pauses, that is, the time between words is marked, but '<Laughter>' is indicated to differentiate the filled pause from unfilled pauses. Aside from keying important thematic material, '<laughter>' helps maintain the 'tightness' of sections where there are few (long) pauses. As laughter is an important oral dynamic in the presentation of the story, it deserves representation in a text which illustrates its oral equivalent.

Another convention used in this presentation is the use of indentations, which, along with periods, delineate grammatical sentences. Hence, each new sentence begins at the left margin and subsequent lines which are part of that sentence are indented. An example of this is the fourth sentence of the text which is a single sentence comprised of four lines: *Niin tahshwiin kaa-kii-ishi-noontawakwaa / cipwaa anihshinaape ohomaa eyaac ahkiink / awiyaashiihshak iko kiih-ayaawak / ninkii-tahtipaacim*. In the single example in the text where one sentence immediately follows another with no pause between the two (sentences 11 and 12), no pause is marked:

Ahpii tahsh waa-ani-maacaac.
Mii hi eh-kii-ishi-pimoweshkitic ihimaa kaa-ishi-ohkohshininici   (1)
'sehfer'   (0.5)

In an attempt to minimize the leap from the Ojibwe text to the English text, the translation follows the Ojibwe text line by line, rather than paragraph by paragraph, as is standard in Algonquian text collections. The line was taken as the fundamental unit of this presentation, and to maintain this integrity in the English, the translation necessarily follows that structure. Because the structures of the two languages are so different, this results in a somewhat awkward English translation. However, this may help the reader in understanding some of the features unique to Ojibwe. This is, after all, an Ojibwe legend spoken in Ojibwe; it was not presented as an English piece of literature. Translating according to Ojibwe lines retains the flavour of the original.

RHETORICAL DEVICES

Swanson began his narrative with a general introduction (sentences 1 to 3) explaining how he came to know the story, an implicit statement of his legitimacy as a storyteller. Notice that this entire section is spoken in the first person.

1 *Tepinaahk iko kekoon mihshiinoyek inaacimikosi Wiihsahkecaahk.*	There are all kinds of stories one could tell about Wiihsahkecaahk.
2 *Kaawiniin maayam tahshiin kaye kahkina ninkihkentahsiin kaa-kii-ishi-noontamaan enaacimaakani-wic, kahkina.*	I don't really know [how to tell] all the ones that I've heard, the ones that were told, all of them
3 *Mooshak ohsha wiin eh-pi-awaashihshiiwiyaan, ninkii-noontaan, ninkii-noontaan eh-aacimaakaniwic ahaawe Wiihsahkecaahk, awiiya e-kii-ishinihkaasokwen.*	When I was a child, I often heard it, I heard it, when a story was told about Wiihsahkecaahk, as this person was supposedly named.

The use of the first person continues into the first sentence of the second part of the introduction (sentence 4) when Swanson makes a metaphorical step back in time to when 'before man was here on the earth.' This marks the beginning of the introduction to the *Wiihsahkecaahk* cycle in which this character is able to talk to and understand all the animals (sentences 5 and 6).

4 <Cough> *Niin tahshwiin kaa-kii-ishi-noontawakwaa cipwaa anihshinaape ohomaa eyaac ahkiink awiyaashiihshak iko kiih-ayaawak ninkii-tahtipaacim.*	*<Cough>* Indeed, I heard them [say], that before man was here on the earth there were only animals, that's what I'm going to talk about.
5 *Taapishkooc tahsh e-kiih-kanoonikoc inweniwa entaso-ohkaanehsinici awiyaashiihshak, 'aanimo.'*	Then it was like they talked to him, every kind of animal, 'animal.'
6 *Kahkina okii-nihsitohtawaan ahaawe Wiihsahkecaahk.*	This Wiihsahkecaahk understood every one of them.

The third part of this introductory section, comprising sentences 7 through 9, introduces the particular *Wiihsahkecaahk* episode. In sentence 7, we have the final use of the first person found in this story. This explicit narration places the action of the story where a modern Swampy Cree village now stands. Swanson's use of the first person here again gives his credentials for telling the story – he had *personally* heard this story told.

7 *Ekwa tahsh eshi-noontamaan weti*
peshik e-waapantamaan 'Poot
Seben' *kaa-ishinihkaatek*
Waashahoowisiipi, <Cough> *okii-*
mihkawaan pahpashkiinhsan.
8 *Mii tahsh — okiih-kanoonaan.*
9 *"Aaanti kimaamaamiwaa,"* okiih-
inaan eshi-pimihshinowaac
ikiweniwak pahpashkiinhsak.

Anyway, so I heard it there [at that
place] I once saw, it's called 'Fort
Severn,' Fort Severn River,
<Cough> that he found the little
partridges.
So then — he spoke to them.
"Where your mother?" he said to
them, to those little partridges that
were lying down there.

In the *Wiihsahkecaahk* story, the audience is not as important as the ori-
gins of the story, and Swanson's right to tell such a story. Laying the foundation for the right to tell a story is very important in the initial frames of
Swanson's stories. Thus the three parts of the *Wiihsahkecaahk* introduction
do not match the introduction of the first-person narrative, where Swanson
was interested in naming his audience and the reason for the storytelling
session. But note that, in the plane crash story, Swanson does make a point
that the accident happened right across from his house where he was an
eyewitness, and hence, an appropriate narrator of that incident.

PRONOUN SHIFTS

The first type of pronoun shift discussed here is from the first to the third
person in subject position. This shift can be seen in sentence 7. This shift
in person marks the progression from the here and now, back to the time
of a previous generation of storytellers, and finally into the time frame of
the story. Other pronoun shifts occur in sections of direct discourse where
first and second persons are once again used but where these pronouns
are pointing to characters within the story (see sentences 9, 10, 17 and 19;
and discussion of direct discourse, below).

TENSE SHIFTS

The tense shifts which best demonstrate metanarrative function are those
that create immediacy within a narrative. In Ojibwe, there are two types of
tense shifts: from an expected past tense into the historical present tense,
and from an expected past tense into a 'future more vivid' tense. In this
short text, we find only one example of a tense shift, into the historical
present, found in sentence 19, where Swanson uses the quotative *ihkitowak*
('they say') instead of the expected *kii-ihkitowak* ('they said'). The histori-

cal present in Ojibwe, as in English, is typically found in particularly compelling parts of a story. The second type of tense shift, to the future ('future more vivid'), is not found in this story but is in most other *aatisoohkaanan* that I collected in Lynx Lake. This shift works very much like the present historical in that it focuses the urgency of a situation.

DIRECT DISCOURSE

Direct discourse is a device commonly used in narrative performances of myths, often with attendant vocal changes denoting stereotyped characters. While the 'taking on of voices' is well attested in trickster narratives in Native North American traditions, it is entirely absent in all the Severn narratives I recorded in Lynx Lake. In the use of direct discourse, both between W*iihsahkecaahk* and the baby partridges and between the mother partridge and her children, there is no evidence of changing vocal quality to mimic some assumed feature of *Wiihsahkecaahk* or the partridges. Swanson's voice maintains the same qualities throughout the narrative, including in these sections. But, while the taking of voices is absent, the 'taking on of words,' the use of direct discourse, remains common in all types of narratives.

Direct discourse is often used by storytellers to set up a storyline. The first use of direct discourse in the Partridge story, found in sentence 9, follows this pattern, setting up the conflict of the episode:

"Aanti kimaamaamiwaa," okiih-inaan eshi-pimihshinowaac ikiweniwak pahpashkiinhsak.

"Where your mother?" he said to them, to those little partridges that were lying down there.

Direct discourse works throughout a story to highlight key sections, indexing the narrator's involvement with his narration. The presence of direct discourse is often the best cue that a story is being performed rather than a storyline being reported. In this brief text, direct discourse occurs in four of the twenty-four sentences, in sentences 9, 10, 17, and 19:

9 *"Aaanti kimaamaamiwaa," okiih-inaan eshi-pimihshinowaac ikiweniwak pahpashkiinhsak.*

"Where your mother?" he said to them, to those little partridges that were lying down there.

10 *"Weti ahpin maacaapan," tahsh — okiih-ikoon ini pahpash-kiinhsan.*

"She went a long way away," — those little partridges said to him.

17 *"Kekonen wenci-ishinaakosiyek?"*   "Why do you look like that?"
19 *"Wiihsahkecaahk ninkii-*   "Wiihsahkecaahk defecated all
   miicinikonaan," ihkitowak.   over us," they say. *<Laughter>*
   <Laughter>

REPETITION

Repetition is another device commonly used in Native American narrative traditions. Swanson used repetition extensively in this story, both as a local structuring device and as a means of adding weight to a statement. As noted earlier, this feature is considered 'old-fashioned' by some younger Severn Ojibwe people, who complain that old people 'repeat themselves all the time.'

Doublets occur throughout this text; the most involved structure of this type is found in sentences 11 through 14 (15), where 11 and 14 (and 15) are parallel, and sentences 12 and 13, embedded within the other doublet, are also paired.

11 *Ahpii tahsh waa-ani-maacaac.*   So then he got ready to leave.
12 *Mii hi eh-kii-ishi-pimoweshkitic*   That's when he defecated on them
   ihimaa kaa-ishi-ohkohshinici ...   there where they were lying
   together ...
13 *Mii hi kaa-ishi-opihpimoweskitic.*   That's what he defecated beside.
14 *<Cough> Mii tahsh ahpii kaa-*   *<Cough>* That's when he left from
   ishi-maacaac ahpin.   there.
15 *Amii tahsh — okii-waapamikoon*   So then — he was seen and then
   tahsh ahpin eni-ishi-aninaakosic.   he [just] disappeared.

The use of such structures highlights important information in the text, and creates a verbal artistry which is essential for a storyteller's reputation.

NARRATOR LAUGHTER

While Babcock classified laughter as a paralinguistic feature (1977: 65), I feel that the narrator's laughter is better analysed as metanarrational; when the narrator laughs at his own story, he provides the audience with a key for understanding both the tone of the story and how particular sections of a story should be interpreted.

The tone of this narrative began quite solemnly: Swanson's voice is slow, deliberate, and low-pitched. This mode was maintained throughout the introductory parts of the narrative, and in fact continued through the first half of the story: only when the mother partridge returns does the tempo pick up. When the mother partridge asks the little partridges how they came to look as they did, the tempo quickens considerably and Swanson's voice rises in pitch and in volume. This pace is maintained through the end of the story, with only laughter and short pauses separating lines.

The laughter of sentence comes at a point in the narrative where the educated (i.e., Native) audience knows that the crux of the tension, the essence of the story, has been set up. In sentences 18, 19, and 23, Swanson's laughter points to an outline of the basic conflict of this episode. As was true in Toelken's analysis of a Navaho Coyote narrative, the laughter here is at an action considered "weak, stupid, or excessive ... to order th[e] moral assessment of it without recourse to open explanation or didacticism" (1976: 162). In this narrative, the laughter occurs when the true recipient of Wiihsahkecaahk's insult, the mother partridge, discovers what has happened to her babies. The little partridges had transgressed the norm by talking to a stranger, and they had gotten the anticipated negative result. Swanson's sober tone of voice in the introduction seems to indicate this seriousness of genre (or perhaps of the seriousness of the narrative event), but the laughter later points out the very funny (albeit negative) outcome of the transgressed norms typical of that same genre. In other stories of this genre, some narrator laughter is unambiguously premonitory in nature: the laughter focuses on an action which will cause the actor's ultimate downfall. This is true even in this story, as it is this foolish act of insulting the partridge that resulted in *Wiihsahkecaahk*'s painful slide down a hill in a later episode.

Both the tempo and laughter by the narrator function to key the audience into the frame for interpretation. Laughter here does not simply mean humour, it also can mean 'watch what results this can have.' Swanson's extralinguistic cues provided emotive evaluation. Such devices border on explicit metanarration.

OTHER DEVICES

The use of the dubitative mode (-*tok* in the independent and -*kwen* in the conjunct verb orders) is a common feature of the *Wiihsahkecaahk* narratives, as is the use of highly specific verbs, usually displaying some degree of noun incorporation, such as *eh-kii-ishi-pimoweshkitic* (literally, 'when-past.tense-there-defecate-3.person.singular') and *kaa-ishi-ohkohshinici* (lit-

erally, 'conjunct.past.tense-there-lying.all.together-3.person.obviative. plural'). The ability to generate and use such forms is considered a sign of a
good storyteller. Hence, the speech style is marked as that of a storyteller,
but it is more a question of degree, i.e., of how many forms there are of this
type, rather than purely the presence of such forms that marks it as good
narrative language.

The final feature discussed here is the use of formulaic expressions. The
best example in this text is the idiomatic *okii-waapamikon tahsh ahpin eni-
ishi-aninaakosic.* The closest English equivalent would probably be the idiom
'he vanished into thin air.' In the same way that the statement in English is
bound to a certain context outside the real world, the Ojibwe phrase is
characteristic of the trickster of legends, not of real people. In this way, the
choice of vocabulary once again marks genre.

DISCOURSE ANALYSIS

Although there is no identifiable hierarchy to the pauses, the use of lines
defined by pauses is a valuable presentational device. In orientational sections, where the sentences are quite complex, the division of sentences
into lines provides manageable units. Most pauses occur at syntactic boundaries so that lines tend to consist of complete clauses, or at least apposi-
tional material. The most consistent exceptions are pauses which occur
after false starts; however, none are found in this text – notable in itself.

This story is exceptionally short; the first-person narrative in chapter 8 is
more typical, with its sixty-four sentences. Because of its brevity, and because it represents only one episode, this text is not well suited for extensive study of form–content parallelism (Hymes 1981, Woodbury 1987, etc.).
However, despite the apparent limitations, this is clearly a complete and
well-structured narrative with subepisodic parallels. On the basis of the
concatenation of features, including discourse particles, temporal shifts,
direct discourse, parallel constructions, laughter, and pauses, the following structure is proposed.

Structural Outline of 'Why the Partridge Is Brown'

		Sentence
I.	INTRODUCTION	(1–6)
	A. Intro to genre and series	(1)
	B. Personal qualification of the storyteller	(2–4)
	C. intro to specific *aatisoohkaan*	(4–7)
	1. Era	(4–5)

The division of parallel sections III (The Offence Given) and IV (The Offence Taken) are based on the independent features of direct discourse and independent verb forms found in both sections. Sections IV through VI should perhaps be grouped together, as the laughter continues throughout these sections, binding them together phonologically.

In the section IB (Personal qualification of the storyteller), the particle *wiin* is found in some abundance. In other narratives (*aatisoohkaanan* and *tipaacimowinan* including first-person narratives), this particle, which often occurs in initial sections, seems to indicate the narrator's personal contact with the story or events within the story. In this text the independent personal pronoun *niin* ('I') is also found. In Ojibwe, this pronoun is redundant and rarely used, giving further weight to the focus of the storyteller in this section.

The Ojibwe speaker has recourse to numerous, untranslatable particles (called 'discourse particles'), the precise nature of which is often difficult to pinpoint. One such is the particle *mii*. While the *mii* has been analysed in a southern dialect as signalling a summary statement (Rhodes 1979), this does not generally hold true in Severn narratives. After studying the structure of this and other texts, it became apparent that *mii* generally begins new sections (see especially sentence 8 in this text), and it is also used to mark sentences or entire sections which are sequentially misaligned with the rest of the discourse. Mii followed by the truncated demonstrative pronoun *hi* (translated 'that is ...' or 'so it is that ...') does appear to mark summary statements on the level of the entire discourse. Thus, presenting the four sentences beginning with *mii hi* in this text gives a basic outline of important events in the discourse:

12 *Mii hi eh-kii-ishi-pimoweshkitic ihimaa kaa-ishi-ohkohshinici* ...	That's when he defecated on them there where they were lying together ...
13 *Mii hi kaa-ishi-opihpimoweskitic.*	That's what he defecated beside.
20 *Mii hi kaa-ishkwaa-nooskwaatahwaac ahaawe pahpashki.*	So then after this partridge licked them off.
22 *Mii hi kaa-onci-osaawisic.*	So that's why it's brown.

The final discourse feature discussed here is the use of the proper names. The name *Wiihsahkecaahk* is used three times times in the introductory sections, but only once in the actual story, in the third person during direct discourse. The partridges, whose proper names are never used, are mentioned throughout using the generic plural noun *pahpashkiinhsak.* None of the characters, including the mother partridge with her little partridges, ever use an address form. In Ojibwe, the verb carries information about both subject and object, making explicit reference (the use of independent nouns) unnecessary. This phenomenon of implicit reference to a character is interesting, and generally consistent with everyday conversational practices. This does create problems for translation; one makes a choice between highlighting the importance of the use of a proper noun (or any independent noun, for that matter) in Ojibwe or being able to keep the actors straight in English. The latter necessarily wins out in English translation.

CONCLUSIONS

This chapter has focused on emic genre, the place of legend-myths in Severn life, the oral nature of storytelling, and structures and linguistic features commonly found in *aatisoohkaanan.* Included in the discussion were interactional dynamics, including those between narrator and audience, and narrator involvement with the story (seen in laughter, in the physical acting-out of sections, in changes of voice during direct discourse). While the primary functions of storytelling are to teach proper modes of behaviour and to entertain, this specific narrative was a demonstration of cultural expertise by the storyteller, and an indexation of friendship which had been formed between the narrator and his audience.

In closing this chapter, it is important to stress that virtually every aspect of the natural world surrounding the northern Ojibwe, each bit of flora and fauna, has a story connected with it. When one sees a brown partridge, the story of *Wiihsahkecaahk* hovers near. Lichen on cliffs testifies to the stupidity of punishing an innocent party, and to the place of revenge, both warranted and unwarranted. And so on. Thus, the dialogue between *aatisoohkaanan* and the contemporary world of the Severn Ojibwe pervades the very atmosphere of the northern Ojibwe.

Chapter Ten

◁ꓵbᑕ⅃ᵇ bꓑᑕꟲᵅᑕ·▽ᵅᑕᒣᵇ·▽∩ ᒧbᵅ

'Work to Create the Future You Want'

Other studies in the ethnography of speaking have profitably taken named discourse genres as the starting-point of investigation and, through these genres, have discovered metaphorical structuring of social action. (For a detailed discussion of ways in which genre has been addressed in anthropology, linguistics, and other disciplines, see Bauman and Briggs 1992.) Especially notable in this regard is Gossen's (1974) study of Chamula speech. However, among the Severn Ojibwe, and subarctic Amerindians in general (Scollon and Scollon 1979), genres tend to be less marked, both linguistically and culturally. As we saw in chapter 9, only the *aatisoohkaan* has overt restrictions placed on its telling.[1] When I elicited an extended list of genres of talk from community members (see appendix 2), the collection held no surprises; the types of talk named were those expected in a society with relatively few traditional ritual speaking forms. Most named genres of talk contained recognizably related bases such as *-aacim* ('relate' or 'narrate'), *-kit* ('say'), and *-wiintam* ('tell something'). Indeed, the great majority of terms for talk were appropriate for classifying and evaluating types of informal, dialogic discourse.

Rather than beginning with a study of genre, I found that a more productive method of inquiry for the community of Lynx Lake was an exploration of social institutions or domains and the linguistic forms most typically used within each. Once a basic correlation of form and domain had been established, I found these now-stereotyped linguistic forms being extended into new domains creating a complex, emergent discourse between and within institutions. Thus, we look within text to discover how and which external social factors are indexed in it and we look to social context to discover the reason for formal linguistic choices that are made within discourse.

As has been demonstrated throughout this book, the study of discourse necessitates concurrent ethnographic research. Additionally, as outlined in chapter 7, ethnographic research must be combined with the study of the discourse in order to hear the contemporary voices of a society. By listening to Native-to-Native discourse, the ethnographer sidesteps the tendency to create an ethnographic agenda which runs the risk of failing to reflect or represent contemporary culture. This issue is becoming increasingly important in Native North American research as many Native communities legitimately complain to the academic world that 'we are not museum pieces,' but in fact people living in the same complex contemporary world as the researcher. Indeed, this has been a motivating factor in my choice of topics to discuss in this book. I hope that I have demonstrated, if only superficially, some of the richness and complexity of current language use in Lynx Lake. This is a Native community whose increased interaction with western society has resulted in even *greater* linguistic resources, including multilingual literacy, new genres, new media, and even new linguistic codes, all of which are manipulated either seriously or jokingly by community members.

A formal linguistic study of discourse indexes crucial aspects of social life, just as cultural context provides keys to understanding the discourse. By focusing on a community's discourse, the anthropologist is attuned to listening to emergent social concerns. With an understanding of community life in Lynx Lake, opportunities for gathering naturally occurring discourses were easily found, and in fact, because of the interest with Native media, my services as an archivist were often solicited by the community.

METHODOLOGIES

An integrated approach to the analysis of discourse-internal structuring (the analysis of formal linguistic features of discourse) combined with discourse-external structuring has yet to be realized. Bauman (1986a) and Feld (1982) have both begun to address these issues with some success, but have been limited by the paucity of metalanguage available to talk about discourse. Jacopin (1988) outlines this dilemma (below) but, even so, fails to carry out discourse-internal analysis in his examination of a Yukuna myth:

In this article, I treat myth as formal speech, designated by the expression *mythical speech*. It is speech, because before being recorded or written down in the ethnographer's notebook, myth is a social event and a performance. It is formal because, although myths may, for example, be expressed in Yukuna language, their specific idiom is *marked* by its social function; that is, it carries marks (mythical words, tense, intonation) that distinguish it from other kinds of speech (simple conversation, dialogue with the elderly, magic and ritual spells). In other words, myth belongs to two different orders of things which, though they are distinct, are inseparable. From the external point of view, myth has a specific social function that depends on the social structure and on the nature of the society in which it takes place. ... In other words, the relationship between the internal structure of myth and its external social function is not mechanical. The two aspects cannot be reduced to each other: the social function of myth does not determine its internal structure, and recipro-cally, the syntax of myth does not determine its social role. This does not mean, however, that the two aspects are not intimately related; for in actual practice any myth stems from problems of social organization. (pp. 132–3; emphasis in origi-nal)

While Jacopin's interest was in myth, the problems he so compellingly sum-marized are just as prevalent in the study of any discourse genre. Indeed, one could easily substitute the term 'discourse' for 'myth' throughout the preceding quotation, making Jacopin's claim all the more relevant.

Like Jacopin, many scholars analysing discourse have focused on a sin-gle genre (cf. Hymes 1977 and 1981; Tedlock 1984 and 1987; and Labov 1972b, who deals with several genres, but each independently of the other), and have built analytic methodologies based upon the particular genre studied. In this exploration of a wide variety of discourse types used in Lynx Lake, I found no single methodology sufficient for either description or analysis, and was compelled to use multiple approaches, including ethnopoetics, conversational analysis, and statistical analysis of code switch-ing. As has been demonstrated in the previous chapters, the Severn Ojibwe speech community differs in important ways from those which gave rise to the methodologies; that is, the speech community I have described is one in which genres are not heavily marked and where boundaries between genres quickly blur. Ritual language is tied into an imported institution, the Anglican church, and to an imported language, Cree. Because Severn discourse is so subtly marked, I was led to study a broad range of genres which reflect and index a correspondingly broad range of social institu-tions and behaviours. Working with these more subtly marked discourses, using methodologies developed for other speech communities, provides simultaneous insight into both the object of study, the discourse, and the methodology. In my critique of various methodologies used in this study of Severn Ojibwe discourse, both strengths and weaknesses are outlined.

The transcription devices used by those studying conversation (Sacks,

Schegloff, and Jefferson 1974) were found to be valuable in the initial transcriptions of the majority of texts I collected in Lynx Lake. For presenting essentially monovocal Severn texts, pauses provided a convenient division of the discourse into lines. While I have used this device extensively in the presentation of discourse throughout this book, I did not discover hierarchical ordering within the discourse marked by pause alone, and therefore consider it more a presentation device than an analytic tool as has been proposed by some researchers working in ethnopoetics (cf. Tedlock 1984). However, when pauses correlate with other rhetorical devices such as particular discourse particles, tenses, modes, and lexical items, I believe that they are meaningful and must be attended to.

The work on form–content parallelism has been particularly helpful in pointing to the interplay of these linguistic devices (Woodbury 1987; Hymes 1981), especially in the more 'artistic' verbal genres such as in the telling of myths. I found this perspective informed my entire research design, although rather than looking for especially numerical patterning in the cultural context to match the patterning in myth, I looked for social patterns which correlated with a concatenation of linguistic forms in the attendant discourse. In the analysis of a legend-myth found in chapter 9, I was able to follow rather closely the lead of those working in this area.

However, when I was working on the analysis of the first-person narrative in chapter 8, I found both the methodology and the terminology somewhat restricting and so used Labov's (1972b) model as a springboard for the current research. While, this type of narrative analysis is too heavily based upon the study of a particular genre of English narrative to be widely usable, the categories discussed differ enough from any of the other discourse perspectives to be both interesting and beneficial. However, because this model is built upon a single English genre, its greatest limitation is also one of its greatest assets: by using the model for studying the same genre in another language, we are afforded an excellent tool for cross-cultural comparison of rhetorical structuring.

The statistical sociolinguistic methodology employed in chapter 4 was yet another analytic tool brought into play in this study. Statistical analysis is typically used with few variables over a large population (cf. Labov 1972a). In this study, I found the methods valuable even in the speech of a small population: here to show both the presence of a given linguistic style or genre (religious talk) and an individual's degree of manipulation of the phonetic variable (the denasalization of nasal clusters) which marked that genre. The person with the most status as a religious leader is shown to demonstrate the highest degree of the phonetic change; other people in

Lynx Lake show variable use of that marker in religious talk, indexing their level of involvement and status within the formal religious hierarchy. This methodology was especially helpful in determining some of the key linguistic forms that determine discourse genre. Coupled especially with the perspective of form–content parallelism, it is a powerful tool for discovering the relationship between form and context. One of the disadvantages of the methodology is that the researcher must discover a likely variable prior to statistical study. This means that statistical analysis can be used only after the researcher has formed a hypothesis about the link between some form and it social meaning. Thus, statistical study is limited by the researcher's understanding of the language/culture intersection. It is an excellent way to test empirically hypotheses about language use, but it is not in itself useful as a discovery tool.

DATA COLLECTION AND TECHNOLOGY

Prior to their analysis data must be collected.[2] In the ethnographic study of discourse, data-collection methodology can be as critical for the final product as is the analytic methodology. In over a decade working with and among Ojibwe people, I have used several different means of data collection with varying degrees of success. In the earliest stages of study in Lynx Lake, I tried to elicit data using a traditional linguistic methodology: I would ask for individual words and sentences in English, and an approximate translation would be offered. Within the first two weeks, I discovered that this was not a particularly effect method of getting *appropriate* data. I had asked for the translation of what I thought of as a standard greeting, 'How are you doing?' and was given the sentence *Aan eshi-ayaayan*. I immediately began to use this with people in the community, but each time I tried the phrase, people would look at me in total bewilderment. My first problem in those first weeks was that I did not hear phonemic differences in vowel length and was actually saying *Aan eshi-ayaayaan* or 'How am I?' Even discovering and correcting this error did not help, however, as the implications of the question included 'I know you have been ill, so how are you now?' People simply did not use words for greetings, nor, for the most part, for leavetakings. Elicitation was surely not the way to learn the language. Shortly after my first rather disastrous attempts to get good linguistic data, Rand discovered that syllabic literacy was being taught in the school several times each week, and he began sitting in the class where the (then) Reverend William Pipoon wrote down hypothetical conversations between two students in syllabics. These dialogues were outstanding: they covered current events in the community, they were always appropriate, and the language was that of the Native speaker. Later we would have these dialogues read by a Native speaker, taped, and translated into English for us to memorize and use in the community as a tool in learning to speak Severn Ojibwe. Also around this time we began taping discourses off the radio, some of which we later transcribed and translated. Aside from copying the dialogues off the school chalkboard, the tape recorder was the primary piece of equipment for gaining competence: elicitation was limited to noun and verb paradigms which were collected after nearly a year and a half of studying naturally occurring discourses.

By 1987, a majority of homes in Lynx Lake had television sets and videocassette recorders (VCRs). When I returned to conduct further research in Lynx Lake in 1987, I used a Sony 8-mm video camera for data collection. With its two-hour metal tapes, it gave better-quality sound and longer, uninterrupted recordings than a cassette-tape recorder. The video capabilities seemed almost secondary – that is, until I brought the camera into the village and used it for the first time. This was a device that people truly appreciated. Before, copies of tapes of sermons or discussions from the radio might be of interest to a couple of people in the community, but everyone was interested in videotapes, and the opportunities they provided to see their neighbours and oneself. As was mentioned in the introduction, the videocamera created a meaningful place for me in Lynx Lake society as, essentially, community filmmaker. Not only was I invited to record a wide array of events (and discourses), but I was also able to give records of the events to those involved almost immediately. Thus, the audience for the tapes was not merely or exclusively some outside anthropologist; rather, it was the local Native community. Further studies of discourse in Lynx Lake need to integrate both the language and the physical actions of the speakers. Currently, studies in this area are in their infancy, better suited to oral and visual presentation than the linear presentation required by books (though work by C. Goodwin and M.H. Goodwin are exceptions). As computer technology advances in its graphical and interactive interfaces, future studies of videotaped discourse will be able to utilize such dynamic means of data manipulation and display: the potential for electronic publication of academic materials is only just now gaining a hearing.

The study of naturally occurring discourse takes the focus away from interviews and elicitation, methods traditionally associated with ethnography, towards actual community events, both large and small. Much anthropological methodology has focused on researcher-directed interviews. The researcher comes into the situation with a hypothesis which he or she intends to prove or disprove, thus delineating the area for study independently of the people being studied. The Native participants who opt to help the anthropologist tend to be those who are comfortable with that situation: among the Ojibwe, the people often chosen as primary sources or translators of information are those who have had the most contact with Euro-Canadians or Americans, and who have a vested interest in being brokers of cultural information which necessarily entails a strong traditionalist framework, if the researcher is leaning in that direction for study. This accommodation of perceived interests also applies to representatives of other Western institutions outside of academia, including governmental and religious workers. This problem is similar to that discussed by Paredes (1977) in his critique of anthropologists studying border Mexican Americans.

Lakoff and Johnson's (1980) 'myth of objectivism' appears closely related to traditional approaches which proceed by means of an *a priori* (universal, etic/objective) framework imposed upon cultures, often entailing value judgments as to the efficacy and import of different aspects of another's culture. In Lakoff and Johnson's words: "In a culture where the myth of objectivism is very much alive and truth is always absolute truth, the people who get to impose their metaphors on the culture get to define what we consider to be true – absolutely and objectively true" (p. 160).

Recently scholars have attempted to address this dilemma by making the dialogic nature of the research endeavour more transparent (Marcus and Fischer 1986; Clifford 1988). These scholars admit the primacy of the anthropologist in the ethnographic product derived from the discourse between anthropologist and informant. This reaction to the fallacy of the omniscient anthropologist is a step forward in understanding the problems of ethnographic research outside of one's own culture, but the approach unnecessarily limits the scope of the study.

This newer approach, which recognizes the objectivism fallacy, at least as it applies to other cultures, turns inward and says that, since the only emic system that we can truly understand is our own, then we should focus on how knowing another's culture reflects on an understanding of our own.[3] While this approach may be valid, it is severely and unnecessarily self-limiting, as it assumes that the interview is primary in ethnographic research. The problem with this view may be illustrated using linguistic research methodology. What constitutes the language of the Ojibwe (or any group) is that language used by Native speakers and not that elicited by even the best sentence grammarian. However, because a linguist is capable of eliciting sentences, and even texts, this in no way precludes the collection of naturally occurring discourse. The latter is much more difficult, to be sure, but rather than accepting this limitation, a linguist concerned with getting at the essence of the Ojibwe language would make the effort to creatively discover means to collect natural discourse. The study of elicited material is, indeed, interesting and can be useful, but it is a far different task from studying language as it is used in natural contexts – even when the linguist is concerned with exclusively sentence-level phenomena. Thus, the study of the naturally occurring discourse is critical even when the concerns are much more limited.

In returning to the question of how to conduct ethnographic research that will not turn the people studied into subjects of the anthropologist (pun intended), the study of Native-centred, as opposed to anthropologist-centred, discourse is critical. Since discourse is the arena in which much of a community's culture is substantiated, reinforced, negotiated, and changed, the collection of discourse is collection of culture. This is not to make the claim that there is a causal relationship between language and culture, but that there is a significant, discoverable relationship between discourse and culture. A discourse-centred approach, in which the discourse being studied is that of cultural insider directed to another cultural insider, that is, naturally occurring discourse, provides an excellent basis for learning about the creation, enactment, and emergence of cultural systems with minimal interference from an outside researcher. The voices of those studied speak independently of the anthropologist, and indeed can speak for themselves long after the anthropologist's voice is made hollow by the vicissitudes of theory.

The discourses presented in this book are offered as unique but representative tokens of language use in Lynx Lake. It is from such naturally occurring data that we can discover many of the core attitudes about social institutions. The traditional anthropological methodology of interviewing comes after the data collection, during the translation process, at a time when the Native discourse is front and centre. The questions elicited here revolve around the Native-to-Native discourse: the discourse provides the domain covered, a real as opposed to hypothetical situation to discuss, and a context which is understandable to the Native expert. This is a far less threatening methodology for the Native research participants, and one that goes a long way to minimize the anthropologist's agenda.

The advantages of a discourse-centred approach are many: the discourses provide an empirical basis upon which theoretical constructs may be based, and by which these constructs may be evaluated; through discourse one can see social change in action; through discourse, the emphasis is on the 'here and now' rather than on reconstruction; as language and social networks are intimately intertwined, discourse brings such networks to the foreground; and the data, the discourses, the words of the people themselves, are available for reanalysis using alternative theoretical models by future anthropologists, among whom we expect to find members of the Native community, and are available for immediate use and analysis by the Native community itself.

Disadvantages of a discourse-centred approach in the study of cultures include: the need to gain access to a wide spectrum of discourse; the time required for analysis of discourse as it necessitates a knowledge of the language; and the fact that each speech community is unique, an agenda for study cannot be predetermined, it must come out of the community itself. Actually, the disadvantages of the discourse-centred approach are also its greatest assets: there is no way to circumvent the time needed to get acquainted with both the language and the culture. 'Fieldwork' cannot be done in three-to-six-month forays into an area. Rather, researchers involved in studying discourse must commit themselves to several years of learning a language and living with the people. In North American Native communities, where researchers are often suspect, the time commitment is important for both sides: when an outsider proves himself or herself a learner over the long haul, the Native community begins to trust and befriend him or her. Conversely, living in a Native community for a long period helps to turn academics into people who understand that being trustworthy and maintaining relationships with others is often more important than publishing another article. In my linguistic work with Amerindians in Canada, I have found as I hired and worked with Native colleagues, that these talented people were typically 'discovered' by the local Band office or school, and whisked away into permanent and prestigious positions. The linguistic training that researches can provide may ultimately prove to have economic, political, and social value far beyond that initially expected. In North America where Native status and land claims are often decided by incredibly misinformed politicians, as was the case with the Menominee in Wisconsin, sophistication about language and culture may be critical for the survival of Native groups.

Malinowski's (1935) 'Language of Magic and Gardening' stands as a testimony to the strength of the association between language and culture in early anthropological research. In North America, Boas and his students were notable for their integration of linguistic and cultural studies among Native American groups. Despite this early union of language and culture in anthropological research, we still do not have a comparative base of discourse in societies, analogous to comparative studies in kinship. This book provides one more piece of the mosaic of discourse patterns found in societies around the world.

In proper Ojibwe fashion, I close this work chiastically, with an explanation of the title of this chapter. The phrase ⊲ᗑbᑕ⅃ᵇ bʃᗫᵃᑕ·∇ᵃᑕ⅃ᵇ ·∇∩ ᗑbᵃ , *Anohkaatamok kaa-ishi-nantawentamek weti niikaan,* first came to my attention in the December 1989 issue of *Wawatay News* at the bottom of a Kelner Airways advertisement. Kelner Airways was one of the several small airlines which had been flying goods into Native communities in north central Ontario for some time. The Lynx Lake Band, along with several other neighbouring Bands, became partners with Kelner Airways[4] in a move to gain control over yet another important area of technology which, until this move, had been the exclusive domain of Euro-Canadians. The quote, which I have used as the title of this chapter, was translated into English as 'Work for your future needs' and attributed to 'Anapat Memekwe 1913–1988 Lynx Lake.' Anapat, a highly respected elder, was the gentleman to whom, in 1987, I was constantly directed as a great storyteller; in December of that year, when the lake was frozen over and the snow lay thick on the ice, Anapat graciously narrated six hours of stories over a period of three nights. I was struck by the coincidence of having been directed to Anapat as a teller of traditional tales and then finding that the words which are most prominently displayed and attended to by the community are those which address the future. The attitude which Anapat so eloquently summarized was precisely that which I found in Lynx Lake: the future begins now; one must work to create the future that is wanted. These people *are* creating their own futures by making considered decisions about the importation of technology and ideas. The aim of this research was to provide an empirically based, synchronic overview of a community in the midst of rapid social change. The changes continue in the lives of the Lynx Lake community, but these are changes that arise out of a solid understanding of what it means to be and live as an *Anihshininiwak*. They are making the future their own.

Postscript

On June 1994, a Euro-Canadian Anglican priest was convicted of sexually abusing numerous children in Severn Ojibwe communities over a period of some twenty years. The trial and conviction of Ralph Rowe marks a turning-point for many Severn people and communities. In the healing that began with laying charges against this man, the role of the Anglican church in some communities has been shaken, especially among the younger generations.

The Severn world is changing – many of the discourses will also emerge in different forms. This book documents a specific era in the Lynx Lake community, a time of transition from the traditional hunting-and-gathering society to a more sedentary lifestyle on a relatively isolated reserve. As outlined in this book, Lynx Lake is and remains a pivotal community in the Severn region: it was a member of the Lynx Lake reserve who gave key testimony that convicted Rowe of his crimes. As a community which views itself as forging the future for many of the Severn Bands, Lynx Lake is also forging the way for community-wide healing, the shape of which is only beginning to emerge. The discourses discussed in this book provide a foundation for understanding some of the forms this healing may take.

Typological Overview of Severn Ojibwe

In this appendix I present some of the major typological features of Severn Ojibwe. Those interested in more detailed Severn Ojibwe grammatical treatments should consult R. Valentine 1994, Todd 1970, and Rogers 1964. Also suggested are the excellent Ojibwe grammars by Nichols (1980) and Rhodes (1976).

Severn Ojibwe shares with its Algonquian congeners a 'mild' polysyntheticity (using Goddard's [1987] term), characterized by quite robust derivational and inflectional morphological process. There are three principal parts of speech in Severn Ojibwe: nouns, verbs, and particles which are not inflected.

Nouns are marked for person, number, obviation, and gender with all categories cross-referenced on the verb. The two genders are animate and inanimate, classifications that are roughly logical, i.e., people, animals, and many plants are categorized as animate whereas things such as moccasins, blankets, and sticks are considered inanimate. There are many systematic exceptions to this generalization, e.g., heavenly bodies (sun, moon, stars), traditional religious articles (tobacco, pipes, drums, etc.), close personal possessions (mitts, spoons, snowshoes, etc.), and an odd assortment of unrelated items, including among many others certain berries, stones, and tires. Note that there is no morphological masculine/feminine differentiation as we find in the English pronouns he and she.

There are four verb classes, differentiated on the basis of transitivity and gender. The first two classes include intransitive verbs, which are further categorized on the basis of the animacy of the subject: inanimate intransitive (II) verbs have inanimate subjects, and animate intransitive (AI) verbs have animate subjects. In this morphologically ergative system, the animacy of the absolutive determines the verbal class of transitive verbs. These last two categories are called transitive inanimate (TI) and transitive animate (TA) verbs. Person, number, and obviation of subjects and objects are also marked on the verb, as noted above.

There are three verbal orders, independent, conjunct, and imperative. In general, independent verbs are found in main clauses, and conjunct verbs are found in dependent clauses and with certain particles. Verbs are also marked as to tense (past, neutral, future, voluntative) and mode (neutral, preterit, dubitative, and dubitative preterit). Other aspects of Ojibwe grammar are discussed as specific in this study as they arise.

PHONOLOGY/ORTHOGRAPHIC CONVENTIONS

The orthographic tradition used throughout this presentation is the Northern Ojibwe roman alphabet, as standardized in the mid 1960s by C.E. Fiero. The values of the alphabet characters are phonemic.

Vowels

Vowel length is distinctive, though short e neutralizes with the short i at some late stage in the phonology and thus never appears on the surface. Because of this, Severn orthography uses a single character, e, to indicate a long, non-high, front vowel. The other long vowels are indicated orthographically, with digraphs, ii, aa, and oo.

Vowel Inventory
   i/ii
   e   o/oo[1]
                a/aa

Consonants

Phonotactically consonant clusters consist of either a nasal or a fricative followed by an obstruent. From Proto-Algonquian (PA) consonant clusters with oral continuants in the first position, hC (preaspirate) clusters arose. These have been changed to /h/ in Severn Ojibwe and are realized or reanalysed as geminates or simple or aspirated voiceless stops in more southerly Ojibwe dialects (R. Valentine, personal communication).

Consonant Inventory
   Stops: p   t   k

Fricatives		s	sh		h
Affricates:			c		
Nasals:	m	n			
Glides:			y	w	(h)

Appendix Two

Terms for Talk

aacimowin	True story, factual account
aacimowinenhs	Brief, funny story/anecdote, often embarrassing
aatanoohke	'One is telling a legend' (rare)
aatihsoohke	'One is telling a legend'
Ahawe pankii ka-kakito.	'That one is going to talk a little,' used when one gives a speech or other address.
ayamihaa	'One is praying'
enahamaasoc	Name of song, singing something
ihkito	'One is saying,' used most often in quotes
ihkitowin	Word, utterance
inaacimo	'One is reporting/telling a story,' a true happening
ishi	'Say to one!'
kaa-ayamihitinaaniwank	Conversation
kakanooso	Arguing (neutral connotations)
kakiinawishke	'One is lying,' (negative connotations)
kakito	'One is talking'
kiih-wanimo	'One said it wrong accidently,' 'one said it differently, accidentally'
kiimooci-kakito	'One is whispering'
kiiwanamo	'One is talking foolishly,' like a dirty old man, about a woman. (can be either negative or funny, depending upon the context)
kikakwecimin	'I am asking you'
kikiih-ayamihin	'I talked to you'

kikiih-kanoonin	'I called you' (on the telephone, over the radio)
kinahkaweshihin	'I am answering you (your request),' used when one has called and asked for something
kinanahkaweshin	'You talk back to me'
mate-kakito	'One is there talking'
mate-kihci-kakito	'One talked in a big way,' boasting, considered negative
mate-wiintam	'One told'
nikamo	'One is singing'
nimihkomaa	'I am mentioning one,' used when talking about one.
nintooshinihkaanaa	'I am naming one.' Old people consider it very important to take a name from the Bible.
otanshimaatiwak	'They are discussing a topic among themselves,' used most often in the context of the Band office
otanshitaan	'One is discussing a subject,' used when answering the question: 'What was his/her topic?'
shahshaakowe	'One is screaming' said of children, or of one calling for a child (reduplicated form of s*haakowe*, 'one is shouting')
tipaacimo nimpi-miinikoo	'I have news'
tipaacimowin	True story (more common than *aacimowin*)
waawiyatwe	'One is joking, kidding around verbally,' considered funny
wiintam	'One is telling a secret,' something that should have remained quiet, that one wanted to be kept quiet
wiintamaakewin	Telling one to do something
wiintamaw	'Tell one!'

Notes

CHAPTER TWO

1 Culturally, most Severn communities continue to demonstrate features which align them more with Swampy Cree people than with other Ojibwe groups.

2 The Laurentian Plateau, also known as the Canadian Shield, is a Precambrian land mass which extends over half of Canada, from the Arctic Ocean in the northwest, southeast around Hudson Bay and northeast to Laborador.

3 The nearest Hudson's Bay post was about thirty-five miles east of Mihshamihkowiihsh, at Kaamiskwaapihkaak Lake.

4 *Shehtak* and *kwaashkwekaneyaap*, 'thread,' are used in the north and south groups respectively.

5 Where there has been long-standing contact between Cree and Ojibwe people, as in the western Saulteaux areas and in the Severn area, intelligibility is much greater between the languages. Severn Ojibwe shares many morphological features and lexical items with Swampy Cree in particular, creating the potential for greater intelligibility between the two. Swampy Cree and Severn Ojibwe people occasionally intermarry, and the offspring of such unions often serve as interpreters between the two groups. When teaching a combined group of Cree and Ojibwe students in the same class, I have observed that the most monolingual of the Severn Ojibwe and Swampy Cree speakers will often pair up, each speaking a mildly simplified version of his or her own language. Younger Cree and Ojibwe speakers who are conversant in English have a much harder time understanding the other language. Hence, mutual intelligibility is a complex issue that cannot be discussed categorically.

6 Many of the southern dialects exhibit vowel syncopation, creating consonant clusters that render syllabics highly inefficient.

7 A widespread indication is that, among the Ojibwe, the northern groups are

regarded as more closely fitting the 'real Indian' ideal. This is seen among the Severn Ojibwe through the acceptance of Swampy Cree as the liturgical language, despite minimal understanding of that language among the Severn people.

CHAPTER THREE

1 Some of the transcription conventions used in this book are: ellipses (...) for material that has been deleted; em dashes (—) for false starts; angle brackets (< >) for non-linguistic textual material; and square brackets ([ ]) for implied information that has been added in the English translation. See chapter 9 for further discussion of transcription conventions.
2 While the article focused on legal definitions and penalties for the perceived abuses caused by overuse, the following statement from the inspector-in-charge of the federal Department of Communications gives a more balanced view in keeping with the stated uses noted earlier: "... personal calls are part of the trapline, says Bonnefoy [the inspector-in-charge], because trappers check-in with their community and family to let them know where they are. 'That type of (call) would be fine, but keep it to a minimum,' he says. 'We don't want to have people out there talking for an hour and a half on the radio (while) somebody else is trying to make an emergency call.'"
3 The statement was given in Ojibwe.

CHAPTER FOUR

1 For exceptional cases in which stable bilingualism is involved between minority languages, see, among others, Jackson 1974 and Sankoff 1980: 34–46.)
2 All pauses were measured using the Macintosh SoundCap program.
3 Tuberculosis was the primary cause of extended hospital visits.
4 Although school lessons in Lynx (grades kindergarten through eight) are taught in English from the first grade, children normally do not speak English beyond the level of isolated words and phrases, even in the classroom.
5 There are several in the Band office and up to two positions at the school which are filled by women and which require some proficiency in English.
6 Uncertain form; as it stands, it appears to be grammatically incorrect.
7 The examples of code switching into English given in this chapter were the only ones in the hour-long discourse where the English used was longer than a phrase.
8 This is the Band councillor who did not show up.

9 Note the absence of the negative.

10 The people of Lynx Lake typically call their language Cree in English, but I have chosen to translated *anihshinaapemowin* ('people's language') as Ojibwe for the sake of consistency. The term 'Ojicree' (also spelled 'Oji-Cree') has recently gained some prominence among Severn people, but is considered misleading by Algonquianists. I apologize to the people of Lynx for the use of the term 'Ojibwe.'

11 In one case that did not comply to the rule of 'over 30,' the chief provided the English for '23,' and then immediately apposited the Severn equivalent.

12 The Algonquin dialect of Ojibwe, spoken in western Quebec and linguistically the most closely related to Severn, also lacks these nasal clusters, but all other dialects have them (e.g., Ottawa, Nipissing, Eastern Ojibwa, Chippewa, Saulteaux, and Northwestern Ojibwe).

13 There are other types of linguistic moves towards Cree in these genres, including lexical and morphological changes, which deserve further study.

14 Ojibwe, a morphologically rich language, distinguishes inflectionally between verbs which occur in main clauses, designated as *Independent order* forms, and those which occur in subordinate clauses and substantive questions (equivalent to English wh-questions), designated as *Conjunct order* forms. Ojibwe also distinguishes between inclusive and exclusive first-person plurals, the former including the addressee(s) and the latter excluding him/her/them. The abbreviation '21' for first-person inclusive encodes the fact of speaker *and* addressee involvement in the action.

15 Obviation is a category found in Algonquian languages which distinguishes between more and less central third person participants. Participants which are possessed by third persons are obligatorily inflected as obviatives.

16 The use of /-ahk/ in place of the expected /-ank/ for the '21' conjunct verbal suffix has been discussed at the phonological level, but, indeed, the presence of the preaspirate carries this change into the realm of morphology as well.

16 This word is itself historically a borrowing from French, *bon jour.*

18 Only the first six minutes of the sermon are provided here.

19 This and other forms below do not have the expected reduplication -*ayamihtoon-*.

CHAPTER FIVE

1 *Kinihtaa-anihshininiiwasinahike na?* The preverb *nihtaa-* means, simultaneously, 'be good at' and 'be able to.' Thus the translation of this sentence is more accurately stated: 'Can you write (or: Are you good at) writing syllabics?'

2 Most of these issues have been addressed previously in articles which deal

with similarly complex literacy situations in which both syllabics and roman are used in essentially complementary distribution. Particularly notable in this respect is Burnaby and MacKenzie 1985, which provides a nicely contextualized discussion of reading and writing in an East Cree community, a community whose literacy situation is strikingly similar to that in Lynx Lake.

3 This is an important political aspect of literacy in a country where English is the majority language as it places all non-standard, and most second-language, English speakers at a distinct social disadvantage.

4 Numbers are written using roman characters.

5 The spelling system used on map 4 is that associated with Southern Ojibwe.

6 The term 'traditional skill' is used here to denote a skill which is considered the venue of the Native community as opposed to that of the matrix society.

7 Indeed, it only took me one day to learn to read and produce syllabics.

CHAPTER SIX

1 See Rogers's (1962) section, 'Round Lake Ojibwe Religion.'

2 Lay readers in this community undergo religious training which invests them with the authority to read portions of the liturgy publicly. Lay readers are often called upon to read long portions of scriptures and thus must be better-than-average readers.

3 Some Ojibwe farther south do have some forms that appear similar to these genres (John Nichols, personal communication). However, I contend that, given the very different historical development of religion in these two regions, the current forms found in the Severn area need not be overlays on an earlier system.

4 The examples using musical notation were initially produced using the ConcertWare program.

5 This is an official church office held by trained members of the laity.

6 The SoundCap and SoundWave programs were used to digitize these and the following samples.

7 For example, there was no attempt to incorporate these genres into List's (1963) schema, although many of the parameters he covers are represented here.

CHAPTER SEVEN

1 The only two titles in the community which are consistently used are The Venerable Pipoon, in reference to the archdeacon, The Venerable William

Pipoon, and the Reverend Pipoon, in reference to his brother, the Reverend Simon Pipoon, a priest. In less formal situations (most in Lynx Lake), these two men are known, respectively, as William and Simon, but befitting the formal nature of written materials, I have used the more formal titles here.

2 A notable exception to this overwhelming trend is Basso's (1970) account of the Cibecue Apache in which both Native and Christian traditions are systematically, and impartially, analysed.

3 The pronominal morphemes in Ojibwe do not distinguish between masculine and feminine.

4 The father-in-law came from an area southeast of the Lynx Lake region which borders the Lac Seul dialect and cultural region. Bear-walking has been noted in more southerly groups of Ojibwe, especially among the Ojibwe on Manitoulin Island. Because there has been no evidence for this type of spiritual activity in the Severn area, it seems probable that this represents a more southerly tradition which has been imported.

5 An extended discussion of methodological and ethical implications of studying spontaneous discourse directed towards in-group members can be found in chapter 10.

6 That text was not included here because of space considerations.

7 Interesting formal features of this text include some degree of nasal-cluster simplification discussed in chapter 4, marked within the text by underlined blanks in the Ojibwe sections, and the use of rhetorical questions. The rhetorical questions *Cwaan awanenan ini kaa-kii-waapamaac, awanenan ini kaa-kii-waapamaac kihci-apiwinink* ('Who was it that John saw? Who was it that he saw on the throne?'), used by the Rev. Simon Pipoon are highly marked in several ways. First, the use of the proper noun Cwaan ('John') prior to the interrogative pronoun *awanenan* is extremely unusual, and, in fact, is not found in any other data that I have collected. Second, the question is repeated, the second question adding slightly more information ('on the throne') to the first. Finally, the use of a question in a formal, public and monologic setting makes this a rhetorical question, a device rarely found outside formal, English settings. This device may have been learned in one of the priest schools that are held for Native people. In this case we can be sure that the Rev. Pipoon learned it from another Ojibwe- or Cree-speaking person as he does not speak English.

CHAPTER EIGHT

1 Swanson Turtle died in the summer of 1991 from a long-standing lung ailment.

2 I respectfully use Swanson's first name throughout this chapter as that is the normal form of address in the community. In Lynx Lake, first or first and last names are used in third-person discussions, unless the person mentioned is a relative or has an established, named role in the community. If a relative is discussed, the kinship term for that person is used and similarly, the name of a role (i.e., *okimaahkaan*, 'chief' or *ayamihewikimaa*, 'priest/minister') is used to refer to those in particularly salient positions. The use of the prefix, Mr, is so foreign to the community that I cannot in good conscience use 'Mr Mekanek' which presents an artificial, Euro-American/Canadian system superficially imposing a degree of respect which often extends only to the name. Here I will risk sounding too informal with the hope that the great respect I have for this elder (*kihchi-ahaa*) will be seen throughout the text while retaining the community standards of address.

3 Transcription by R. Valentine and Lydia Mamakwa.

4 In only one narrative of those I have studied did Swanson not feel comfortable with the particular story. This was heavily marked in the initial narrative frame by an admission of some confusion as to the genre of the story, and by the lack of the personal connection with the tale itself. Swanson made a point of distancing himself from the narrative within the introductory frame by attributing the story to others. (See discussion under 'Metanarration.')

5 This is true, except for religious discourse, where many of the Christian terms used are taken from the Cree Bible, which was translated from English and has an inordinate number of nominalized verbs reflecting the original Greek forms.

CHAPTER NINE

1 Thanks to Richard Bauman and John Minton for pointing this out in an earlier analysis of the text.

2 The title is given only for referential convenience. The only story collected in Lynx Lake that was titled was one given in writing by a young woman who had been educated in public (i.e., English-language) schools through high school.

3 Later, in another community, after listening to this tape, an elder retold this and the revenge episode of the story. In this version, the partridge is called by its other name, 'the startler.' When *Wiihsahkecaahk* defecates on the baby partridges, he makes the statement '*That* is startling!' Later, after several other escapades, the mother partridge gets even when she flies up in *Wiihsahkecaahk*'s face, causing him to slide down a cliff on his bare, badly

scorched behind, leaving his scabs on the cliff. Her response: 'Now *that* is startling!'

CHAPTER TEN

1 In Lynx Lake, *aatisoohkaanan* are told exclusively by men, and optimally during evenings after the snow has covered the lake.

2 This is in no way to claim that data collection is atheoretical. Indeed, any selection of data to collect involves theoretical decisions which must be attended (cf. Ochs 1979; Becker 1974; and Rouch 1974).

3 This is essentially the same methodological paradox underlying Chomsky's linguistic research paradigm which suggests that, since language is innate, all languages will share a large core and that the study of any particular language, and indeed any particular speaker, will equally reveal the core. But only those very familiar with a language (perhaps ultimately only native speakers) are capable of making the subtle judgments of grammaticality required for more refined aspects of the grammatical model and for distinguishing errors of performance attributable to such factors as fatigue from the structures (competence) underlying those.

4 The slogan 'A First Nations-Kelner Partnership Adventure,' is displayed prominently across their full-page advertisement.

APPENDIX ONE

1 It may be that rounded back vowels are underlyingly high. Since the status of this vowel is not of concern in this presentation, I will represent it with a value consistent with its traditional orthographic representation.

References

Abu-Lughod, Lila, and Catherine Lutz. 1990. Introduction: Emotion, Discourse, and the Politics of Everyday Life. In *Language and the Politics of Emotion*, eds. C. Lutz and L. Abu-Lughod, 1–23. Cambridge: Cambridge University Press.

Babcock, Barbara. 1977. The Story in the Story: Metanarration in Folk Narrative. In *Verbal Art as Performance*, ed. Richard Bauman, 61–79. Prospect Heights: Waveland Press.

Basso, Keith H. 1970. *The Cibecue Apache*. New York: Holt, Rinehart and Winston.

– 1972. 'To Give Up on Words': Silence in Western Apache Culture. In *Language and Social Contexts*, ed. Pier Giglioli, 67–86. Markham: Penguin Books.

– 1979. *Portraits of 'the Whiteman': Linguistic Play and Cultural Symbols among the Western Apache*. Cambridge: Cambridge University Press.

– 1983. 'Stalking with Stories': Names, Places and Moral Narratives among the Western Apache. In *Text, Play and Story: The Construction and Reconstruction of Self and Society*, 19–55. Proceedings of American Ethnological Society.

– 1988. 'Speaking with Names': Language and Landscape among the Western Apache. *Cultural Anthropology* 3, 99–132.

Bauman, Richard. 1977. *Verbal Art as Performance*. Prospect Heights: Waveland Press.

– 1986a. *Story, Performance, and Event: Contextual Studies of Oral Narrative*. Cambridge: Cambridge University Press.

– 1986b. Disclaimers of Performance. Unpublished manuscript.

Bauman, Richard, and Charles Briggs. 1992. Intertextuality and Social Power. *Journal of Linguistic Anthropology* 2/2, 131–72.

Becker, H.S. 1974. Photography and Sociology. *Studies in the Anthropology of Visual Communication* 1, 3–26.

Blom, J.–P., and J. Gumperz. 1972. Social Meaning in Linguistic Structures: Code-switching in Norway. In *Directions in Sociolinguistics*, eds. J. Gumperz and D. Hymes, 407–34. New York: Holt, Rinehart & Winston.

Bloomfield, Leonard. 1958. *Eastern Ojibwa: Grammatical Sketch, Texts and Word List*, ed. Charles F. Hockett. Ann Arbor: University of Michigan Press.

Bourdieu, Pierre. 1991. *Language and Symbolic Power*, ed. John. B. Thompson. Cambridge: Polity Press.

Bricker, Victoria. 1973. *Ritual Humor in Highland Chiapas*. Austin: University of Texas Press.

Bright, William. 1982. Poetic Structure in Oral Narrative. In *Spoken and Written Language: Exploring Orality and Literacy*, 171–84. Norwood: Ablex.

Brody, Hugh. 1981. *Maps and Dreams: Indians and the British Frontier.* Vancouver: Douglas and McIntyre.

Brunvand, Jan Harold. 1968. *The Study of American Folklore*. New York: W.W. Norton and Company.

Burnaby, Barbara. 1981. Language Shift in Northern Ontario. In *Papers of the Twelfth Algonquian Conference*, ed. Wm. Cowan. Ottawa: Carleton University Press.

Burnaby, Barbara, and Marguerite MacKenzie. 1985. Reading and Writing in Rupert House. In *Promoting Native Writing Systems*, ed. Barbara Burnaby, 57–81. Toronto: OISE Press/The Ontario Institute for Studies in Education.

Casagrande, Joseph B. 1952. Ojibwa Bear Ceremonialism: The Persistence of a Ritual Attitude. In *Acculturation in the Americas*, ed. Sol Tax, 113–17. Proceedings and Selected Papers of the 29th International Congress of Americanists, Chicago.

Chafe, Wallace L. 1962. Estimates Regarding the Present Speakers of North American Indian Languages. *International Journal of American Linguistics* 28, 162–71.

– 1965. Corrected Estimates Regarding the Present Speakers of Indian Languages. *International Journal of American Linguistics* 31, 345–6.

Chambers, J.K., and Peter Trudgill. 1980. *Dialectology*. Cambridge: Cambridge University Press.

Clifford, James. 1988. *The Predicament of Culture: Twentieth-Century Ethnography, Literature, and Art*. Cambridge, MA: Harvard University Press.

Cole, M., and S. Scribner. 1981. *The Psychology of Literacy*. Cambridge, MA: Harvard University Press.

Darnell, Regna. 1974. Correlates of Cree Narrative Performance. In *Explorations in the Ethnography of Speaking*, eds. R. Bauman and J. Sherzer, 315–36. Cambridge: Cambridge University Press.

Densmore, Frances. 1910. *Chippewa Music* [1]. Bureau of American Ethnology Bulletin 45. Washington.

– 1913. *Chippewa Music* [2]. Bureau of American Ethnology Bulletin 53. Washington.

– 1929. *Chippewa Customs*. Smithsonian Institution, Bureau of American Ethnology, Bulletin 86.

Dicks, Dennis. 1977. From Dog Sled to Dial Telephone: A Cultural Gap? *Journal of Communication* 27, 120–9.

Diringer, David. 1962. *Writing*. London: Thames and Hudson.

Dolby-Stahl, Sandra K. 1985. A Literary Folkloristic Methodology for the Study of Meaning in Personal Narrative. *Journal of Folklore Research* 22, 45–69.

Feld, Steven. 1982. *Sound and Sentiment: Birds, Weeping, Poetics, and Song in Kaluli Expression*. Philadelphia: University of Pennsylvania Press.

Finnegan, Ruth. 1988. *Literacy and Orality: Two Forms of Information Technology*. Oxford: Blackwell.

Gal, Susan. 1978. Variation and Change in Patterns of Speaking: Language Shift in Austria. In *Linguistic Variation: Models and Methods*, ed. D. Sankoff, 227–38. New York: Academic Press.

Geertz, Clifford. 1973. Deep Play: Notes on the Balinese Cockfight. In *The Interpretation of Culture*, 412–54. New York: Basic Books.

Gill, Sam. 1987. *Native American Religious Action: A Performance Approach to Religion*. Columbia: University of South Carolina.

Givon, Talmy. 1980. *On Understanding Grammar*. Perspectives in Neurolinguistics and Psycholinguistics Series. New York: Academic Press.

– 1985. *Topic Continuity in Discourse*. T. Givon, ed. Philadelphia: John Benjamins.

Goddard, Ives. 1978. Central Algonquian Languages. In *Handbook of North American Indians, Northeast* 15. Washington, DC: Smithsonian Institution.

– 1988. Post-Transformational Stem Derivation in Fox. In *Papers and Studies in Contrastive Linguistics* 22, 59–72.

Goffman, Irvine. 1974. *Frame Analysis: An Essay on the Organization of Experience*. New York: Harper and Row.

Goodwin, Charles. 1981. *Conversational Organization: Interaction between Speakers and Hearers*. New York: Academic Press.

Goodwin, Marjorie H. 1982. Instigating: Storytelling as a Social Process. *American Ethnologist* 9, 799–819.

– 1990. *He-Said-She-Said: Talk as Social Organization among Black Children*. Bloomington: Indiana University Press.

Goody, J., ed. 1968. *Literacy in Traditional Societies*. Cambridge: Cambridge University Press.

Goody, J., and I. Watt. 1963. The Consequences of Literacy. In *Comparative Studies in Society and History* 5, 304–45.

Gossen, Gary. 1974. *Chamulas in the World of the Sun: Time and Space in a Maya Oral Tradition*. Cambridge, MA: Harvard University Press.

Gumperz, John J. 1982. *Discourse Strategies*. Cambridge: Cambridge University Press.

Gumperz, John J., and Eduardo Hernández-Chavez. 1970. Cognitive Aspects of Bilingual Communication. In *El Lenguaje de los Chicanos*, eds. E. Hernández-Chavez, A. Cohen, and A. Beltramo, 154–63. Virginia: Center for Applied Linguistics.

Gumperz, John J., and Dell Hymes, eds. 1974 [1972]. *Directions in Sociolinguistics: The Ethnography of Communication*. New York: Basil Blackwell.

Halliday, M.A.K. 1985. *An Introduction to Functional Grammar*. London: Edward Arnold.

Halliday, M.A.K., and Ruqaiya Hasan. 1976. *Cohesion in English*. London: Longman.

Hallowell, A. Irving. 1934. Bear Ceremonialism in the Northern Hemisphere. *American Anthropologist* 28, 1–175.

– 1936. The Passing of the Midewiwin in the Lake Winnipeg Region. *American Anthropologist* 38, 32–51.

– 1939. Sin, Sex, and Sickness in Saulteaux Belief. *The British Journal of Medical Psychology* 18, 191–7.

– 1942. *The Role of Conjuring in Saulteaux Society*. Philadelphia: Publications of the Philadelphia Anthropological Society, 2.

– 1971. [Review of] *Missionary Linguistics in New France*, by Victor E. Hanzeli, 1969. *American Anthropologist* 73, 408–9.

Heath, Shirley Brice. 1978. Bilingual Education and a National Language Policy. In *Georgetown University Round Table on Languages and Linguistics* 1978, ed. J.E. Alatis. Washington, DC: Georgetown University Press.

– 1982a. Protean Shapes in Literacy Events: Ever-shifting Oral and Literate Traditions. In *Spoken and Written Language: Exploring Orality and Literacy*, ed. Deborah Tannen, 91–118. Norwood: Ablex.

– 1982b. What No Bedtime Story Means: Narrative Skills at Home and School. *Language in Society* 11, 49–76.

– 1983. *Ways with Words*. Cambridge: Cambridge University Press.

Heller, Monica, ed. 1988a. *Codeswitching: Anthropological and Sociolinguistic Perspectives*. Berlin: Mouton de Gruyter.

– 1988b. Strategic Ambiguity: Code-switching in the Management of Conflict. In *Codeswitching: Anthropological and Sociolinguistic Perspectives*, ed. Monica Heller, 77–96. Berlin: Mouton de Gruyter.

Hines, H.E. 1948. *A Cree Grammar*. Toronto: The Missionary Society of the Church of England.

Horden, John. 1970 [1929]. *The Book of Common Prayer in the Cree Indian Languages*. Toronto: The Anglican Book Centre.

Hudson, Heather. 1977. The Role of Radio in the Canadian North. *Journal of Communication* 27, 130–9.

Hymes, Dell. 1964. Introduction: Toward Ethnographies of Communication. In *The Ethnography of Communication*, eds. J.J. Gumperz and D. Hymes, 1–34. *American Anthropologist* 66, part 2.

– 1974. Studying the Interaction of Language Use and Social Life. In *Foundations in Sociolinguistics*, ed. Dell Hymes, 29–66. Philadelphia: University of Pennsylvania Press.

– 1977. Discovering Oral Performance and Measured Verse in American Indian Narrative. *New Literary History* 8, 431–57.

– 1981. *'In Vain I Tried to Tell You': Essays in Native American Ethnopoetics.* Philadelphia: University of Pennsylvania Press.

– 1985. Language, Memory, and Selective Performance: Cultee's 'Salmon's Myth' as Twice Told to Boas. *Journal of American Folklore* 98, 391–434.

Jackson, Jean. 1974. Language Identity of the Colombia Vaupes Indians. In *Explorations in the Ethnography of Speaking*, eds. Richard Bauman and Joel Sherzer, 5–64. London: Cambridge University Press.

Jacobson, Roman. 1960. Concluding Statement: Linguistics and Poetics. In *Style in Language*, ed. T.A. Sebeok. Cambridge, MA: MIT Press.

Jacopin, Pierre-Yves. 1988. On the Syntactic Structure of Myth, or the Yukuna Invention of Speech. *Cultural Anthropology* 3/2, 131–59.

James, Bernard J. 1961. Social-Psychological Dimensions of Ojibwa Acculturation. *American Anthropologist* 63, 721–46.

Jenness, Diamond. 1935. *The Ojibwa Indians of Parry Island: Their Social and Religious Life.* Ottawa: Canada Department of Mines Bulletin 78, Anthropological Series 17.

Jones, David J. 1976. *Extracts from a Basic Algonquin Grammar* [1977, *sic*]. Maniwaki, PQ: River Desert Band Council.

Jones, William. 1917. *Ojibwa Texts,* ed. Truman Michelson. American Ethnological Society Publications 7.1, Leiden/New York; 7.2, New York, 1919.

Josselin de Jong, J.P.B. 1912. A Few Otchipwe Songs. *Internationales Archiv fur Ethnologie* 20, 189–90.

Kaye, Jonathan D., and Glyne L. Piggott, eds. 1973. *Odawa Language Project, Second Report.*

Kaye, Jonathan D., Glyne L. Piggott, and Kensuke Tokaichi, eds. 1971. *Odawa Language Project, First Report.*

Kegg, Maude. 1976. *Gii-ikwezensiwiyaan/When I Was a Little Girl: Memories of Indian Childhood in Minnesota,* ed. John D. Nichols. Minnesota: Onamia.

– 1978. *Gabekanaansing/ At the End of the Trail: Memories of Chippewa Childhood in Minnesota,* ed. John D. Nichols. University of Northern Colorado Museum of

Anthropology, Occasional Publications in Anthropology, Linguistic Series 4. Greeley, CO/Thunder Bay, ON: self-published.

– 1983. *Nookomis Gaa-inaajimotawid/What my Grandmother Told Me,* ed. John D. Nichols. Saint Paul: Minnesota Archaeological Society.

Labov, William. 1972a. *Sociolinguistic Patterns.* Philadelphia: University of Pennsylvania Press.

– 1972b. *Language in the Inner City: Studies in the Black English Vernacular.* Philadelphia: University of Pennsylvania Press.

Lakoff, George, and Mark Johnson. 1980. *Metaphors We Live By.* Chicago: University of Chicago Press.

Landes, Ruth. 1968 [1937]. *Ojibwa Religion and the Midewiwin.* Madison: University of Wisconsin Press.

List, George. 1963. The Boundaries of Speech and Song. *Ethnomusicology* 7, 1–16.

– 1964. Acculturation and Musical Tradition. *International Folk Music Council Journal* 16, 18–21.

Longacre, Robert E. 1976. *An Anatomy of Speech Notions.* Lisse: The Peter de Ridder Press.

Lutz, Maija M. 1978. *The Effects of Acculturation on Eskimo Music of Cumberland Penninsula.* Canadian Ethnology Service Paper No. 41. Ottawa: National Museums of Canada.

McConvell, M. 1988. MIX-IM-UP: Aboriginal Code-Switching, Old and New. In *Codeswitching: Anthropological and Sociolinguistic Perspectives,* ed. Monica Heller, 97–150. Berlin: Mouton de Gruyter.

Mailhot, Jose. 1985. Implementation of Mother-Tongue Literacy among the Montagnais: Myth or Reality? In *Promoting Native Writing Systems,* ed. Barbara Burnaby, 17–26. Toronto: OISE Press/The Ontario Institute for Studies in Education.

Malinowski, B. 1935. The Language of Magic and Gardening. Reprinted in *Coral Gardens and Their Magic* (1978). New York: Dover Publications.

Marcus, George E., and Michael M.J. Fischer. 1986. *Anthropology as Cultural Critique: An Experimental Moment in the Human Sciences.* Chicago: University of Chicago Press.

Merriam, Alan P. 1967. *Ethnomusicology of the Flathead Indians.* Chicago: Aldine Publishing.

Moerman, Michael. 1988. *Talking Culture: Ethnography and Conversation Analysis.* Philadelphia: University of Pennsylvania Press.

Nettl, Bruno. 1989. *Blackfoot Musical Thought.* Kent, OH: Kent State University Press.

Nichols, John D. 1975. *Northwestern Ontario Dialect Survey Research Report.* Paper read at 7th Algonkian Conference, Niagara-on-the-Lake, ON.

– 1980. Ojibwe Morphology. PhD dissertation, Harvard University.

– 1988. *An Ojibway Text Anthology*, ed. John D. Nichols. London: Centre for Research and Teaching of Canadian Native Languages.

Ochs, E. 1979. Transcription as Theory. In *Developmental Pragmatics*, eds., E. Ochs and B. Schieffelin, 43–72. New York: Academic Press.

Ong, Walter J. 1982. *Orality and Literacy: The Technologizing of the Word*. London: Methuen.

Paredes, Americo. 1977. On Ethnographic Work among Minority Groups: A Folkorist's Perspective. *New Scholar* 6, 1–32.

Philips, Susan U. 1983. *The Invisible Culture: Communication in Classroom and Community on the Warm Springs Indian Reservation*. New York: Longman.

Phillips, Sondra B. 1985. Aboriginal Languages in Canada: A Research Report. Manuscript for the Department of the Secretary of State.

Plummer, Ken. 1990. Staying in the Empirical World: Symbolic Interactionism and Postmodernism. *Symbolic Interaction* 13/2, 155–60.

Poplack, Shana. 1977. *The Notion of the Plural in Puerto Rican Spanish: Competing Constraints on /s/ Deletion*. Philadelphia: Academic Press.

– 1979. Sometimes I'll Start a Sentence in Spanish y Termino en Espanol: Toward a Typology of Code-Switching. *Centro Working Papers* 4. New York: Research Foundation of CUNY.

Quill, Norman. 1965. *The Moons of Winter and Other Stories*, ed. Charles E. Fiero. Red Lake, ON: Northern Light Gospel Missions.

Rhodes, Richard A. 1976. The Morphosyntax of the Central Ojibwa Verb. PhD dissertation, University of Michigan.

– 1979. Some Aspects of Ojibwa Discourse. In *Papers of the Tenth Algonquian Conference*, ed. William Cowan, 102–17. Ottawa: Carleton University Press.

Rhodes, Richard, and Evelyn M. Todd. 1981. Subarctic Algonquian Languages, ed. William C. Sturtevant, *Handbook of North American Indians* 6, 52–66.

Rice, Keren. 1985. Some Notes on Native Literacy Programs. In *Promoting Native Writing Systems*, ed. Barbara Burnaby, 175–9. Toronto: OISE Press/The Ontario Institute for Studies in Education.

Rogers, Edward S. 1962. *The Round Lake Ojibwa*. Royal Ontario Museum: University of Toronto, Art and Archaeology Division, Occasional Paper 5. Toronto.

Rogers, Jean H. 1964. Survey of Round Lake Ojibwa Phonology and Morphology. *National Museum of Canada Bulletin* 194, 92–154.

Rothenberg, Jerome. 1972. *Shaking the Pumpkin: Traditional Poetry of the Indian North Americas*. Garden City, NY: Doubleday.

Rouch, J. 1974. The Camera and Man. *Studies in the Anthropology of Visual Communication* 1, 37–44.

Sacks, Harvey, Emanuel Schegloff, and Gail Jefferson. 1974. A Simplest Systematics for the Organization of Turn-taking for Conversation. *Language* 50, 696–735.

Sankoff, Gillian. 1980. On the Acquisition of Native Speakers by a Language. In *The Social Life of Language*, ed. G. Sankoff, 195–210. Philadelphia: University of Pennsylvania Press.

Sapir, Edward. 1949 [1921]. *Language.* New York: Harcourt, Brace and World.

Scollon, Ronald, and Suzanne B. K. Scollon. 1979. *Linguistic Convergence: An Ethnography of Speaking at Fort Chipewyan, Alberta.* New York: Academic Press.

– 1981. *Narrative, Literacy, and Face in Interethnic Communication.* Norwood: Ablex.

Sherzer, Joel. 1983. *Kuna Ways of Speaking: An Ethnographic Perspective.* Austin: University of Texas Press.

Sherzer, Joel, and Greg Urban, eds. 1986. *Native South American Discourse.* Berlin: Mouton de Gruyter.

Shimpo, Mitsuru, and Robert Williamson. 1965. *Socio-cultural Disintegration among the Fringe Saulteaux.* Saskatoon.

Speck, Frank G. 1935. *Naskapi: Savage Hunters of the Labrador Peninsula.* Norman: University of Oklahoma Press.

Street, Brian V. 1984. *Literacy in Theory and Practice.* Cambridge: Cambridge University Press.

Stubb, Michael. 1980. *Language and Literacy: The Sociolinguistics of Reading and Writing.* London: Routledge and Kegan Paul.

Tedlock, Dennis. 1971. On the Translation of Style in Oral Poetry. *Journal of American Folklore* 84, 114–33.

– 1977. Toward an Oral Poetics. In *A Journal of Theory and Interpretation.* New Literary History offprint, vol. 8.

– 1984. *The Spoken Word and the Work of Interpretation.* Philadelphia: University of Pennsylvania Press.

– 1987. Hearing a Voice in an Ancient Text: Quiche Maya Poetics in Performance. In *Native American Discourse: Poetics and Rhetoric*, eds. J. Sherzer, and A.C. Woodbury, 140–75. Cambridge: Cambridge University Press.

Thibault, Paul J. 1993. *Social Semiotics as Praxis: Text, Social Meaning Making, and Nabokov's Ada.* Theory and History of Literature, vol. 74. Minneapolis: University of Minnesota Press.

Timm, L.A. 1975. Spanish-English Code-Switching: El Porque y How-Not-To. *Romance Philology* 28, 473–82.

Todd, Evelyn M. 1970. A Grammar of the Ojibwa Language: The Severn Dialect. PhD dissertation, University of North Carolina.

Toelken, Barre. 1976. The 'Pretty Languages' of Yellowman: Genre, Mode and Texture in Navaho Coyote Narratives. In *Folklore Genres*, ed. Dan Ben-Amos, 146–70. Austin and London: University of Texas Press.

Urban, Greg. 1991. *A Discourse-Centered Approach to Culture: Native South American Myths.* Austin: University of Texas Press.

Valentine, Rand. 1994. Ojibwe Dialectology. PhD dissertation University of Texas at Austin.

– 1986. Western Ojibwe Rhetorical Structure. Unpublished manuscript.

Valentine, Rand, and Ruth Spielmann. 1982. The Man Who Married a Beaver: Narrative Structuring in an Algonquin Text. Unpublished manuscript.

Vecsey, Christopher. 1983. *Traditional Ojibwa Religion and Its Changes.* Philadelphia: American Philosophical Society.

Vogt, Evon Z. 1988. Indian Crosses and Scepters: The Results of Circumscribed Spanish-Indian Interactions in Mesoamerica. Paper prepared for the Symposium 'In Word and Deed: Interethnic Images and Responses in the New World,' Trujillo, Spain.

Wawatay News 16/5 (May 1989).

Winterhalder, Bruce. 1983. Boreal Foraging Strategies. In *Boreal Forest Adaptations: The Northern Algonkians,* ed. A. Theodore Stegmann, Jr, 9–54. New York: Plenum Press.

Wodak, Ruth, ed. 1989. *Language, Power and Ideology: Studies in Political Discourse.* Amsterdam: J. Benjamins.

Woodbury, Anthony C. 1987. Rhetorical Structure in a CAY Eskimo Tale. In *Native American Discourse: Poetics and Rhetoric,* eds. J. Sherzer. and A.C. Woodbury, 176–239. Cambridge: Cambridge University Press.

Woolard, Kathryn. 1988. Codeswitching and Comedy in Catalonia. In *Codeswitching: Anthropological and Sociolinguistic Perspectives,* ed. Monica Heller, 53–76. Berlin: Mouton de Gruyter.

Index